FAILURE OF A
REVOLUTION

FAILURE

OF A

REVOLUTION

GERMANY IN
1918–1919

BY

RUDOLF COPER

CAMBRIDGE
AT THE UNIVERSITY PRESS
1955

PUBLISHED BY
THE SYNDICS OF THE CAMBRIDGE UNIVERSITY PRESS

London Office: Bentley House, N.W. I
American Branch: New York

Agents for Canada, India, and Pakistan: Macmillan

Printed in Great Britain at the University Press, Cambridge
(Brooke Crutchley, University Printer)

To
Freda

CONTENTS

PREFACE

The German Revolution of 1918 left militarism to dominate the German scene. Therefore it was a failure. This book shows and explains how this failure came about.

The German Revolution of 1918 set up a political democracy. A political democracy is a mere form if there exists no democratic social and economic substance to support it. In Germany, the State has never had a democratic substance; government has always been the prerogative of certain groups and individuals. Hence democratic political forms could not maintain themselves.

The failure of 1918 manifested itself most visibly in 1933 and in 1939. In 1945, these manifestations were expunged by Germany's defeat. But the seed of the old substance remained.

The German democratic forms of 1918, like real democracy wherever it exists, comprised the division of the functions of government into three branches, legislative, executive and judicial. The latter branch of government became particularly important in Germany because it was the only branch that functioned there after the defeat of 1945 and thus had not only substantial but also unbroken continuity. We shall see a number of examples of its earlier functioning, in the Revolution, in the following pages. As the writing of history serves (or should serve) a purpose, it is instructive to give here also two examples of the working of the German judiciary after the downfall of Hitler.

The first of them is connected with the Revolution of 1918. Matthias Erzberger, a progressive leader of the Centre Party in the Revolution, was murdered by two young men, Schulz and Tillessen, in 1921. They found sanctuary in Hungary and returned to Germany in 1933 to be *fêted* as national heroes. At the end of the Second World War both were apprehended by the Allied authorities in the Western Zone of occupation. Tillessen was handed over to the German judiciary authorities. Although

Hitler had, in 1933, passed an amnesty for offences against the Weimar Republic, a German court of justice in Freiburg in Baden tried Tillessen, thus placing him in double jeopardy. As his case was thrown out of court on the grounds of that amnesty it is possible that the whole procedure served the purpose of exonerating him formally. However, the French occupation authorities ordered a re-trial by a different German court, and this court not only tried Tillessen, placing him in triple jeopardy, but sentenced him to fifteen years in a reformatory.

Then again, in March 1954 a court of justice in Dortmund in Westphalia tried some twenty former Nazis who had confessed to having killed an undetermined number (running, however, into hundreds) of Jews in the Warsaw ghetto in the Second World War. All of them were acquitted on the grounds that they had acted under orders from officers who were long since dead, and that 'because of their scant formal education they failed to realize that they committed a misdeed'.

A revolution is an enormous event. He who lives through a revolution cannot forget it. The events of the German Revolution of 1918 are imprinted on my memory, more vividly so than the events of three other enormous happenings, two world wars and the Nazi revolution. As for the latter, I ran away from Germany shortly after it started. As for the First World War, I was too young to fight, and that was good, for I would have been forced to fight on the wrong side. As for the Second World War, I was too old to fight. Somebody called my generation the lost generation. I do not agree. Only individuals are lost, not generations. To be sure, it is great to fight with arms to repel an aggressor; it is tragic to have to sit at home. But there are other ways of fighting, too. The writing of history, the telling of the truth is one of them.

The teller of the truth cannot tell all the details of the truth. The historian must select his material. But the truth is indivisible. No matter what other pertinent material I might have selected, the lesson would be the same. Nor have I allowed myself to be influenced in my selection by what I saw with my eyes and heard with my ears. I saw and heard much of what is described here in so far as it took place in Berlin. I saw and heard in action most of the men and women who speak from these pages and of whom these pages speak. I knew many of them. I am not an actor in this book, though you might have found me in many of the crowds I describe. I am passive in every respect. It is not the historian's right to utter opinions. But it is his duty to provoke opinions by drawing conclusions from the facts he describes. Otherwise he would be a chronicler with a scientific apparatus. And it is his right (if he was not an actor and has no axe to grind) to add colour to the drabness of the scene by spreading the tints of his memory. But I have not relied on my memory for any facts, not even those facts that everybody knows. And I have not relied on German or any other newspapers of the period. The following pages show, among other things, of how little value the German newspapers are as a source of factual information, revealing though they are in other respects. Instead, I have used an excellent German chronological compilation[1] and, of course, the writings listed in the bibliography. Many of them are memoirs of the main actors in this book. It is part of the historian's task to check and judge their reliability. This task is especially important in the present case because there are many details that cannot be verified from any other source; it is complicated by countless contradictions among the multitude of confessions, accusations, lies, and protestations of innocence. But just this multitude contributes to a satisfactory result, if the task be undertaken seriously.

One technical remark. The numerous page-references in the text refer invariably to pages of this book. This technique has been chosen to relieve the reader's memory in a welter of detail that might otherwise be bewildering.

RUDOLF COPER

NEW ORLEANS, LA.
Spring, 1954

[1] See Bibliography, Horkenbach.

I. SURRENDER

Canadian, Australian, and French divisions broke through the German lines between Albert and Moreuil on 8 August 1918. Under the cover of a dense fog that had been intensified artificially their tanks took large numbers of prisoners and captured whole staffs of German divisions and documents of incalculable value. Three days later, the Kaiser drove to Avesnes to see Hindenburg at his quarters. The Marshal led him into a small cabinet. First Quartermaster-General Ludendorff was waiting for them. He began: 'We must realize that we have suffered a grave defeat.' The Kaiser grew pale. Ludendorff went on with his report on the military situation. A discussion followed. The Kaiser concluded: 'I see we must strike the balance. We have reached the limit of our ability to resist. The war must be terminated.' The Kaiser was the Supreme War Lord with power to declare war and make peace. Such was the Imperial Constitution; its eleventh article read: 'The Kaiser represents the Reich internationally, declares war and concludes peace in the name of the Reich....'

Another three days later the three men met again, at the Kaiser's headquarters in Spa. The Kaiser had also summoned the Crown Prince; the Imperial Chancellor, Count Hertling; the Foreign Secretary, His Excellency von Hintze; and three of his personal advisers.

The Chancellor reported on the internal situation; the people were war-weary, nutrition was inadequate, the lack of clothing was worse. Ludendorff and the Crown Prince declared the home front must be ruthlessly organized. The Kaiser declared that a propaganda commission must be created in order to weaken the enemy's confidence in victory; flaming speeches must be made for consumption abroad and at home. The Chancellor declared that there was no dearth of material for such speeches; diplomatically, the ground must be prepared for an understanding with the enemy at the right moment. The right moment would be after the next success on the Western Front. The next military success—this did not mean victory; it meant the stopping of the rout of the German armies.

No success was achieved at the Western Front. On the contrary, there were more reverses. And there were reverses on the political front; Austria-Hungary and Bulgaria, allies of Germany, collapsed. Ludendorff grew panicky. 'It seems clear that Ludendorff actually feared a break-through. He may have known of gaps in his line where one could occur if the enemy discovered them. The fear of such discovery might well have occasioned his "loss of nerve" and his pressure for an immediate armistice.' Anyway, on 28 September 1918, he demanded that the government immediately ask the enemy for peace and request an armistice; every hour counted. This demand came as a blow to the Kaiser. Six weeks earlier he had said that the war must be terminated because of the hopeless military situation. Now he was surprised to learn that the military situation was hopeless. Was there no other way out? He would try. He proclaimed, a day later, that it was his will that 'men who have the confidence of the people participate in a large measure in the rights and duties of government'.

2

A new government had to be formed because the Chancellor, Count Hertling, and his cabinet would not be trusted at home and abroad if they suddenly posed as a peace cabinet; they had meekly sailed in the wake of the General Staff, and this meekness had been demonstrated most strikingly when, against their better judgement, they allowed the German militarists to inflict the savage peace of Brest-Litovsk upon Russia, a peace that did as much for the promotion of Bolshevism there as Lenin and Trotsky. The new government had to be *de jure* responsible to the Reichstag, for the

same reason; a government that held office merely through and
during the Kaiser's pleasure offered no guarantee of the stability of
its peaceful intentions. *De facto*, the Reich government had been
semi-responsible to the Reichstag since November 1917 when
Count Hertling became Chancellor. The majority parties (we
shall learn who they were as we proceed) forced him to submit his
programme to them for approval before he took office. Of course,
the Reich government always had to have the support of a majority
in the Reichstag in order to get any bills enacted, but under the
system that was inaugurated by Bismarck the Chancellor and his
cabinet could obtain the necessary majority regardless of what
parties it consisted of. Sometimes, of course, they did not obtain it,
and then there was nothing left to them but to resign. This system
could produce a clear-cut policy only if the will of the Kaiser was
clear cut, or else if the will of the Chancellor was so and the
Chancellor dominated the Kaiser. It was a system that suited the
peculiar talents of Bismarck, but with lesser chancellors and at the
same time an emperor of the incalculable and intractable temperament of the last Kaiser it could, and did, produce a great deal
of confusion in internal as well as external politics.

The change towards parliamentary government when Count
Hertling took office meant that the Chancellor had to have the
support of a stable majority (not just any majority), and that this
stable majority confirmed or rejected the Kaiser's nominee for
Chancellor and could force him out of office if they no longer
agreed with him. They could not yet present a candidate of their
own choosing and have him confirmed or rejected by the Kaiser,
and the Imperial Constitution still forbade a member of the Reichstag to be a member of the Reich government or the government
of any of the States in the federation; the Reich was a federation of
monarchies, much as the American Union is a federation of
republican States. Moreover, this new system had no constitutional basis. It was the outcome of the political situation of the
time and might change with the time. In fact, the Chief of the
Kaiser's Privy Council, Rudolf von Valentini, who conducted the

negotiations with the leaders of the majority parties that led to the formation of the Hertling government, declared that this 'whole parliamentary circus would last no more than a few months'; after the war, His Majesty would govern as he saw fit.

This dictum of Valentini's was not so vulgar as it might appear when one considers that it was indeed only under the stress of a great war that there was really serious pressure for changes in the form of Germany's government. Richard Müller-Fulda was a Reichstag deputy of the Centre Party at that time, a man as influential behind the scene as he was self-effacing on it. Taking a newly elected member under his wing he gave him the following advice that deserves to be quoted at some length from that member's memoirs: 'Attach no importance to the noisy declarations and tragic gestures of speakers on the occasion of the first reading of a bill.... Our party leaders are augurs who have learned to look at each other in public assembly without laughing. But surrounded by the mystery of their private confabs they are hand in glove. I know it because I am one of them. We set up a noisy opposition only in order to obtain privileges. The Chancellor plays on winnings with parties that are quarrelling over his favours and with leaders who are always ready to sell themselves.... The Reichstag is composed of three dozen clever and skilful manipulators and three hundred and fifty idiots who are indifferent to the progress of business. Our leaders endeavour to surround themselves with mediocrities in order to have no rivals.... All of them are in continuous relations with *Wilhelmstrasse* [the seat of government] which knows their ambitions and consequently knows how to play with them. People abroad believe we have a national representation. But we have only a handful of operetta conspirators whom an enlightened stage-manager directs as he pleases. With us, such big words as ministerial responsibility, liberty, and democracy have no meaning.... We are a nation of lackeys and slaves whose mind has been prepared for all forms of servitude by intellectuals who have been domesticated by the government and are greedy for honours and distinctions.'

4

3

Count Hertling's government had to step down, then, and a new government had to be formed that had 'the confidence of the people'. In other words, it was to be responsible to the Reichstag, not the Kaiser; and it was to ask the enemy for peace. It was headed by His Grand-Ducal Highness, Prince Maximilian of Baden, heir apparent to the throne of that Federal State. At first, the reigning Grand-Duke of Baden, Friedrich II,[1] refused to give Prince Max permission to accept the chancellorship because he believed that the liquidation of a lost war by a member of their dynasty would react unfavourably on that member and that dynasty. The personal intervention of the Kaiser was necessary

---

[1] Even when discussing so grim an event as the German Revolution of 1918 we may relax for a moment to smile at the freaks of dynastic policy and dynastic history. Friedrich II had no children. Prince Max was the son of the elder of Friedrich's two younger brothers and as such, according to the constitution of Baden, heir apparent. His mother, Princess Marie, was a *née* Duchess of Leuchtenberg. The Duchy of Leuchtenberg, in Bavaria, was created by Napoleon for his stepson, Eugene Beauharnais, the son of Josephine, Napoleon's first wife, by her first marriage. Princess Marie was a granddaughter of Eugene, and Prince Max thus was a great-great-grandson of Josephine. Napoleon married Eugene to Augusta, daughter of Maxmilian Josef, King of Bavaria. In order to make possible this marriage, which was of great political advantage to Napoleon, Princess Augusta had to dissolve her betrothal to Prince Karl Ludwig of Baden. But Napoleon had to take care to keep Baden in his fold, too. Therefore, he compensated Karl Ludwig for the loss of Augusta by marrying him to his adopted daughter, Stephanie Beauharnais, a cousin of Eugene. When the then reigning Grand-Duke of Baden, Karl Friedrich, died in 1811 he left only sons by his second marriage to a Countess Hochberg. This marriage had been below his station, and the sons who sprang from it could not succeed to the throne. Thus, Karl Ludwig, who was a nephew of Karl Friedrich, became Grand-Duke. He and Stephanie had several children but none of them was surviving when he died in 1818. Consequently, as no other successors were available, the throne fell to the Hochberg line after all. Prince Max sprang from this line. It was perhaps from conscious or unconscious revenge for the contempt in which they had been held in the first place that the Hochbergs made Baden the 'liberal model country', as which it was known in Germany. Had Karl Ludwig and Stephanie had a surviving son, the 1918 heir of the Baden throne would have had Beauharnais blood in him just the same. As matters were, Prince Max's blood was neither quite 'blue' nor quite German.

to induce the Grand-Duke to give the consent required by the constitution of Baden.

Prince Max had become President of the Baden House of Lords in December 1917. As such he had made a number of speeches that earned him the reputation of being a democrat. His hobby-horse was 'ethical imperialism'. He had recently acquired a foundation for his ethics at Dr Johannes Müller's soul sanatorium for applied Christianity at Elmau Castle near Partenkirchen in Bavaria. In one of his speeches he said in December 1917: 'Even in war love for the enemy is the symbol of those who are faithful to Germany.... If the world is to become reconciled to the greatness of our power it must feel that there is a world conscience behind it.' This was ethical imperialism. The Kaiser, too, was an ethical imperialist; he wired the Prince that his speech was an achievement. The Kaiser found himself in strange company on this occasion; Democrats and Socialists cheered the speech as loudly as he. When the Prince read his praise in the Leftist Press he awoke with a shock and wrote to his cousin, Prince Alexander von Hohenlohe, a pacifist who lived in Switzerland: 'The... [leftists] should leave me alone, and the pacifists, too. I am not an ideologist....Naturally, I want to see our military success exploited to the full....I desire as much compensation as possible in order that we be not too poor after the war.' This letter was published, first by the Swiss and then by the German Press, about a week after the Prince took office as Chancellor. It caused a grave cabinet crisis. But in the end the majority parties decided to forget the matter; there was more at stake than personalities and uncontrolled impulses: peace was at stake.

At the beginning of October 1918 the majority parties were willing to accept the Prince as Chancellor. Knowing this, Hertling's Vice-Chancellor, Friedrich von Payer, suggested the Prince's candidacy to the Kaiser. Consequently, the leaders of the majority parties were informed by his Excellency von Berg, who had succeeded the impossibly outspoken Privy Councillor von Valentini (p. 3) as Chief of the Kaiser's personal advisers, that the Prince

Surrender

was 'the best candidate'. His Excellency von Berg then went on
to recommend that the parties of the Right, who did not form part
of the majority, be taken into the cabinet. He did not actually
address the party leaders but 'talked to the walls in the tone of a
lieutenant of the Guards, pacing up and down in uniform with
boots that reached above his knees, saying that the majority
should not imagine that they could govern by themselves'.

The most urgent task with which the new government had to
deal was Ludendorff's demand for armistice and peace. Until this
demand arrived in Berlin the (outgoing) government, the Reichstag, and the German people had been kept in ignorance of the
seriousness of the military situation. Now that this seriousness had
become apparent the Vice-Chancellor deemed it advisable that
the party leaders should be given detailed military information
before the new government presented itself to the Reichstag.
Upon his request the Supreme Command sent Major von dem
Bussche to Berlin. He addressed the party leaders on 2 October.
The effect of his address was shattering. But in spite of the gloom
it spread, and in spite of his intimate knowledge of the situation
at the front (or perhaps because of this knowledge) the Prince
fought bitterly to obtain a respite from Ludendorff. He argued
that if he were to ask the enemy for an armistice before he made his
declaration of policy in the Reichstag, the enemy would see that
Germany's military situation was desperate. He implored Ludendorff to wait a few days. But Ludendorff would not wait. The
Prince approached the Kaiser with the same request. The Kaiser
said to him: 'The Supreme Command considers it [the immediate
dispatch of the request for an armistice] necessary. You have not
been brought in to cause difficulties for the Supreme Command.'

The new government held its first meeting on the evening of
3 October and decided to send a note to President Wilson asking
him 'to take in hand the restoration of peace...and to arrange
the immediate conclusion of an armistice on land, by sea, and in
the air'.

When, in later years, it came to blaming Germany's debacle on

7

'democracy', Ludendorff reproached Prince Max for asking for an *immediate* armistice whereas Supreme Command had demanded that he *immediately ask* for an armistice. Ludendorff seriously believed that if the enemy imposed harsh conditions Germany could reject them and continue the war. In this case, he calculated, the armistice would provide him with an opportunity for regrouping his armies and giving them the sorely needed rest.

4

Prince Max was also an expert on America. His speech about the world conscience (p. 6) contained the following passage: 'We must not deceive ourselves; the American people really believe that the war must continue in order to make the world safe for all the great ideals. It is a tragic fact of this world war that Europe is historically, psychologically, and politically an undiscovered land for the broad masses in America.'

His expert knowledge of American affairs was put to the test when President Wilson's reply arrived and several more notes were exchanged. Two days after the President's third note arrived on 24 October 1918, Ludendorff was dismissed by the Kaiser upon the insistence of the government. The government had lost all confidence in him because he suddenly declared that the German army, though unable to defeat the enemy, was able to continue the war until better terms could be obtained than were obtainable then. A number of constitutional reforms had been carried out in the Reich meanwhile. Especially, Article XI of the Constitution had been changed to the effect that the Federal Council (p. 107) and the Reichstag, not the Kaiser, were to declare war and conclude peace.

In his third note the President said: 'It is evident that the power of the King of Prussia to control the policy of the Empire is unimpaired.' This meant that the President was not satisfied with the constitutional reforms that had been made. Beyond this, did it or did it not mean that the President was demanding the abdication of the Kaiser? Prince Max did not know. He felt that he must supplement his expert knowledge by direct methods. He asked for information to be gathered in neutral countries.

The neutral capitals were full of diplomatists and semi-official and private representatives of all the belligerents. These men and women explained to each other what was going on in their respective homelands, but most of them believed they knew more about the opposite countries than they actually knew about their own. Consequently, the reports that came in from Holland, Denmark, Switzerland and Sweden were contradictory. Some of them said that a few more parliamentary reforms would satisfy the President. Others said the President was demanding the abdication of the Kaiser and the Crown Prince. Still others said that the President was demanding a German republic. All of them agreed that the President was fighting an uphill battle against the Allied jingoes. An American diplomatist besought the German ambassador in Copenhagen, Count von Brockdorff-Rantzau: 'For God's sake, do something to make Wilson strong against the Entente militarists who are in power in France and England.'

Prince Max could not make up his mind. Very soon the German people made it up for him.

5

The dilemma of Prince Max's government arose from the question: What were the German people thinking about the situation? If the enemy imposed conditions that the majority of the German people would reject, a 'struggle of national desperation' could be proclaimed and the Kaiser retained. But if the majority of the German people felt that the Kaiser's abdication would satisfy the enemy, such a struggle could not be proclaimed.

The demand for the Kaiser's abdication came first from Junker circles. They condemned the monarch because he had asked the enemy for conditions; this was undignified, it desecrated the throne. Another anti-Kaiser source flowed in Bavaria; separatism flared up violently there. Prince Max's War Minister, General von

Scheüch, informed the cabinet that the Bavarian troops would not hold out any longer. There was much talk in Bavaria of a separate Bavarian peace with the Entente. The Reich threatened to fall to pieces.

The Kaiser, who was in Berlin, would not hear of abdication. As soon as the slightest murmur became audible he forestalled any discussion of the question by declaring that he would not desert his armies. Prince Max approached a number of persons who were intimate with the Kaiser and requested them to enlighten the monarch about the urgency of the situation. All of them refused; it was disloyal to speak of the obvious. The Prince would not undertake the mission either; he was the heir apparent to a German throne and felt that for this reason he could not propose abdication directly to the Emperor. At last, however, he realized that he had to fulfil the unpleasant duty himself. But he was told suddenly, on 29 October, that the Kaiser was on the point of leaving the capital for army headquarters behind the front. The Prince, according to his memoirs, thought 'this was a bad joke'. He went to the telephone and implored His Majesty to stay; the political situation made his presence in the capital imperative. But His Majesty said: 'Now you have got rid of Ludendorff I must install Groener.' He was very friendly. But when he arrived at headquarters in Spa he said to His Excellency von Hintze (p. 1), who was now the representative of the Foreign Office attached to General Headquarters, that the government of Prince Max was working towards his removal, and that he had come to military headquarters because he could resist better in the midst of his troops than in Berlin.

II. REVOLUTION

I

A dull morning ushered in the ninth of November 1918 in Berlin. The streets looked as they had looked for many months past. Men, most of them middle-aged and old, all of them weary, were hurrying to the factories. Women were hurrying to the factories. Many of them had a lemon-coloured complexion; they worked in munitions plants and handled picric acid. There were other women; they carried the morning newspapers from door to door. Other men; they carried long poles with which they turned out the gas-jets high up on the lamp-posts. There were no bakers on their rounds with rolls (the Berliner's traditional breakfast food), no milkmen on their rounds with milk; there were no rolls, there was no milk.

The street-cars were driven by women; the conductors, too, were women. The street-cars, the city trains, the underground trains clattered along noisily; their bearings were worn out and there was not enough metal to replace or repair them, not enough grease to lubricate them properly. The people clattered along noisily; they were ill-clad and their shoes had soles of wood and their heels had rims of steel.

Everywhere in the streets of the capital were soldiers in groups of three. The one in the middle was unarmed, the other two had rifles, their bayonets fixed. The unarmed soldier had been on leave from the front and had stayed at home until he was picked up and taken to police headquarters. When several hundred like him had been collected they were put in a train and the train was sealed and sent to the front. Thus the soldiers extended their leave by a few weeks. They knew that they would not be punished unless they resisted arrest; they were needed.

11

The cheeks of all the men and women were hollow. Ration coupons for a tiny quantity of butter and milk per head were not much help when one could not buy any butter and milk. The coupons for a weekly morsel of meat, too, were gaudy to look at, but there was hardly any meat to be had for them. Sickening saccharine took the place of sugar. Boiling water was poured over roasted barley; the brew looked black, it was 'coffee'. The bread, of which there was a small loaf per head per week, never grew hard; the rye was ground out almost one hundred per cent, that is to say, the flour contained almost the entire sticky shell of the rye. Moreover, it was stretched by adding potatoes, barley bran, wheat bran, and oatmeal. A few things were obtainable in sufficient quantities; artificial honey and turnips, the former made from the latter. The turnips were often frozen, and then they smelled and tasted horrible.

There were also people whose cheeks were round. They were not to be found in the streets between five and seven in the morning. They were to be found between five and seven in the afternoon, for instance, in the hotels Adlon and Bristol, Unter den Linden, and afterwards in the many night-clubs. To be sure, they had difficulty in obtaining butter on fatless days and meat on meatless days; about as much difficulty as one had in obtaining whiskey in New York during Prohibition. The luxury hotels and night-clubs were well supplied, not for German war profiteers but for international journalists and visiting businessmen. It was a matter of national representation. Naturally, the German war profiteers could not be kept out. This was deplorable, but it was not undesirable, for these profiteers were very patriotic and they talked to the foreigners, many of whom wrote home gloomy reports about the unbreakable will of 'the Germans' not to give in.

2

Outwardly, then, the world of Berlin looked no different from what it had looked like for many months past, on this dull morning of 9 November 1918. But hundreds of thousands of the hollow-cheeked men and women who were hurrying to the factories that morning had thoughts in their minds very different from the thoughts they had on any other morning, before and after. Would the Kaiser abdicate? Would there be a revolution? A republic? And a more immediate thought: shop stewards, men whom they all knew well, men whom most of them trusted—shop stewards had told them the day before that they should be ready for a walk-out, a general strike, a political general strike. Would it come off? The aim of the general strike was to force the Kaiser to abdicate, to enforce an armistice, to enforce peace. The trade union leaders had got to know of it. They had appealed to the workers not to strike, had entreated them to think of the Fatherland. But five days ago the sailors had mutinied at Kiel. On the next day Bremen and Hamburg had gone revolutionary. Then, the whole north of Germany and Hanover, Cologne, and Bavaria. And yesterday, Württemberg and Saxony.

The mutineers at Kiel at first had no intention of becoming the firebrands of revolution. But they had learned that the fleet was to put out to sea in an attempt to change the fortunes of war; and they believed the attempt was hopeless, the war was lost. Their chief demand was that the expedition be abandoned. When the navy command yielded on this point the sailors advanced new demands that were of a political character though quite immature (p. 68).

One of the admirals at Kiel was Prince Heinrich, the Kaiser's brother. When things became turbulent he tied a red ribbon round his arm and fled in an automobile. His flight made the sailors nervous and suspicious.

In Brussels, the army commander, Crown Prince Rupprecht of Bavaria, abandoned his post without a moment's hesitation. He drove away in a red-flagged motor-car that was put at his disposal by the soldiers' council. (Soldiers' councils, or soviets, sprang up everywhere when the German army collapsed. They assumed the power of command and usually deposed the officers.)

Prince Adalbert, one of the Kaiser's six sons, was an officer at the naval base of Swinemünde on the Baltic Sea. Two cruisers and a garrison of some two thousand men were at Swinemünde, all of them loyal to the old régime. When they learned that revolt was spreading they were prepared to march against the rebels. When Prince Adalbert learned what the garrison was prepared to do under his command he enthusiastically donned civilian clothes and disappeared.

Prince Friedrich Leopold of Prussia, another Hohenzollern, was in residence at Glienicke Castle near Potsdam on 9 November 1918. With dignified calm he ordered a red flag to be hoisted on the palace.

A single officer in the whole of Germany's armed forces remembered his pledges and his honour as he saw it. Captain Weniger was commander of the battleship *König* at Kiel. He placed himself before his ship's flag when the sailors went to haul it down. One of the men tried to get past him. He shot the man. The men shot him.

Was Berlin lagging behind? the workers of Berlin asked themselves on that dull morning of 9 November. Many of them had grown impatient when things began to happen in the other cities. They were angry because their shop stewards were restraining them. Berlin was the heart and brain of the Reich, said the stewards, if anything went wrong there all would be lost, for the time being at least. But yesterday the stewards had told the workers of Berlin to be ready.

Yesterday, too, the Naumburg Rifles had arrived in the capital. They were said to be the regiment most loyal to the old régime. They came from the Ukraine where they had helped the German puppet, Hetman Skoropadski,[1] to keep down the revolution.

[1] In the years after 1933, Hetman Skoropadski became *persona grata* with Hitler. His storm troopers, wearing white shirts and black trousers and swastika

They came from Finland where they had done the same job for General Mannerheim. Count Rüdiger von der Goltz, the German commander in Finland, was dismayed when Baron Mannerheim had many thousands of prisoners executed after they had been handed over to him by the Germans who took them.

How did they stand now, the Naumburg Rifles? What would they do? Was something to happen in Berlin today?

3

Between 8 and 9 a.m. the factory gates opened. The workers streamed out, hundreds of thousands of them, formed processions, endless. They marched to the inner city, to the squares by the Palace and the Reichstag, quiet, in good order.

A captain of the Naumburg Rifles appeared at headquarters of the Social Democratic Party. He begged that a deputy be sent to the Alexander barracks where the Naumburgers were quartered; the troops had got out of hand and the worst was to be feared if they were not enlightened. The Social Democratic Reichstag deputy, Otto Wels, hurried to the barracks, accompanied by a Rhinelandish party comrade of his, Heinrich Schäfer. The commander of the troops, an old major, told the two that the soldiers intended to go into the streets and fight against the revolution. He added that they might try to kill Wels if he tried to address them. But Wels said he was not afraid. A military vehicle was turned over on the parade ground, and he mounted it. At first, the soldiers refused to listen to him and threatened to kill him if he did not go. He persisted, and made them listen. Wels was a convincing though by no means outstanding orator, quite untheatrical. When he finished, the troops declared that they would not only refrain from fighting against the revolution but would join it. Proudly, Wels marched to the Reichstag at the head of the Naum-

armbands that matched those of the brownshirts, were often to be seen in Nazi parades in the streets of German cities. When his hopes had reached their zenith, before the Nazi invasion of Russia, his *Führer* put him a concentration camp.

burg Rifles. The other regiments in the capital declared themselves for the revolution, too. Wels was made commandant of Berlin, the highest local military authority.

By noon the inner city was packed with people who clamoured for abdication, armistice and peace. There were a few clashes but no real fighting. Fifteen of the revolutionaries were killed, one woman among them. A few more victims, but less than fifteen, fell on the other side. In this respect the events of the day were almost another Glorious Revolution.

Shortly after noon leaflets were distributed; the Kaiser had abdicated, the Socialist Republic had been proclaimed, a socialistic government had been formed. It would immediately sign the enemy's conditions for an armistice.

'The bankruptcy of the State and the helplessness of the bourgeois society became clearly evident. Workers' and soldiers' councils took over the government with such ease that it seemed the most natural thing in the world, and as if it were a mere trifle to dissolve the State order in the country of Frederick the Great and Bismarck in the moment of the gravest crisis through which Germany had gone in centuries.'

The Revolution was victorious. The war was ended. What was going to happen?

III. SOCIALISTS

At one of the last cabinet meetings of the old régime Ludendorff was present. He suggested, 'Get hold of the people. Work them up. Can't Ebert manage this?'

Friedrich Ebert was chairman of the Social Democratic *Fraktion*, that is to say, the parliamentary section of the Social Democratic Party. When war broke out in August 1914 the Reichstag had 397 members. The last election had been held in 1912. The electoral districts were established by the Electoral Law of 1873 on the basis of delineations made in 1869. Since then, the urban population had grown enormously in relation to the rural population, but the electoral districts were not adjusted. Thus it happened that Berlin, which sent five Social Democrats to the Reichstag in 1912, had six members for four million people. But in eastern Germany, the Junker land *par excellence*, there were districts where fewer than 10,000 people elected a representative. The Social Democrats, moreover, would not have obtained as many seats as they did had it not been for their electoral alliances sometimes with Catholics and sometimes with the Progressive Liberals in many constituencies.

The Social Democrats were the largest *Fraktion* with 110 deputies. The Social Democratic Party had a million members. Its press had a million and a half subscribers. The 'Free Trade Unions', so closely connected with the party that they were often called Social Democratic trade unions, had $2\frac{1}{2}$ million members. And then there was a mighty organization of co-operative societies and cultural and other associations that, too, were closely connected with the party.

The Reichstag of 1912 comprised, further, 87 Liberals, 91 Catholics (Centre Party), 18 Poles, 9 Alsatians, and 57 Conservatives. The rest was made up of various small parties, none of them to the left of the Social Democrats.

The Reichstag was elected by the male vote of Germans of 25 or more years of age. In 1912, the number of those entitled to vote was 14·4 millions out of a population of over 65 millions. Almost 85 per cent of the voters went to the polls. Close on 35 per cent of the vote was cast for the Social Democrats. Thus they would have had 138 members had the vote been direct. Other parties would have had correspondingly fewer members. The Conservatives, for instance, gained 12 per cent of the vote but 14 per cent of the members.

2

The first German workers' party was founded by Ferdinand Lassalle in 1863. Six years later, a second workers' party was established by Wilhelm Liebknecht and August Bebel. When 22 years old, Liebknecht had proclaimed the Republic in Baden, the country of Prince Max, during the ill-fated revolution of 1848. The failure of this revolution and the subsequent reaction forced him to flee. For the next thirteen years he lived in London in close contact with Karl Marx.

Another six years later, in 1875, the two workers' parties held a combined meeting at Gotha. They merged to form the Social Democratic Party of Germany. Its programme was a compromise between Marxian and Lassallean ideas. But the Party Congress at Erfurt, in 1891, adopted a new programme. It was entirely Marxian, that is, revolutionary socialist. Its chief author was Karl Kautsky. Nominally, it remained in force until after the revolution of 1918. The Erfurt Programme is one of the most famous documents in the history of socialism. Some knowledge of it is necessary to understand the events of the Revolution of 1918. The following points comprise its essence.

Private ownership of the instruments of production formerly secured to the producer his own product. But it had become the means of expropriating peasant proprietors, manual workers, and small traders. It had become the means of putting the non-workers (capitalists and large landowners) in possession of the product of the workers. Private ownership of the means of production had grown incompatible with their rational use and their full development. It was the aim of the working class, politically represented by the Social Democratic Party, to establish a society without any kind of exploitation whether it be exercised against a class, a party, a sex, a race, or a creed. For this purpose it was necessary to abolish all classes. And as classes were determined by the relation of people to the instruments of production it was necessary to transfer the instruments of production from private ownership to social ownership. This 'social transformation means the liberation not only of the proletariat but of all mankind; for all mankind suffers from present-day conditions'. Then came the following sentences that are especially important for the understanding of the revolution of 1918: 'The struggle of the working class against capitalistic exploitation is of necessity a political struggle. . . . It [the working class] cannot bring about the transfer of the instruments of production to social ownership *without having first come into possession of the political power*' (my italics).

The interpretation which Ebert and his friends gave to the last sentence had a great deal to do with the maintenance of the militaristic substance of the German State in November 1918. This interpretation held (consciously or unconsciously) that the immediate goal of Social Democracy was political democracy in the capitalist State while its next goal was political power, achieved by the processes of democracy, as a precondition for reaching the ultimate goal, namely, the social revolution that would establish socialism. In other words, political power was expected to come to Social Democracy as the culmination of democratic political evolution, not by political revolution. But this last was what happened in Germany in 1918. Therefore the conclusion was drawn that political democratic evolution had not run its full course and that, consequently, Germany was not yet ripe for Social Democrats to hold the political power, let alone for social revolution and socialism.[1] All this will become evident from the actions of the Social Democratic leaders as our narrative proceeds. Beyond referring occasionally to what has been discussed here we shall not find it necessary to return to Social Democratic theory and its interpretation. But one other theoretical point must be mentioned for the understanding of those events.

In 1900 another *émigré*, Eduard Bernstein, returned to Germany to become an important leader of the Social Democrats. He too had spent many years of exile in London, but unlike Wilhelm Liebknecht he did not fall under the influence of Karl Marx (who died in 1883). Instead, he imbibed the ideas propagated by a society founded in England in 1884, the Fabian Society. Bernstein held that socialism could be achieved by transferring the instruments of production to social ownership in a gradual process of social reform, and that political power, though not to be despised, was not a precondition of this transfer.

The social Democratic Party at first rejected Bernstein's ideas that were called Reformism (or Revisionism). It retained the Erfurt Programme. However, Reformism infiltrated deep into the Party's leadership and through the leadership into the ranks. This development was accompanied by violent convulsions of the Party which were clearly visible at the annual Party congresses. Among the many questions debated again and again at these congresses was the important problem of the mass strike. At the Congress at Jena, in 1905, Bebel moved that the mass strike be officially included in the list of political weapons to be used by the Party. The motion was carried. In the following year, at the Congress at Mannheim, Bebel declared himself against the mass strike, but he agreed to a motion that confirmed the resolution of Jena. At the 1911 Congress, however, again at Jena, Bebel de-

---

[1] This point was bluntly stated by Albert Grzesinski in his memoirs (see Bibliography, p. 283) which show a greater understanding of and greater regret for what happened in November 1918 than the memoirs of any other Social Democrat who took a leading part in those events.

clared that 'the mass strike or a military strike to prevent a war was madness'. This Congress of 1911 stood under the shadow of the approaching elections of 1912, and Bebel wanted to attract large numbers of sympathizers who were not radical. The Congress of 1915, also at Jena, concluded sadly that 'the masses did not show the least inclination to embark on a mass strike in order to gain universal suffrage for Prussia' (p. 120). At this Congress, Bernstein's Reformism won a complete victory.

There were then three groups in the Social Democratic Party whose viewpoints were as day and night. The Reformists, who were generally called 'opportunists', were under the leadership of Bernstein. They were the right wing of the party. The revolutionary socialists (Marxists) were under the intellectual leadership of Kautsky, the main author of the Erfurt Programme, and the political leadership of Karl Liebknecht, son of the Party's cofounder Wilhelm Liebknecht. The son was the most popular German workers' leader of his time. His group was the left wing of the Party. And then there were the 'centrists' who vacillated between Marx and Bernstein. Their head was Hugo Haase, chairman of the whole *Fraktion*. Friedrich Ebert, a Reformist, was second in command. He was equalled in importance in the Party by Philipp Scheidemann and Otto Landsberg, both of them 'opportunists' too. These three men formed the first government of the Republic after the Revolution of 1918. We shall hear a great deal of them.

3

Political parties, party programmes, interpretations of such programmes, political, economic, and social trends, events, and conditions: all of them are the work of men. They cannot be explained without reference to the psychological make-up of the men behind them, particularly the men who are leaders.

Speaking of socialism it is well known that Karl Marx held that the 'liberation of the working class' could only be the work of that class itself. Although he and his lifelong friend and collaborator,

Friedrich Engels (and also many outstanding Marxians of later days, notably Lenin), were of bourgeois origin, they regarded bourgeois intellectuals as a curse of the labour movement, and all intellectuals are bourgeois to Marxism.

The Reichstag of 1912 contained a mere three working men, only one of whom belonged to the Social Democratic *Fraktion*. Of course, there were in this *Fraktion* a great number of former workers, such as Ebert and Scheidemann for instance; but they had long since become intellectuals, usually editors and professional politicians. And there were among the Social Democratic deputies many who had never been anything but bourgeois. Some of them were lawyers, such as Karl Liebknecht, Haase and Landsberg.

It is interesting to note that Müller-Fulda indulged in the same wholesale condemnation of intellectuals as many Marxists (p. 4). But it may safely be said that the experience of the Imperial Reichstag, especially between 1900 and 1918, shows that there was little to choose (with regard to socialists and from the socialists' own viewpoint) between leaders who had always been intellectuals and those who were of working class origin and had become intellectuals. On balance there is perhaps justification for holding that the 'native' intellectuals were less of a curse to the German Social Democrats than the upstart intellectuals.

The Social Democratic Party Congress at Dresden in 1903 debated the question whether or not the Party should demand the post of a deputy speaker in the Reichstag. Bernstein moved, Bebel opposed. This, of course, was a Reformist demand; Socialist parties at that time rejected participation in bourgeois governments and office in bourgeois parliaments. It was typical of the confusion among the Social Democrats already at that early date that this Reformist motion was carried but that the Congress resolved simultaneously that it 'most decidedly condemned Reformist tendencies'. In order to be entitled to the post of a deputy speaker the Social Democrats naturally would have to be a major party in the Reichstag. Now, the elections of 1912 returned them not only as a major party but as the largest party, and this entitled them according to the tradition of the House not only to a vice-presidency (the speaker of the Reichstag was called president) but to the presidency itself. Of course, it was unthinkable that this key post should be given to the Social Democrats in the Imperial German Reichstag. After hectic wrangling that lasted four weeks the Social Democrats were kept out of any presidential post whatever. But during this period Scheidemann (p. 21) was a deputy speaker. Another member of that Reichstag wrote later in his memoirs: 'During four weeks we saw Scheidemann occupy the presidential chair of the Reichstag for an hour or two at each sitting. His glory was ephemeral, but one cannot eat the pleasant fruit of fame with impunity. After his short acquaintance with honours this former compositor was to retain a taste for high rank and influential relations. Whosoever has not heard him say, with a rising gorge, "I call upon His Excellency, the Chancellor of the Empire, to speak", cannot penetrate the mystery of the soul of an upstart.'

Bebel (p. 18) grew eccentric through the political influence he wielded. When Scheidemann was elected a deputy speaker Bebel was much concerned about the new dignitary's having a frock coat. This Bebel of 1912 was the same, yet not the same, as the Bebel of 1903 who had opposed the motion that Social Democrats accept public office. For himself, he accepted a decoration from the King of Prussia, the last Kaiser, not long before his death in 1913.

Ludwig Frank, a brilliant young man, Reichstag deputy for a constituency in Baden, bade fair to become a leader of the Social Democrats. He was received at the court of the Grand-Duke and struck up an intimate friendship with Prince Max.[1]

Beginning in 1904, some Social Democratic *Fraktions* in various southern German State legislatures voted for the budgets of their respective governments, in clear violation of resolutions of Social Democratic Reich congresses, in order to obtain concessions in various fields. In Bavaria, the Social Democratic *Fraktion* of the Diet went to the heretical length of voting for the civil list of the

[1] Frank was killed in action shortly after the outbreak of war in 1914.

reigning house. (The civil list was the income of a monarch and certain members of his family out of public funds. Incidentally, the Kaiser had no civil list as Emperor, but he had a substantial one as King of Prussia.)

The Reichstag followed the custom of having the speaker call for three cheers for the Kaiser at the end of each legislature. The Social Democrats used to remain seated on these occasions. But then, in order to escape the vilifications of the Right, they took to leaving the chamber before the event. In 1911, however, a number of Social Democratic deputies stayed and rose for the cheers.

After all, these leaders and minor parliamentarians were human beings and Germans and, as Müller-Fulda put it, greedy for honours and distinctions. The prospect of gaining them in and through a revolution must have appeared bleak to many of them, seeing that they could not interest the masses of their followers in such a fundamental undertaking as the reform of the feudal Prussian suffrage. Conditions in this respect had changed little in the sixty years preceding the First World War, since the time when Lassalle (p. 18) said that while one could discuss with the English worker how to improve his situation he had to persuade the German worker that his situation was depressed by the privileges of other classes. Of course, if these leaders despaired of the masses it was also true that the masses despaired of these leaders. However, many of the latter remained revolutionary, and among them there were workers and intellectuals just as there were workers and intellectuals among those of them who became Reformists.

The psychological make-up of these men naturally influenced their intellectual attitude towards their programme. Scheidemann may again serve as an example. When, in 1917, a provincial politician approached him with the suggestion that he 'should personally make a bold move, throw out the government, and take command', and 'that he did not know how great his influence was among the middle classes', he blustered: 'I would stick at nothing if I were convinced that I was doing something to stop the war and end the misery of our people.' But he added cautiously that he had no such conviction. The connexion between the auto-suggested timidity of these men and their political views was always striking. This timidity was most unblushingly expressed by the same Scheidemann when, a few days before 9 November 1918, he had a conversation with Count Bernstorff, the former German ambassador in the United States, who was then a confidant of Prince Max. The Count relates: 'He was as anxious as I to prevent the revolution, but at the same time he laid great stress on the fact that his party was not yet capable of governing and must first learn to do so.' Generously, the Count adds: 'In this regard he was only too right, though that incapacity was more of a national failing than the infirmity of a party.' The Count overlooked the fact that the national failing he had in mind was bad government, whereas Scheidemann seemingly was afraid, not of governing badly, but of governing altogether. In reality Scheidemann was nothing of the kind. But that he said he was, and that he said so to the Count, was revealing. His words indicated the secret admiration he and his like had for Germany's then ruling and governing groups. He wanted to govern. But he did not want to become a cabinet minister in a government of his peers. It was obvious to him that he would be called upon to govern within a few days, there was only his party that could take over, unless it were the Spartacists (for whom see pp. 52 ff.), and he wanted to take over as a Secretary of State to His Imperial Majesty, the Emperor (not, however, Wilhelm II against whom he, like most Social Democratic leaders, had many personal grudges). When he cringed before a Count he intimated that he wanted to learn the art of governing under the counts. And when this miserable pettiness, this boundless ambition, this toadying self-degradation was translated into programmatic language it said grandiloquently that political democratic evolution had not run its full course and that, consequently, Germany was not yet ripe for the Social Democrats to hold the political power in a republic (p. 19).

4

Divided against itself on fundamental principles and by conflicting personal ambitions, the Social Democratic Party was not capable of any consistent political action. Its imposing organization concealed its weakness, however, and party discipline prevented an open split for a long time. But an open split was bound to come. It came in 1917 when a number of Social Democratic members of the Reichstag formed the Independent Social Democratic Party (p. 47). Haase became chairman of the Independents. Ebert succeeded him as chairman of the Social Democratic *Fraktion* which from then on was usually called the Majority *Fraktion* just as the party it represented was simply called the Majority Party.

On 9 November 1918 Prince Max of Baden handed over his office of Chancellor to Ebert. Through Ebert the Majority Party 'came into possession of the political power'.

What did they do with it?

IV. COLLUSION

When the powers that be decided upon responsible government on 30 September 1918 (p. 2), a Reichstag majority could have been found without the Social Democrats. But such a majority would have had to include the Conservatives, and the Conservatives were impossible; they would not even then renounce annexations, and Prince Max would have no annexationists. Moreover, the Social Democrats would not work with the Conservatives, and Prince Max would not work without the Social Democrats; he felt sure that without them a 'summons to national defence would not awaken an echo among the masses'. It did not help the Conservatives that they suddenly informed the Prince of their willingness to abandon their annexationist plank in order to be taken into the government. They were left out, and consoled themselves by declaring that it would make a disastrous impression at home and abroad if they renounced annexations in order to be taken into the government.

The eighty-seven Liberals in the Reichstag were divided into two parties, the National Liberals and the Progressive People's Party. The former were right of Centre, the latter left of Centre. The National Liberals had forty-five members. Their leader was Gustav Stresemann. Flatteringly, Prince Max informed Stresemann that he needed him in the Opposition. In fact, however, he rejected him because Stresemann too had been quite insane in his demand for annexations throughout the war. It helped Stresemann as little as the Conservatives that he forswore his annexationism in the twinkling of an eye in order to be taken into the cabinet. But he was wise enough to keep his new conviction during the next five weeks, the last five weeks of the Empire that

27

was dear to him. And later on, of course, he became a champion of world understanding.

It was necessary then to induce the Majority Social Democrats to participate in the government. There is irony in the thought that if the Prince had been consistent in his exclusion of former annexationists he could not have accepted the Social Democrats either. To be sure, there is no record of any annexationist utterance by Ebert. But Ebert was discreet and subtle; he allowed himself to be 'interpreted' by the Social Democratic Press. And this Press interpreted him as holding the view that while the annexation of people was objectionable there was nothing to be said against the annexation of territory. Scheidemann was less cautious. He made at least one utterance that was ambiguous in form but decidedly annexationist if considered in connexion with the circumstances in which it was made. Landsberg went on record with outright annexationist demands in the early part of the war. However, the Prince had to forgive the Social Democratic leaders their annexationist lapses in order to be able to form a government. Perhaps he had a premonition that a week later they would have to forgive him his letter to his cousin Hohenlohe (p. 6).

2

On 2 October 1918, the Social Democratic *Fraktion* held a meeting to discuss the question of their going into the cabinet. Ebert did not state his views in this discussion, but Scheidemann urgently warned his colleagues not to join a 'bankrupt concern': the masses would desert them if they did. The *Fraktion* held another meeting the next day. This time Ebert insisted on participation. The vote went in his favour. Scheidemann was chosen to represent the Party in the inner war cabinet.

Prince Max formed his government of Progressives, National Liberals, Catholics (Centre), and Social Democrats. The latter were represented, apart from Scheidemann, by Eduard David (Secretary of State without Portfolio, like Scheidemann), Gustav Bauer who took the newly created post of Minister of Labour, and two under-secretaries. The Progressive People's Party was represented, among others, by Friedrich von Payer who remained Vice-Chancellor. He had held this office since the Prince's predecessor, Count Hertling, became Chancellor in 1917. Its functions were not defined, and depended on the ability of its incumbent. Payer made as much of it as any man could have made. The Centre was represented, among others, by Matthias Erzberger. Payer and Erzberger were among the most capable parliamentarians in the history of the German Empire. They towered above their colleagues.

The inner war Cabinet consisted, apart from the Prince of course, of Erzberger, Scheidemann, Groeber, and Friedberg. Adolf Groeber, the chairman of the Centre *Fraktion*, was as staunch a believer in political authority as Erzberger, the Centre's *enfant terrible*, was a disrespecter of tradition. However, Groeber always opposed the Conservatives.[1] Robert Friedberg was the representative of the National Liberals, Stresemann's party. He had never held any post in the Reich; his entire career was in Prussian politics, where he rose to high office. It was probably due to this fact that he remained insignificant in Prince Max's cabinet.[2]

Ebert was the shrewdest political tactician of Germany in his day, as shrewd a tactician as Payer and Erzberger were solid parliamentarians—though the latter's shrewdness, but not, unhappily, his personal integrity, left nothing to be desired either. To swing a great party into a measure that was distasteful to the majority of its rank and file, and to have the most vigorous opponent of this measure, Scheidemann, chosen to carry it out, was indeed a remarkable achievement. If things went wrong, Scheidemann would be the scapegoat. If things went right, Ebert was still the

[1] Groeber died in 1919 aged 66.
[2] Friedberg was at first on the right wing of his Party. But during the war he became an advocate of universal suffrage for Prussia and was therefore regarded as a traitor by his friends. After the war, he joined the Democrats and led their *Fraktion* in the Prussian Diet. He died in 1920 aged 69.

leader of the Party and as such entitled to the greater honours that
would follow. Ebert declared later that he would have joined the
government of Prince Max if the *Fraktion* had asked him to join.
But he did not explain why he was not asked and Scheidemann
was.

Prince Max wrote home: '...The Conservatives speak quite
openly of abdication. Thank God, I have allies in the Social
Democrats...with whose help I hope to save the Kaiser.' But a
few weeks later things looked different to him. Towards the end
of October, Ebert told the Prince that he was a convinced republican, and 'not only in theory', but that he would put up with a
'monarchy on a parliamentary basis with a social-reformist tinge'.
Yet when he spoke in the Reichstag in the great debate on the
armistice demand he expressed his utter dissatisfaction with the
parliamentary reforms that had been accomplished so far. Sadly,
Prince Max recorded in his diary that Ebert obviously wanted to
play before the masses the part of the pushing labour leader. But
the Prince's disappointment was not without relief; 'Ebert struck
the patriotic note that comes naturally to him.'

Scheidemann, too, had 'republican leanings'. Yet like Ebert
and the Conservatives he repeatedly told the Prince that the Kaiser
must be enlightened; abdication was necessary if the monarchy
were to be saved. When the Prince asked Scheidemann outright
what the people would say if the enemy demanded abdication he
received the reply: 'If the question were put: war or desertion of
the Hohenzollerns, the people would be for peace, even at this
price. But I shall take up my stand for rejection; then success will
be possible.' This was the same Scheidemann who ridiculed the
Liberal and Catholic members of the cabinet for suggesting that
he should force his will upon his followers; they had such silly
notions of what the leaders of the masses could do; the Social
Democrats were a democratic Party.

But those other gentlemen in the cabinet were not silly; they
were merely ignorant of the mood of the masses. Intelligent
enough to realize their own ignorance, they relied on their Social

Democratic colleagues for information. The Social Democrats knew the mood of the masses very well, but they did not like it; the masses were deserting them for joining an Imperial cabinet. And their leaders including Scheidemann tried to do the very thing Scheidemann called silly when others asked them to do it; they tried to swing the masses back to the Party without removing the cause for which the masses were swinging away from it. Prince Max, and through him the non-Social Democratic rest of the cabinet, came to recognize that the Majority leaders had a false idea of their power over their followers. On 31 October 1918, the cabinet held a meeting. The Social Democratic members (so parliamentary was the government) were not invited. The meeting agreed that the masses would return to the Social Democrats if the latter withdrew their members from the government. The Social Democrats did not withdraw their members.

But their leaders had to do something; complete desertion by their followers in Berlin was in sight. And Berlin was everybody's key to everything at that time. Scheidemann was obsessed by the fear of Bolshevism. The masses were deserting the Party, he reasoned, not because they wanted peace, the Republic, and socialism (to want which he and his co-leaders had trained them for decades) but because they were being misled by Bolshevist propaganda that emanated from the Russian embassy in Berlin. This was certainly true, but that the masses of the people wanted peace only because of that propaganda was not true. Anyway, Scheidemann suggested that one of the Russian embassy's mail cases be made to go to pieces 'accidentally' at a railroad station. Accordingly, a case was said to have gone to pieces and to have been found to contain insurrectionary propaganda material. On the evening of that day, 4 November 1918, a cabinet meeting decided to expel the Russian ambassador, Joffe, and his staff.

Scheidemann had a competitor in the affair of the mail case. Lieutenant-Colonel Alfred Niemann, Liaison Officer between the Kaiser and the General Staff, was constantly around the Emperor in those days. He relates in his memoirs that the suggestion to drop the case was made by His Majesty. And there was a third competitor. Major von Roeder was Chief of the Counter-Espionage Department of the General Staff during the war. He said later that the case was dropped upon his initiative. To introduce some variety into this friendly controversy of three minds that were thinking alike, Roeder named a different railroad station in Berlin from that named by Scheidemann and Niemann.

But the masses of the followers, mostly workers, did not return to the Social Democrats upon the drop of a box. They grew more and more angry, their mood more and more ugly. The trade union leaders and functionaries were tireless in their efforts to restrain the workers of Berlin. Almost the entire Reich outside of Berlin had gone revolutionary. But the course of events in the capital was not yet clear. The unionists never left the factories, ceaselessly harangued the workers, shouted in the din of the machines. The workers shouted back, called them funks, black-legs, traitors. General strike was in the air.

3

Twenty-six mass meetings had been arranged in Berlin for the evening of 7 November (p. 72). Scheidemann calculated that these meetings would give the Social Democrats a chance to bring the workers to their senses—that is, bring them back to the Party, perhaps. On the other hand, if the workers could not be brought to their senses, if they enforced abdication through a general strike, social revolution would be the consequence and the Social Democrats would be in a hopeless situation. It was a difficult dilemma. Suddenly Scheidemann was informed that the military authorities had forbidden the meetings. This gave him an idea. The Social Democrats would demand that the ban on the meetings be lifted. At the same time they would put an ultimatum to Prince Max: If the Kaiser refused to abdicate within twenty-four hours the Social Democrats would resign from the government. The ultimatum would be read out at the twenty-six meetings. The workers would see that the Social Democrats were putting themselves at the head of the revolution. They would return to the Social Democrats.

Without informing Ebert in advance Scheidemann put his idea before the *Fraktion* which was in almost constant session in its rooms in the Reichstag building. Ebert was present. The proposal was adopted without dissension. The ultimatum was telephoned to the Prince in the late afternoon of 7 November. Ebert looked subdued. He took Scheidemann aside and told him that he had seen the Prince early that morning. He had told the Prince that the Kaiser must go; the Prince must make him go. In this case the abdication would be voluntary, not enforced by the workers, and the monarchy saved. If the Prince succeeded with the Kaiser, Ebert would try to bring the masses round to the government. This was what Ebert told Scheidemann about the pact he had made with the Chancellor. But now, he added, he had come to realize that Scheidemann was right; it was too late for voluntary abdication, the Republic was inevitable. But Scheidemann's idea was good, it would forestall Bolshevism.

Ebert did not tell Scheidemann, or anyone else at that time, all that had passed at his *tête-à-tête* with the Prince. The Prince asked: 'If I succeed in convincing the Kaiser, can I count on your support in fighting the social revolution?' Ebert replied: 'Unless the Kaiser abdicates social revolution is inevitable. But I will have none of it. I hate it like sin.'

Whether or not Ebert intended to tell Scheidemann of the pact he had made with the Prince is conjecture. But whatever his intentions were, Scheidemann unwittingly forced his hand. Ebert knew that the Prince had informed the cabinet of the pact (that is, excluding the Social Democratic cabinet members). The cabinet, too, might not have told Scheidemann, but in view of the ultimatum they were sure to tell him, sure to accuse Ebert of double-dealing (in fact, they accused him of reaching out his hand for the leadership of the State). Therefore Ebert had to inform Scheidemann.

Scheidemann left the session of the *Fraktion* and went across to

Wilhelmstrasse to join a meeting of the cabinet. There he was informed that Prince Max had telegraphed to the Kaiser, in consequence of the ultimatum, asking for leave to resign. Scheidemann had not expected this. He was crushed; social revolution was certain if the country were without a government at this moment and he, too, hated social revolution although he, like Ebert, constantly proclaimed that he was serving it. He went to the telephone, came back, said he had been talking to Ebert who told him that the ultimatum had been spread by broadsheet among the masses and was having an extraordinary effect in calming the workers (actually, few workers took it seriously). Scheidemann begged: 'I am exceedingly sorry the Chancellor has taken this step. We arrived at our decision [the ultimatum] after mature consideration.' Another cabinet member asked him indignantly: 'If you were going in for abrupt action of this kind, why did you not tell us so?' Scheidemann replied: 'That was simply due to want of time.... The pace of events has been overwhelming.' Everybody was too excited to notice the contradiction between want of time and mature consideration. Scheidemann continued: 'Your step [the Prince's resignation] has been decided on in five minutes.' In reality, several hours had passed. 'You, gentlemen, must admit that we have done everything we could to keep the masses in hand.... The government need not break up if only the Chancellor remains.' Scheidemann begged. Payer, the Vice-Chancellor, roared at him: 'You can't behave like this among decent people.'

Prince Max did not change his mind about his resignation. He felt bitterly hurt; he had trusted so unreservedly in the Social Democrats. Ebert, implored by the non-Social Democratic members of the cabinet to withdraw the ultimatum, did not change his mind either; the ultimatum remained in force. The ban on the meetings, too, remained in force, by accident. The cabinet had been discussing it when Scheidemann appeared about the ultimatum, and afterwards everyone forgot about it. Night fell on the seventh of November.

The ultimatum expired at noon on 8 November. The Kaiser telephoned from Spa that he would consider abdication after the armistice was concluded. He knew the opinion of the majority of the cabinet that the enemy would not grant the armistice unless and until he abdicated. The telegram also requested the Prince to stay in office for the time being.

The Social Democratic *Fraktion* passed a resolution: 'The *Fraktion* has taken note of the Chancellor's statement that he has communicated its ultimatum to the Kaiser. In order not to jeopardize the armistice negotiations the *Fraktion* does not desire the resignation of the Chancellor; nor would it approve the withdrawal of its members from the government unless and until the armistice is a fact.' The resolution did not mention abdication. But it forbade Scheidemann to resign; he had said he would. *Finis ultimati*. What did Müller-Fulda say? 'We set up a noisy opposition only in order to obtain privileges.' The privilege the Social Democrats sought to obtain in this case was the continued existence and the leadership of the old State that was threatened with disaster from its own incompetence.

4

The Prince had for some time past frantically negotiated with General Headquarters for troops to quell the impending revolution. There were, broadly speaking, three kinds of troops in Germany: those on active service at the front, the reserves at home and behind the front, and the *ersatz* troops at home. The *ersatz* troops consisted largely of men above front-line age and of others of low medical categories. They were, as a body, of no military value, but they substituted for regular troops because somebody had to be kept under arms in the barracks at home to represent the authority of the State. Hardly any reserves were left in the country by November 1918, and it was evident that the *ersatz* troops were useless, for political as well as physical reasons, if it came to putting down disorders.

Since the end of 1917 the War Ministry too had urged Supreme

Command to hold front-line troops in readiness for use at home in case of unrest, but Supreme Command needed every available unit at the front. When the situation appeared grave, however, Supreme Command informed the War ministry, on 2 November 1918, that an especially reliable infantry division was being pulled out of the front line to be sent to a place near Berlin. The War Ministry was not satisfied with one division, and Supreme Command prepared a second. When the troops arrived on the Rhine, the Revolution had just broken out there. The transports were stopped to reestablish order, but the soldiers joined the revolutionaries as soon as they were out of the trains. A few trains, however, could not be stopped in time and reached the interior of Germany. Prince Max took new hope. It was short-lived. On the evening of 8 November the War Minister, General von Scheüch, informed him that a mere three battalions of Naumburg Rifles were all the military force at his disposal, and this force which was just marching into Berlin from other quarters (p. 14) was utterly inadequate.

On the previous day, the City Council of Berlin had instructed the Lord Mayor, Wermuth, to get in touch with the War Ministry. The idea was to create a *Bürgerwehr* (citizen's guard) after the model of a force in the 1848 revolution. The Prussian cities had no police authority, not even in emergencies. The fact that this authority was vested in the Prussian State caused one of the bloodiest episodes of the Revolution of 1918, as we shall see (p. 197). Wermuth called on the deputy of the War Minister, Colonel von Wrisberg. The Colonel said that a motley crowd of citizens could not cope with a well-prepared insurrection and would only hamper the military. He added: 'We shall easily stamp out the little fires that have flared up in the Reich if we succeed in holding Berlin, and Berlin will be held, you may rely on that. The local troops are loyal, and new transports of other reliable troops are constantly arriving from outside.'

The Prince did not believe it. He turned once more to the Social Democrats, suggesting that a deputation of cabinet ministers be sent to General Headquarters to speak with absolute frankness to the Kaiser. Would the Social Democrats keep the masses quiet until then?

Landsberg (p. 21) declared: 'We have no intention of proclaiming a republic, because though republicans we are also democrats, and will not force the will of a minority upon the majority.' Scheidemann too was in favour of the ministers' journey; it appeared to him the only way out after his idea of the ultimatum had not worked. But Ebert surprisingly declared that the Party had called upon the workers to go into the streets unless abdication were announced in the early morning papers of tomorrow, 9 November. He kept to himself that he knew that the workers had already been called out for the next day by other forces of which we shall hear more as we proceed. Having been outmanoeuvred by Scheidemann yesterday, in the matter of the ultimatum, he retaliated with a vengeance today.

The ministers' journey was abandoned in view of Ebert's declaration. Despairingly the Prince went to the telephone to make another attempt at persuading the Kaiser without being too outspoken. He was told that His Imperial and Royal Majesty could not be disturbed; His Majesty had gone to bed.

On the front, fighting was going on, soldiers were being killed on both sides. In the factories of Berlin the workers were seething. In the building of *Vorwärts*, the Central Press organ of the Social Democratic Party, a meeting was taking place late on 8 November at which the Party leaders, against strong opposition, pledged their functionaries to prevent the outbreak of revolution. The Progressive Liberal, Haussmann, like Scheidemann a Secretary of State without Portfolio, did not know of that meeting, and while it was going on he recorded in his diary: 'Everything is in the hands of the Social Democrats. It depends on their decision whether or not the workers stay at home or go into the streets. Quite coldly we must at the close of this day ask ourselves whether Germany will be governed in the future with or without the bourgeois parties.'

Night fell on the eighth of November.

V. REPUBLIC

On the morning of 9 November Ebert had another *tête-à-tête* with the Chancellor-Prince. The first private meeting between the two (p. 33) was recorded by the Prince in his memoirs. The second meeting was never referred to in public or in writing by either of the two men concerned. The only account of it is to be found in a novel written by Ebert's personal friend and admirer, the Rev. Emil Felden who had his knowledge from Ebert himself.[1] But even if there were no such book, the events that followed tell the story clearly.

While this second *tête-à-tête* was taking place, Scheidemann sent in his resignation as Imperial Secretary of State.

At noon, Prince Max, unable to get any sense from General Headquarters and seeing that 'the street' would enforce abdication at any minute, issued a manifesto: 'The Kaiser and King has resolved to *renounce the throne*. The Chancellor remains in office until the problems that are necessarily connected with the Kaiser's abdication, with the Crown Prince's renunciation of the thrones of the German Empire and of Prussia, and with the setting up of a regency have been solved. He intends to propose to the Regent the appointment of Herr Ebert as Chancellor and the bringing in of a bill to enact that election writs will be immediately issued for a *German Constituent National Assembly* charged with settling finally the future constitution of the German people....'

This manifesto drew upon the Prince the accusation of high treason from those reactionaries who were not content merely to

---

[1] Felden's book was published after Ebert's death. Historians, politicians, and interested parties checked with him concerning the above story, and accepted his account.

retain the all-important substance of the militaristic German State (which substance was left intact in November 1918), but who wanted to retain, or regain, its monarchic form as well. They abused the Prince incessantly for his actions on that fateful day. He died in bitterness in 1929. It was a minor though befitting irony of history that the first copy of the manifesto accessible to the public appeared in a store window of the Conservative newspaper *Lokalanzeiger*, Unter den Linden.

When the manifesto became known, a deputation of Social Democrats headed by Ebert and Scheidemann went to the Chancellery. Ebert told the Prince: 'We have been instructed by our Party, for the preservation of peace and order to declare to the Imperial Chancellor that we regard it as indispensable...that the government be now entrusted to men who possess the full confidence of the people. We therefore consider it necessary that the Chancellorship...should be held by a representative of our Party.'

Scheidemann opened his mouth to say something. The Prince curtly reminded him of his position as Secretary of State; he thought it best to ignore Scheidemann's resignation at this moment. As a member of the government the man was under his control; without such responsibility he was dangerous, his fiery temper might carry him back to the revolutionary convictions he had forsworn years ago. Ebert, on the other hand, was dependable, the Prince knew it: he had seen him only that morning.

The Prince said to Ebert: 'I have already recommended to the Kaiser the introduction of a bill in the Reichstag, proposing the issue of writs of election to a German Constituent Assembly; this National Assembly shall then decide how Germany is to be governed in the future.'

Ebert said that he could agree to such a National Assembly in principle.

The words 'in principle' contained a lead. It was taken up by the Secretary of State, the Progressive Liberal Conrad Haussmann who said: 'Should the assembly be called at once, in the midst of the revolutionary movement, it would let loose a turbulent election campaign and give no true picture of the public mind.'

Ebert said he would consider. What Haussmann meant by an 'untrue picture' was that a Constituent Assembly called at once might well have a republican majority. But if the assembly were postponed until the people were sick of the necessarily chaotic aftermath of defeat in the war they would blame the chaos on the party in power, and they might even come to long for the retention of the monarchy, if the monarchy could be kept going until then, no matter how feebly. The party in power would be the Social Democrats. Thus, to postpone the assembly now seemed to insure the downfall of this party later on, unless the Social Democrats succeeded in entrenching themselves so firmly as to prevent reaction from raising its head. They could entrench themselves so firmly if they changed the substance of the State at least to the extent of uprooting militarism. How this was practical at the time without going to the full length of socialism is another question that will demand our attention in various places of this book. Here, we must point out that the Social Democrats never made any serious attempt at change at all because they professed to be democrats of the type that condemned any use of power as undemocratic. The reactionaries saw through this Social Democratic attitude. If, as they hoped, reaction should come to attract the majority of the nation, it could be stopped only by means that the Social Democrats held to be non-democratic; and the reactionaries relied on the Social Democrats not using such means even if to be formally democratic meant to kill democracy. This, then, was the problem and the prospect of the Social Democrats if the assembly were postponed. To repeat the main point: postponement of the assembly meant an attempt to ward off the republic.

On the other hand, if the Social Democratic Party did not come out vigorously for the Republic that day, 9 November 1918; if instead it came out for postponement, it might be wrecked right then, because the majority of its followers were beyond the shadow of a doubt in favour of the Republic. If Ebert, faced by this alternative, said he would consider, this could mean one thing only, namely, that he was prepared to see his party wrecked right then, if necessary, in order to save the monarchy. But with the impulsive Scheidemann at his elbow he could not say so; he had told him only two days earlier that the republic was inevitable (p. 33). Therefore, he would 'consider'. Yet both of them wanted to save the monarchy at heart; they had worked untiringly for many weeks past to save it. Truly, they had learned to look at each other without laughing.

2

In his manifesto the Prince had declared that election writs would be issued immediately. Speaking to the Social Democratic deputation he employed almost exactly the words of his manifesto, but he omitted the word 'immediately'. Like Ebert he wanted postponement. Like Ebert he did not dare to say what he wanted.

The cabinet retired to deliberate. Scheidemann was not asked to retire with them; his resignation suddenly became valid. The deliberations of the cabinet were as superfluous as the preceding discussion with the Social Democratic deputation; everything had been rehearsed at the matutinal *tête-à-tête* of the Prince and Ebert. The Prince told the cabinet that he had decided to hand over the Chancellorship to the leader of the Majority Party. Nobody protested against the unconstitutional enormity of this procedure. The Constitution said (responsible government or not) that the Chancellor was appointed and dismissed by the Kaiser. But the Prince's suggestion was the nearest thing to constitutionality in view of the fact that the Kaiser had been dismissed by the Chancellor; for, as we shall see, the Kaiser had not abdicated at all at the time as far as *he* was concerned. And the Prince who had proclaimed the abdication told the Social Democratic deputation that he had recommended the introduction of a bill (p. 39) to the Kaiser who no longer was Kaiser as far as the Prince was concerned.

The War Minister, General von Schcüch, arrived at the cabinet meeting. The cabinet turned to discussing the military situation in

Berlin. Scheüch reported that the majority of the troops would not shoot upon the masses. Should the rest shoot? He suggested that orders be issued to use fire-arms only to protect the lives and the property of citizens and of the government when directly threatened. Suddenly the inevitable Scheidemann rose to speak. Nobody knew how he had got in. Ignoring his own resignation for a change he declared that the new government did not need to be protected. Before the cabinet made up its mind, the military commander of Berlin, General von Linsingen, sent word that he had issued a general order against any shooting.

The Social Democratic deputation was called in once more. The Prince said: 'If anyone is able to save our Fatherland from disaster at this moment it is your Party. You have the widest organization and the greatest influence. Herr Ebert, take over the office of Chancellor.' Ebert and the Prince obviously had rehearsed this scene in the morning. Ebert looked at his colleagues in the deputation and said: 'I must first consult my Party.'

The unrehearsed Scheidemann broke in: 'Nonsense. Just say yes.' Ebert said: 'It is a hard task, but I am ready to take it on.'

Suddenly the equally unrehearsed Foreign Secretary Wilhelm Solf almost upset everything by asking: 'Are you prepared to carry on the government in accordance with the Constitution?'

'In accordance with the Constitution,' echoed Ebert.

'Even with the monarchical Constitution?' persevered Solf. (One wonders which constitution he meant in the first place.)

This was awkward. If Ebert said no, the Prince would reproach him for breaking the promise he had given in the morning, the promise to uphold the monarchic form of State. If he said yes, Scheidemann would explode, not because he wanted the Republic (which he did not), but because of his fear that Ebert was wrecking the Party. Ebert said: 'Yesterday I could have given an unconditional affirmative to this question. Today I must consult my friends first.' (Hundreds of thousands of workers were out in the streets, and away from them at that moment Ebert could not be sure which way things were going.)

The Prince looked up and said: 'We must now solve the question of the regency.'

Ebert said: 'It is too late for that.'

This reply was not rehearsed either. The Prince knew that Ebert wanted to save the monarchy. If the question of the monarchy was left open (as it was by Ebert's evasive reply about the constitution) the question of the regency must be logically left open, too; there could be no monarchy without at least a regent. Yet Ebert was closing the question of the regency. This meant that he was protecting himself in the eyes of both the monarchy and the Republic. The Prince understood, and said nothing. They were another pair that did not laugh.

Ebert and Scheidemann returned to the Reichstag to inform their *Fraktion* of what had passed. Then they went to the restaurant of the Reichstag and sat down to a bowl of watery soup. The *Fraktion* stayed behind in their rooms and began to negotiate with a high official of the ministry of the interior to 'regulate the setting-up of a regency'. Half an hour earlier Ebert had declared that it was too late for that.

A crowd of workers and soldiers, many of them armed, rushed into the restaurant. They demanded that Scheidemann speak to the crowd ouside. He refused. 'You must', they yelled. 'Liebknecht is already speaking from the balcony of the Palace.'

3

Karl Liebknecht, sentenced to four years' hard labour in 1916 (p. 54), had been released at the end of October 1918. He was released by Prince Max upon the insistence of Scheidemann and against the protests of the President of the Supreme Court-Martial and the War Minister. Scheidemann had insisted because he thought that Liebknecht was more dangerous in prison than out of it; he knew that the masses of the workers regarded Liebknecht in captivity as a martyr for peace and socialism. When the prisoner was released he went to Berlin. A huge crowd met him at the Potsdam station. The outstandingly intelligent yet over-impulsive Scheidemann exclaimed in the cabinet that day: 'Liebknecht has been carried shoulder-high by soldiers decorated with the Iron Cross. Who would have dreamed of such a thing happening three weeks ago?'

Liebknecht, then, was speaking from the balcony of the Palace, the historic balcony from which, in August 1914, the Kaiser had told a huge crowd that he knew no parties, only Germans. 'The man who can bring the "Bolshies" from the Palace to the Reichstag or the Social Democrats from the Reichstag to the Palace wins the day', thought Scheidemann according to his memoirs. He knew of course that there was no clear distinction along party lines between the masses at the Reichstag and those at the Palace, and that much depended, not on the masses, but on the speakers who addressed them. All of them were men and women who wanted peace, the Republic and socialism. They did not care who was to bring it to them, although they trusted Liebknecht and did not trust Scheidemann.

He went to a window. The multitude shouted: 'Hurrah, Scheidemann. Peace. Republic. Socialism...Silence.'

Scheidemann spoke. 'Workers and soldiers...the cursed war is at an end...the foes of an industrious people, the real foes in our midst who have caused Germany's downfall...the real foes in our midst are silent and invisible. They were the warriors who stayed at home and demanded annexations....The people has triumphed...Prince Max of Baden has handed over his office as Chancellor to Ebert. Our friend will form a worker's government...miracles have happened...stand united and loyal, and be conscious of your duty.' This was not enough. The man who brings the Bolshies here, away from Liebknecht—'Nothing must be done to dishonour the worker's movement. The old and rotten has broken down....Long live the new! Long live the German Republic!' Shouting. Roaring. Enthusiasm. 'Long live the German Republic!' People standing next to Scheidemann bawled into the restaurant: 'Scheidemann has proclaimed the Republic.'

Scheidemann turned, and went back to his table. Ebert rose, livid[1] with rage. 'Is it true?' he asked. Scheidemann began: 'I had to get the ——' Ebert tried to pounce upon Scheidemann; friends restrained him. He gasped: 'You had no right to proclaim the republic. What becomes of Germany, whether she becomes a republic or something else [*sic!*] must be decided by a constituent assembly.'

In its rooms, the *Fraktion* was still 'regulating the setting-up of the regency' with the high official of the Royal Ministry of the Interior.

Scheidemann has gone down to history as the man who proclaimed the German Republic. In later years, he declared that his shout of 'Long live the German Republic' was intended to be no more than a profession of faith in the principles of his party, just as one would shout, for instance, long live liberty. This is not the only error (if an error it was) that assisted history as a midwife in the birth of the German Republic. Scheidemann made his speech at 2 o'clock. Liebknecht spoke from the balcony of the Palace at 4 o'clock. The workers who urged Scheidemann to speak must have been misinformed themselves or deliberately misinformed him for fear there would be no republic if they did not lead their leaders (although, of course, they could not have known that Scheidemann would proclaim the Republic).

Ebert and Scheidemann went back to the Chancellery. Ebert declared that he would take the Independents into his government; they were dangerous in opposition.

He had a last *tête-à-tête* with the Prince, in the office where Ebert was now host and the Prince a visitor. Ebert said: 'I should like you to remain as Administrator of the Empire.' The republic had been proclaimed, yet even then he did not give up the monarchy for lost. An administrator was in principle the same as a

---

[1] It is immaterial to the historian, yet interesting with respect to the problem of witnesses' statements that some observers of this scene described Ebert as having been purple with rage. This writer, who was one of the witnesses of the scene, seems to remember a purple Ebert.

regent, the difference being that a regent was of the hitherto reigning dynasty, and an administrator was not.

The Prince replied: 'I know you are on the point of concluding an agreement with the Independents, and I cannot work with the Independents.' Down with the Fatherland, if it was to be governed by a party he did not like. At the door he turned back: 'Herr Ebert, I commit the German Empire to your care.'

Ebert said: 'I have lost two sons for this Empire.'

VI. INDEPENDENTS

Ninety-two of its one-hundred and ten members were present when, on 3 and 4 August 1914, the Social Democratic *Fraktion* deliberated its attitude toward credits to finance the conduct of the war. A minority of fourteen were against the credits, among them Liebknecht and Haase, but not a single member dared to oppose the majority of the *Fraktion* on the floor of the House. The *Fraktion* voted unanimously with the other parties, all of whom were, of course, to the right of it. Floor-leader Haase read a declaration to this effect into the record.

The dissenters inside and their followers outside the *Fraktion* held many meetings, secretly, after August 1914. In December of that year Liebknecht voted against further war credits in the Reichstag. He wanted to make a statement but was not recognized by the Speaker. In March 1915 he was joined by another member of the *Fraktion*, Otto Rühle. Rühle's vote was not, however, a revolutionary action, as was Liebknecht's; his rather petty reason was that the war credits on this occasion, otherwise than in August and December of 1914, were part of the budget; that former party congresses had resolved always to oppose the budget (p. 23); and that he felt himself bound by those resolutions. Thirty more Social Democrats left the chamber before the vote of March 1915 was taken. Thus, the opposition actually were thirty-two. A majority of them, however, disapproved of Liebknecht's and Rühle's action; they did not want to split the Party outwardly. Liebknecht's followers, on the other hand, demanded that those who had abstained from voting stand by their conviction and declare themselves against credits in the Reichstag. This discussion among the dissenters was not carried into the open, for the time being. They appeared united in their agitation among the workers.

This agitation was by no means revolutionary in the beginning; the opposition realized that a revolution had no chance of success then. They condemned the annexationist policy of the Reich government; they pointed out that the war was senseless and that no matter who won mankind would lose; they demanded a policy that would be acceptable to the enemies as a basis for peace.

The Party Executive and the Central Commission (that is, executive) of the Trade Unions furiously combated the dissenters. But the dissenters steadily gained ground among the masses of the workers, organized as well as unorganized workers. There was no difference between these two groups in their desire for peace.

In the Reichstag debate of 24 March 1916, Haase delivered a declaration on behalf of the opposition. Its gist was that the opposition remained even in war true to its principles of world peace and the emancipation of the proletariat. Haase's speech was accompanied by unprecedented scenes of tumult. Ebert was purple in the face and roared inarticulate threats. Scheidemann gesticulated and danced like a madman.

Vorwärts, the Central Press organ of the Party, published the declaration of the opposition. The Executive thereupon pushed aside the constitution of the Party and imposed a party censorship on *Vorwärts* in addition to the military censorship. This party censorship was extended to cover all of the important newspapers of the Social Democrats. It enabled the Majority Party to retouch the wrinkles, or rather cracks in its face, and it permitted the concealment of the discrepancy between the Party's professions and its policy.

Vorwärts was a daily newspaper published in Berlin. Its editorial staff happened to be composed of followers of the Party's anti-war group, but military censorship prevented them from coming out openly against the war. However, their attitude could be clearly read between the lines of the paper. Soon after the outbreak of war, the General Commission of the Trade Unions demanded that the Party Executive swing *Vorwärts* in line for the war. Negotiations took place between the Executive, the General

Commission, and the Press Commission of the Party. The editors refused to change their policy. They were supported by the Press Commission and opposed by the Executive and the General Commission. The opposition won, for the time being. *Vorwärts* remained anti-war, for the time being. The leading Social Democratic papers in most of the other cities, too, were anti-war. Moreover, *Vorwärts* was read all over Germany. But the Party and the *Fraktion* and the trade unions, as bodies, supported the war. The workers everywhere in Germany realized that a battle was being fought within the Party.

In January 1915, the chairman of the General Commission of the Trade Unions, Carl Legien, convened a congress of functionaries to protest against the policy of *Vorwärts* in particular, and of the opposition in general. Fifteen hundred delegates met in Berlin. They duly registered a protest. Legien told the delegates much about Germany's invincibility. Many of the things he told them were speedily proved untrue by events. Moreover, the assembled functionaries received an intimate picture of the size and scope of the opposition. They took this picture home, and it made the workers think. The opposition felt indebted to Legien.

After the Reichstag debate of 24 March 1916 (p. 48), the opposition formed the Social Democratic Working Association. The Association remained within the Party. Its leaders were Haase and Ledebour (p. 62). It had only some twelve members in the Reichstag, but its following among the masses was proportionately much greater as we shall see presently.

In October 1916 *Vorwärts* was suppressed by the military authorities. The Party Executive dismissed the entire editorial staff and gave abject assurances of good behaviour in the future to the military. These assurances went so far beyond the requirements of the official censorship that the military hesitated to accept them for fear they would be accused of violating the freedom of the Press. (The official censorship concerned only security, not opinions, unless opinions concerned security, such as, for instance, anti-war utterances.) Eventually, *Vorwärts* was allowed to appear again. It was 'in line'. The revolutionary workers, who were the majority of the workers in Berlin, never ceased to protest against this action of the Executive. They regarded it as a crime committed against them, a theft of their rightful property, the material assets of *Vorwärts*. This attitude led to great bloodshed in 1919 (p. 198).

In January 1917 the Social Democratic Working Association convened a Reich conference in Berlin. The subject of their debate was whether or not the opposition should split away from the Party. The conference rejected a split, but the Party Executive declared that the Association had put itself outside the fold by holding the meeting. In other words, the opposition was expelled. It constituted itself the Independent Social Democratic Party. The constituent meeting took place in Gotha on 9 April 1917. Gotha was the Thuringian place where, back in 1875, the Marxians and the Lassalleans met to constitute the unified Social Democratic Party of Germany (p. 18).

Haase became chairman of the Independents. The new party rapidly acquired a broad basis among the masses of the workers. But the vast majority of the masses were too unrevolutionary in their thinking to follow overnight a practical revolutionary-socialist programme. Therefore the Independents had to confine themselves to working towards a goal that did not require long and arduous theoretical explanations. The limited understanding of the masses was not the only reason that compelled the leaders to move cautiously. The leaders themselves were confused, and divided against each other. They were Haase, the 'centrist'; Kautsky, the former Marxist who had become a centrist too (in 1912); and Bernstein, the Reformist. All this constituted a great weakness in the ranks of the Independents. Nevertheless, from their inception to the end of the war they were the political representatives of the revolutionary workers. Their position as a recognized political party, however, made it impossible for them to carry out all the activities that were necessary for the reaching of their goal. Moreover, like everything that appeared suspicious to the military authorities they were thoroughly supervised.

That which they could not do themselves was done by two other organizations which had come into being earlier. One of them concentrated (without being exclusive in this respect) on the task of re-educating the broad masses of the workers in the theory of revolutionary socialism. This organization, the theorists, was the Spartacus League. It became, as a body, a section of the Independent Party but had no representatives in the Reichstag. The other organization, the Activists, undertook the task of organizing for mass actions. They were party members as individuals and formed the left wing of the Independents. Their leaders in the Reichstag, as Independent deputies, were Georg Ledebour, until then a 'centrist', and Ernst Däumig.

Thus, there were two workers' parties comprising five wings in Germany after the Independents split away from the Social Democratic Party. The Majority Party consisted of the 'rightists' and the 'centrists'. The Independents consisted of a right wing (the former left wing of the Social Democrats); a left wing, the Spartacists; and the Activists who were ideologically close to the Spartacists but tactically worlds apart from them, as we shall see. As for theory and tactics, each of these five groups claimed to be the sole rightful guardian of the Erfurt Programme.

VII. SPARTACISTS

An illegal leaflet was circulated in great numbers among the German workers early in December 1914. It began: 'The present war was not willed by any of the nations participating in it and is not waged for the interests of the German or any other people. It is an imperialist war, a war for capitalist control of the world market, for the political domination of vast territories in order to give scope to industrial and banking capital.'

This leaflet caused a great stir among the workers. Its effect was enhanced by its history. It was the statement that Karl Liebknecht had intended to make in the Reichstag in support of his vote against war credits (p. 47). But he had not been allowed to speak, nor had his declaration been written into the record. However, it was copied in longhand and circulated by hundreds of Berlin workers, and was finally printed. Beginning in January 1916 it was followed, at intervals of one to three weeks, by 'Political Letters' which likewise appeared clandestinely and illegally. Typed and mimeographed, they were distributed so efficiently that they were available in all parts of the Reich. They were collected afterwards and published under the name of 'Spartacus Letters'. Spartacus was a slave who organized a revolt of the slaves in Rome in 73–71 B.C. The demand for this underground publication grew to such proportions that the mimeographed letters could no longer satisfy it. In September 1916 they were complemented, and from December 1916 replaced, by a printed journal, *Spartakus*, which continued at irregular intervals until the outbreak of the revolution in November 1918.

In February 1915 Liebknecht was drafted into the army. He was sent from unit to unit, staying everywhere for a short time only because he made the soldiers revolutionary wherever he appeared. Instead of leaving him where he was, every unit wanted to get rid of him. While he was in the army the Spartacus Letters were mostly written by Rosa Luxemburg who probably was the best brain in the German workers' movement at that time. Her purpose in writing these letters was 'not to discredit or paralyse [the Independents] but to drive them on, to clarify and strengthen the movement'. The declaration of the dissentient Social Democrats (the later Independents) in March 1916 (p. 48) discouraged her, but she did not give in. She held that the valour of these dissenters in voting against war credits was not so great as might appear; their negative vote, she held, was explained by a reason that deprived their action of its sting. This reason was that war credits were no longer necessary because the frontiers of the Reich were secure. In other words, according to Rosa Luxemburg, they did not vote against the régime that plunged Germany into the war; they voted merely against the aggressiveness of this régime; they were prompted by the militarily childish notion that it was enough for the purposes of defence to sit still to prevent the enemy from invading the country. Scorning this attitude Rosa Luxemburg wrote a pamphlet entitled *Either—Or*, in which she said: 'What distinguishes them [i.e. the dissenters under Haase's leadership] from the majority of the Social Democratic *Fraktion* is not their fundamental conception of the war, but merely a different appraisal of the military situation.' The pamphlet had a motto that was more distinct than elegant: 'Oh, that thou wert cold or warm, but because thou art lukewarm I will spit thee out.'

On 1 January 1916, the Liebknecht-Luxemburg group constituted itself as the Spartacus League. The main point of the League's programme was the 'application of the Erfurt Programme to the present problems of revolutionary socialism'. The main task of socialist movements was 'to fuse the proletariat of all countries into one living revolutionary force, to give it a strong international organization with a uniform conception of its interests and tasks, with uniform tactics and political capacity to act, and thus to make it in peace and war that decisive factor of political life which history has singled it out to be.'

Now, the Internationale, an association of socialist parties of various countries one of whose main preoccupations had been the problem of how these parties could prevent their respective capitalist governments from starting a war, had failed miserably in August 1914. The German Social Democrats declared that it was their duty to defend Germany against Russian autocratic invasion, and the socialists in the Western Allied countries declared that they had to support their governments in fighting against German imperialist invasion. Therefore, the programme of the Spartacus League laid down the principles on which a new Internationale was to be established. As the Independents were an utterly heterogeneous group many of whom still believed in the old Internationale, violent ideological clashes between them and the Spartacists were inevitable.

On 1 May 1916, Liebknecht called a mass meeting in the Potsdam Square of Berlin. Several thousand people appeared, mostly women. The workers at large were not yet ready for any mass action. In the Potsdam Square Liebknecht shouted, 'Down with the war! Down with the government!' He was sentenced to four years' hard labour. Shortly afterwards, Rosa Luxemburg was taken into 'protective custody'. Both of them were released in October 1918 (p. 43).

Its two leaders eliminated, the Spartacus League was carried on by two other veteran international socialists, Franz Mehring and Clara Zetkin, who also wrote the Spartacus Letters from then on. They lacked the driving force of Liebknecht and the intellect of Luxemburg. The League failed to make headway although it acquired some following in several districts around Berlin, in Bremen, and in a number of other cities.

Because there was no one who wielded as formidable a pen as Rosa Luxemburg, the ideological clashes between Independents and Spartacists died down. But with the leaders' release from prison they flared up again, and in January 1919 the Spartacus League formed itself into a political party, the Communist Party of Germany (p. 190).

VIII. STEWARDS

Both the Spartacists and the Independents carried on a vigorous anti-war propaganda in the factories and especially the war plants. They were handicapped because the broad masses of the workers clung to the Social Democrats in the beginning of the war and could not be roused by illegal calls to illegal actions. A further handicap was the attitude of the trade union leaders who held that the task of their organizations was to improve the position of the proletariat in the existing order; it was not to change this order. They forbade political discussions at trade union meetings. They subscribed to the war. They decreed that there must be no demands for wage increases for the duration. Strikes naturally were out of order.

Shortly after the outbreak of war the members of the Imperial government paid a visit to the Berlin headquarters of the Metal Workers' Union. The metal workers were in the most important of trades, and the secretaries of State felt that it paid them to be condescending. By way of acknowledging the courtesy, the president of the Metal Workers' Union, Adolf Cohen, promptly forbade all disputes whatsoever. The most important branch of the metal workers was that of the turners. Richard Müller, the president of the turners' branch, refused to recognize the decision of the Metal Workers' Union.

By the middle of 1916 the prices of foodstuffs had risen on the average by 50 per cent. Wages lagged behind; the industrialists had the guarantee of the trade union leaders that there would be no strikes. But there were many wild actions of a local and purely industrial, unpolitical character.

Soon, however, the trade union leaders themselves carried

politics into the plants. They exhorted the workers to stand united behind the Social Democrats. They felt this exhortation was necessary because the workers were hotly discussing the struggle of the opposition within the Party (p. 49). Müller's turners gained a great influence upon the workers of the capital.

Liebknecht's trial (p. 54) was on 28 June 1916. At 9 o'clock in the morning of that day the turners stopped the machines in most of Berlin's plants. The workers marched to the court-house, 55,000 of them. Considering that Liebknecht himself had never been able to achieve demonstrations of nearly that size, it is clear that the government by trying and imprisoning him did more to promote the revolutionary movement than he. Another demonstration took place in the city of Brunswick. The Press was forbidden to report the strikes. Thousands of workers who had struck were drafted into the army and sent to the front. The trade union leaders and their Press bemoaned the misery the strike had brought upon so many women and children through the drafting of the strikers for service in a war they supported.

The Executive Committee of the Social Democratic Party and the General Commission of the Trade Unions issued a joint proclamation. It ended: 'Our most important task is to aid in the speedy coming of peace. The competent organizations in the labour movement are conscious of this great duty and are working untiringly for it. *Workers, remain loyal to your organizations and repulse all attempts to split them!*' The workers grew more suspicious than they had been before; they concluded from this proclamation that the Social Democrats and the trade unions were helping the German annexationists win the war.

2

In November 1916 the government, assisted by the General Commission of the Trade Unions, drafted the 'Bill Concerning Patriotic Auxiliary Service'. This bill froze the workers in their jobs and placed them at the disposal, not of the State, but of their employers. The government wanted to get the bill quietly through a committee of the Reichstag, not through the House. But the trade union leaders were afraid that this procedure would provoke greater opposition than was to be expected in any case. They began to sugar the bill by declaring that Patriotic Auxiliary Service was giving new rights to the workers. The bill was passed and became law.

Consternation reigned among the ranks of labour. It was increased by the inception of unrestricted U-boat warfare in February 1917; the workers feared that the United States would declare war against Germany. Matters were made worse by the announcement that the bread ration was to be curtailed by one-fourth because of the bad harvest of 1916. Added to the unrest caused by these events came the news of the first Russian revolution.

The rank and file of the workers pressed for action. Now they were ahead of their unofficial leaders; circumstances had made them restless. These unofficial leaders, for the most part turners, were well known to the workers, each in the factory in which he worked. They called themselves, and the workers called them, Revolutionary Shop Stewards. They formed the organization (the Activists, p. 51) to carry out the illegal tasks that the Spartacists and the Independents could not carry out; the former because they were chiefly educational theorists and unable to acquire a broad following among the workers; the latter because they were a recognized political party and had to watch their step carefully.

The Revolutionary Stewards 'used the trade unions and the Independents as the basis of their organization, while the ideological connexion was provided by the policy propagated by the Independent Party and the Spartacus League'. However, the Revolutionary Stewards were not the only, though they were the main, source and channel of action. Richard Müller (p. 55) was their leader.

By the spring of 1917 the Stewards, and also the trade union functionaries, felt that the workers could not be kept quiet much longer. The trade unions convened many meetings to open a valve for their members to vent their anger; they hoped this would suffice to calm them. The Stewards opened another valve; they gave the workers action. They decided to make a test on the occasion of the annual meeting of the Berlin Metal Workers' Union. This meeting took place on 15 April 1917, a day before the cut in the bread ration came into force, and a week after the Independents constituted themselves as a new party. Two days before the meeting Richard Müller was drafted into the army; the trade union executives knew that he was the head of the Revolutionary Stewards.

Between 200,000 and 300,000 workers struck in Berlin on 16 April. The official trade union executives, because they were unable to suppress it, assumed the leadership of the strike. It was to make this possible that Müller had been removed. The Stewards had realized that the strike could succeed only if political demands were raised and the action were prolonged. But the *ersatz* leadership talked of nothing but food. In the afternoon they told the workers that they had been assured by the authorities there would be more bread, meat and potatoes in the ensuing weeks. Then they called off the strike. The workers had suffered a grave defeat. There followed the usual mass drafts into the army although the military had declared that there would be no conscriptions if the strike were ended immediately. Müller, however, was released from the army upon the insistence of the rank and file.

Concurrent with the action in Berlin there were strikes in Brunswick, Halle, Leipzig and Magdeburg. All of these cities were important centres of the war industry.

Vorwärts, which had been brought into line in October 1916 (p. 49), warned: 'Undoubtedly the desire for peace plays a decisive role.... The occurrences of yesterday should be understood and considered by everybody in this light. Yesterday did not bring forth any event capable of doing much harm to the nation. Thus, its experiences should be considered as a note of warning for both sides.'

Hindenburg wrote a letter to the Chief of the War Supplies Agency, General Groener, saying that the workers must be properly enlightened. The General issued a proclamation to the munition workers: '...Our army needs arms and ammunition. Have you not read Marshal von Hindenburg's letter?...Who dares to defy Marshal von Hindenburg's call?...I herewith order that high-spirited workers, courageous men and women, immediately co-operate in munition works of all kinds to explain to their comrades what the needs of the hour and the future of the Fatherland demand of all of us....Read and re-read Marshal von Hindenburg's letter again and again, and you will recognize where our worst enemies are. Not out there near Arras, on the Aisne, in Champagne, not in London...our worst enemies are in the midst of us...namely, the strike agitators.' The stupidity of this proclamation was appalling. It said in so many words that the enemy was not the enemy. The workers who wanted enough to eat, who wanted peace and wanted peace to be maintained, the workers who provided the bulk of the armies that were fighting at the fronts, they were the worst enemy. The Stewards were pleased; the spirit of the workers had threatened to be crushed by the defeat of the strike, but the General's proclamation changed their downheartedness to fury.

In September 1917 all the union branches of Berlin passed a resolution. The branches were presided over by the Revolutionary Stewards, not their regular functionaries who were nominally in office. 'The terrible suspicion rests on our administration [i.e. the official administration of the trade unions] that it is in the confidence of the police and the military authorities. Had our administration the necessary proletarian honour it would have been their duty to dispel this suspicion by every means. They would have had to do so not only to safeguard the interests of the organization but also their own integrity....'

The Independents and the Spartacists pressed for new action. The Stewards objected. They knew that immediate action was impossible, if only because the most vigorous of the Stewards and workers had been drafted into the army. However, the Independents and the Spartacists believed that the revolutionary will of the workers would be strengthened by a more or less continuous chain of political actions. The Stewards on the other hand held that this would be a frittering away of the movement's strength. The German workers, the Stewards maintained, were by the tradition of their political struggle and their trade union struggle better capable of united mass action.

This difference of opinion was more than a disagreement on tactics. It marked an unbridgeable gulf concerning the question of organization. We have pointed out (p. 57) that the Stewards used the trade unions and the Independents for their own purposes. But the latter were closely knit mass organizations. This type of industrial and political organization did not lend itself to continuous partial actions such as the Spartacists suggested. If such actions were undertaken upon orders of the central leadership, the units that did not participate felt nervous and wondered what was going on, and those that did participate felt let down by those that did not. At worst, the whole organization disintegrated. At best, lengthy explanations by the leadership were necessary, and revealing their intentions was apt to thwart them.

On the other hand, the organization of councils (soviets) was suited to the tactics of continuous partial actions. But the German workers were not suited to being organized in soviets. The Stewards realized this point clearly. The Spartacists did not realize it. Of course, workers' and soldiers' councils did become prominent in Germany in November 1918 under the stress of events, but only to prove the correctness of the Stewards' argument by their complete failure, as we shall see.

Not agreeing with the argument of the Stewards the Spartacists tried their hand in August 1917. They organized a strike in Brunswick. It broke down after four days without spreading to any other place.

4

A Reich conference of all metal workers had taken place in Cologne in July 1917. It integrated the organization of the Revolutionary Stewards, at secret meetings, to cover the whole Reich. In October 1917 a Revolution Committee was formed in Berlin. It consisted of Revolutionary Stewards of the capital, about eighty in number, as a nucleus. Added to this nucleus were a group of Independent members of the Reichstag and the Prussian Diet. The Revolution Committee held a meeting in the middle of January 1918. Haase suggested a resolution that was adopted and distributed in large numbers by leaflet. 'If the working population now fails to demonstrate its will, it might appear as if the masses of the German people aquiesced in the doings of the ruling classes, as if they had not yet had enough of the appalling misery of the war. ...The hour has struck for you to raise your voice for a peace without annexations and indemnities on the basis of the self-determination of the peoples. You have the floor.' This was not revolutionary. But the Independents were to the end convinced that Germany, or rather the German annexationists, were going to win the war, and they dreaded this prospect that at the same time made them despair of the possibility of social revolution.

On 27 January 1918, a Sunday, Richard Müller convened a meeting of turners' delegates in Berlin. Fifteen hundred of them attended. They resolved to call a strike for the next day. On Monday, 400,000 workers struck in Berlin. Their delegates, four hundred in number, met in the afternoon. Müller was in the chair. The meeting demanded, among other things, peace without annexations and indemnities and the democratization of the entire State organization beginning with the introduction of the universal, equal, direct, and secret vote of all men and women of over twenty years of age for the Prussian Diet. These demands, too, were not revolutionary-socialistic. They were liberal and democratic.

The meeting elected an action committee of eleven. The independents were asked to add three delegates from their party. They sent Haase, Ledebour, and Dittmann, Georg Ledebour was an immature firebrand of seventy. Next to Liebknecht he was the favourite of the workers of Berlin. He had the face of a nineteenth-century character actor and stirred his audiences as few orators did. The venom and sarcasm of his oratory were unbelievable, and he was extremely intelligent. Wilhelm Karl Dittmann was a former trade unionist and became an important figure in the Revolution; we shall meet him frequently in the following pages.

A trade union member who attended the meeting asked that the Social Democrats, too, be invited to send three delegates. The motion was carried. The Social Democrats sent Ebert, Scheidemann and Otto Braun.[1]

Ebert insisted that the demands of the strikers be reconsidered because the Social Democrats could not agree to all of them. Suddenly someone shouted: 'The police are coming.' Ebert and Scheidemann disappeared like lightning. The demands remained as they were. The meeting broke off. The police padlocked the building which, ironically, was the headquarters of the Trades Union Congress, that staunch supporter of the government.

The military proclaimed an 'increased state of siege'. Extraordinary courts-martial were set up. All meetings were banned, particularly any session of the action committee. *Vorwärts* published a calculation, factory by factory, of the numbers of workers striking. The calculation added up to 300,000. The military suppressed *Vorwärts* temporarily for overstating the number and thus spreading alarm.

The third day of the strike brought severe clashes with the

---

[1] Braun (born in 1872) became Prime Minister of Prussia in 1920 and held this post (with a few short interruptions) as the head of different coalition governments until 1932. When Hitler came to power, he went into exile in Switzerland. In spite of his long tenure of one of the most important political offices in the Weimar Republic he modestly disclaimed any influence on German developments not only for himself but for all Germans when he wrote in his memoirs (see Bibliography, p. 282): 'Politicians of various countries often ask me: how was it that the Hitler dictatorship could arise in Germany? I can only answer again and again: Versailles and Moscow.'

police. The streets were teeming with excited workers. The Action Committee met. Scheidemann appeared, dishevelled, crying defiance and revenge. He had blundered into one of these clashes and the police had beaten him up.

The three Social Democrats and Haase advocated negotiations with the government. But the government demanded that the General Commission of the Trade Unions participate in the negotiations. This Commission had seen that the strike was coming. They did not dare to oppose it, but they found a compromise. The strike was political, and politics were taboo in the unions. Therefore the leadership declared the unions 'neutral'. The government could hardly have been sincere in demanding that the General Commission of the Trade Unions participate in the negotiations; they must have seen that the workers were out of the control of the trade union leaders and that these leaders were therefore not competent to speak for the strikers. However, their competency was not put to the test; the Action Committee refused to have anything to do with them. Negotiations with the government could not take place.

On the following day, 1 February 1918, the strikers overturned the few street-cars still operating in Berlin. Ebert addressed an open air mass meeting. His speech was carefully empty and emptily careful. The workers heckled him many times. Dittmann spoke after him. He was arrested before he got very far. He was arrested not for what he said but for participating in a meeting that was illegal. Ebert was not arrested. An extraordinary court-martial sentenced Dittmann to five years' detention in a fortress. This type of punishment was meted out for offences that did not spring from base motives.

The Action Committee met again. The three Social Democrats did not attend. It was useless for them to attend; they had no influence over the masses of the workers, let alone the Action Committee. The meeting assessed the mood of the workers. They agreed that the rank and file would regard the calling off of the action as a retreat, not a defeat. Retreat was necessary; the strike had reached the point where it would at any moment change to civil war, and the strikers had no arms.

While this was happening in Berlin, mass strikes occurred in Brunswick, Cologne, Danzig, Hamburg, Mannheim, Munich, Nürnberg, Leipzig, and in many other cities.

The Action Committee terminated the strike. Many of the participants were sentenced to terms of hard labour and imprisonment. Nearly all the Revolutionary Stewards were drafted into the army. So were thousands of workers, 60,000 in Berlin alone. The revolutionary organization was shattered. It did not recover readiness for action until November 1918. Richard Müller was again forced into uniform although he was physically unfit for military service. He was soon discharged, however, because the Independents nominated him as their candidate for a Reichstag by-election. In order to devote himself fully to this campaign he did not resume the chairmanship of the Revolutionary Stewards but left it in the hands of the man to whom he had turned it over upon being drafted. This man was Emil Barth, a metal worker with whom we shall meet frequently as we proceed. Barth had been at the front from 1915 to January 1918 when he was discharged from the army as '100 per cent invalid through war service' (tuberculosis).

5

The strike of January 1918 had a sequel in the Magdeburg Trial six years later. Ebert was President of the German Republic then. An insignificant newspaper in an insignificant town in central Germany published an open letter by an insignificant National Socialist (Nazi) member of the Reichstag, Rothart. The letter accused Ebert of treason committed by speaking at that outdoor meeting. The public prosecutor charged the editor of the paper with libel of the President. Rothart was protected by parliamentary immunity. The trial took place in Magdeburg in December 1924. It became a scandal. Ebert, in the witness stand, denied that he had said the strikers should disobey the draft orders to be expected.

The editor was sentenced to three months in prison on the technical grounds that the open letter contained insulting language. He was not sentenced for libel because Ebert did commit treason, as the judge said in his reasons for judgement. Thus, the writer had stated something that was true, and to do so was not libel. From the historical or political viewpoint, the judge admitted, Ebert had joined the Action Committee for the purpose of throttling the strike (this was Ebert's defence). But a judge was not concerned with politics, only with facts. It was a fact that Ebert did join the Committee and made that speech, and this was treason.

Stresemann called the judgement outrageous. He pointed out that Ebert had lost two sons in the war and that he did not withdraw his third son[1] from the front although the Kaiser requested him to do so. This was a well-meant apologia, but it could not efface the fact that there was a ban on meetings at that time, and that Ebert's participation in a meeting was a criminal offence. Of course, it was an offence only under the law of the Empire. But this law had been maintained by Ebert and his Party when they had the power to repeal it in the Revolution. He could not reasonably expect to be exempt from its application, belated though it came. He was fortunate that no public prosecutor had the courage directly to charge him with treason.

Ebert died on 28 February 1925, two months after the Magdeburg Trial. Those who were around him said that the trial contributed to his death at the age of 54 (he postponed a needed appendectomy in order to attend the trial, and this neglect caused his death when the operation was finally carried out). Hindenburg was elected his successor in April. The public prosecutor appealed from the Magdeburg verdict. President von Hindenburg (styled the 'Saviour' by his campaign managers) saved the guilty editor as well; he pardoned him before the second trial could take place.

[1] Upon the division of Berlin into three Western Sectors and one Eastern Sector after World War II this third son, Friedrich Ebert Jr., became Lord Mayor of the Russian Sector.

6

In the summer of 1918 Barth, the new chairman of the Revolutionary Stewards, organized shock troops in all important factories. Their task was to 'make themselves masters of the streets of Berlin and the other large cities upon the outbreak of the revolution, to drive forward those who were hesitant, and to draw over to them the soldiers who would be ordered to operate against the revolution'. The shock troops were provided with arms from various sources. Part was supplied by soldiers who were home on furlough and were let into the secret. Part was bought from other soldiers on furlough who did not know what the arms were to be used for. And the rest came from army depots. Supreme Command were aware of this traffic but unable to stop it. When the revolution broke out these arms, like Barth's minutely detailed plan, were not used; the monarchy fell without offering any resistance. There were also other reasons why Barth's plan was not used (p. 73). The money to supply the munitions and to finance the activities of the organization in general came from sources that were not revealed. Barth declared later that they were nobody's concern. Other people declared that they were Russian.

In addition to the Independents, the Revolutionary Stewards and the Spartacists, there was a fourth group that worked for the downfall of the German monarchy. It was an infamous organization and came to a befittingly odious end in the Revolution (p. 192). It operated independently of the three others and concentrated on the front line army. But in spite of its concentration on this field it made no headway; the front-line soldiers were too busy and in too dangerous a position to take much interest in politics. Many of its members had formerly belonged to the international revolutionary youth movement. Liebknecht was the moderator of this movement up to the war. One of its leaders was a certain Wolfgang Breithaupt. He recanted immediately after the war and wrote accounts of his war activities in the German reactionary press. These accounts were later collected in a book that is as vile as one would expect of the man considering his actions. This gang systematically organized desertions with the aim of demoralizing the German front. The deserters fled in two streams across the frontiers, one to Holland and one to Denmark. At the receiving end was the British Secret Service. Such was the anti-militaristic ardour of these deserters that they shirked the open fight against the militarists and their laws at home, corrupted large numbers of innocent men into committing what was a heinous crime under these laws, and exposed all German soldiers to dangers of life and limb beyond the normal chances of war.

7

While the German front-line army remained, generally speaking, untouched by revolutionary activities until the military situation grew manifestly hopeless, there occurred a mutiny in the German Navy in 1917. This mutiny became one of the parade horses of the German monarchists. They blamed it on the Independents because Independent leaflets were found in the possession of some of the mutineers who had also been in contact with Haase and Dittmann (p. 62) and another Independent deputy, Vogtherr. The Imperial Chancellor, Michaelis, who had succeeded Bethmann-Hollweg less than three months earlier, and his attorney-general found no grounds for taking action against those deputies, but two sailors, Reichpietsch and Köbis were executed as a consequence of the mutiny.[1] Many others were sentenced to penal servitude. One of the mutineers was the sailor Eglhofer of whom we shall hear more.

In November 1918 the sailors mutinied again, and then their mutiny became the spark that touched off the revolution. Their

[1] That the revolutionary events of that time are living in the memory of the German workers is attested by the fact that, after World War II, streets were named after these two sailors in many Western German cities, including staunchly anti-Communist Western Berlin. Michaelis was another victim, a political victim, of the mutiny. His Secretary of the Navy, Admiral von Capelle, speaking in the Reichstag, accused those three deputies of complicity, but a majority of the Reichstag protected them, and forced Michaelis to resign because of Capelle's blundering. He was succeeded by Hertling.

leader on this latter occasion was the rating Artelt, a 'fiery under-dog with a booming voice'. The discrepancy between the demands of the Independents and the Spartacists on the one hand, and those of the sailors on the other hand makes it doubtful that the sailors had any really close connexion with these political groups even then. These groups postulated, among other things, a thorough transformation of the army and navy. But the sailors postulated the following ridiculous, and at the same time moving, trans-formation: 'The form of address, *Herr Kapitän*, should occur only at the beginning of a sentence; thereafter superiors may be addressed as "you".' (Soldiers and sailors were not allowed to say 'you' when talking to a superior. To give an example, a soldier could not say, 'I did not hear you, sir'. He had to say, 'I did not hear the *Herr Kapitän*', or whatever the rank was.)

8

An American historian, commenting on the 1918 Revolution, wrote in 1932: 'It was part of the German tragedy that the working-men in the essential war industries were not organized so that their lowered morale could be strengthened and their powers of resistance prepared for the final struggle.' This state-ment, which is typical of many, contains a fault of reasoning as well as one of fact. As for the former, it is inherent in the free-enterprise method of production that not all workers can be organized in unions (and even the industrial unions, as distinguished from the trade unions, were much less developed in 1918 than they are now). As for the latter, the Revolutionary Stewards were almost without exception intelligent, highly skilled, organized workers, and leaders of the same kind of men.[1] History shows that unskilled, unorganized people may at best bring about a revolt of slaves. Revolutions, whatever their causes, are made by strong, and often rising, classes, not by down-trodden masses.

[1] There were only two intellectuals among them, Ledebour and Däumig (p. 51).

In this background of the Stewards lay the strength of their movement, but also its weakness. In Germany, like all other industrially developed countries, the trade unions consisted of an aristocracy of workers. In Germany, this aristocracy of workers like any other aristocracy anywhere was interested in the maintenance of existing conditions. In Germany, as elsewhere, the trade unions tried to stay clear of politics. This attempt failed, as it was bound to fail. Where both a trade union movement and a political workers' movement exist, the question is not which of them can stay clear of the other; the question is which of them dominates the other. In Germany, the trade unions came to dominate the political workers' movement. The latter was originally revolutionary. As it came to be dominated by the workers' aristocracy, the princes among this aristocracy, the Eberts and Scheidemanns, called the tune of the Social Democratic Party while the 'native' intellectuals, the Liebknechts and Haases, went on mouthing revolutionary phrases that had become meaningless (there were of course exceptions among trade unionists as well as among intellectuals). Naturally, the rank and file listened to their own social kind, those princes, rather than to the intellectuals. Bernstein, the Reformist, another of those princes, did not think up an idea that was divorced from reality; it represented reality.

Of course, the war was an existing condition that few Germans wanted to maintain. Those who wanted to end it differed greatly about the means to achieve this aim. The socialist groups, that is to say, the Independents, the Spartacists, and the Revolutionary Stewards, wanted to end it by establishing socialism, or what each of them regarded as socialism. The Majority Social Democrats wanted to end it by persuasion, and they were prepared to include in the bargain some constitutional reforms that would protect the monarchy from itself. The progressive bourgeois went further than the Majority Socialists. To be sure, they did not want to overthrow the monarchy, they liked it. But like the Socialists and unlike the Majority Social Democrats they realized that militarism was a social, not a political, phenomenon. Thus, there was a common ground on which revolutionary socialists and progressive bourgeois could have joined forces (in fact, when the Social Democratic Party was still intact, including its revolutionaries, it often co-operated with another party that on the surface seemed to be most unsuited for the purpose, the Catholic Centre). A union of these two groups might, in the conditions of that time, have fashioned a German State that was neither militarist nor socialist. That they distrusted each other and therefore did not join forces, because they made a faulty analysis of the political situation and especially of each other's objectives, was the real German tragedy. The attitude of the Majority Socialist leaders made social revolution to establish socialism impossible. More than that, their attitude and their actions during the Revolution precluded any social change whatever, and therefore they shared with the Conservatives and the reactionaries the responsibility for preserving German militarism.

Of course, an analysis of future social and political developments, though it may serve as an adequate basis for immediate social and political action, can never be quite accurate. As events unfolded they made possible what would have appeared impossible beforehand; they brought certain chances of success for a socialist revolution. That these chances presented themselves was due to actions, not reasoning, on the part of the Revolutionary Stewards. That they did not materialize was due to Spartacist blundering. All this will be shown as we now proceed with our narrative of events.

IX. 'ÉLITE'

I

On 3 November 1918, Ebert telephoned to the permanent head of the Reich Chancellery, Under-Secretary of State Arnold Wahn-schaffe, to tell him that riots were planned for the next day. He added that the trade union leaders 'were doing everything they could to keep the masses in hand, but his impression was that the local authorities [i.e. the military in Berlin] were underrating the seriousness of the situation'. Wahnschaffe thanked Ebert for the information and notified Prince Max. Prince Max 'alarmed the proper authorities'. The proper authorities prepared, as far as they were able to in view of their inadequate resources, for action against the prospective rioters. But nothing happened the next day.

Ebert's story had, however, a basis in fact. The Revolution Committee (p. 61) had met on 2 November. It now consisted of Revolutionary Stewards, Independents, and Spartacists. The ideas represented by these three component groups clashed sharply at the meeting. Ledebour, the leader of the Independent left wing which was the political arm of the Revolutionary Stewards, and Barth, the chairman of the latter, demanded action on 4 November. Haase, the chairman of the Independents and leader of their right wing, objected determinedly. He, who was later accused more persistently than anyone else of promoting the Revolution, saw no chance of success even at this date. He declared it to be criminal folly to speak of revolution; any attempt would be put down bloodily. He had always counselled caution. If Germany won the war, he reasoned, revolution was impossible and those who had propagated it would be the objects of cruel retribution. Such caution had become senseless. Haase knew as well as anyone else that Germany could not win the war and that revolution was on the march. It became apparent that his caution was due not only to political calculation but also to a hesitancy that was so ingrained in him that he could not shed it when it had lost all foundation in reality. Dittmann supported Haase.

Liebknecht, the leader of the Spartacists, also opposed Barth, but for reasons different from Haase's. In his opinion Barth wanted to 'make revolution', and he held that this was impossible. He propagated his old idea of working up a revolutionary mood in the masses through constant demonstrations and partial strikes that would develop into general strike and revolution. In spite of the successful mass actions the Stewards had organized in response to the mood of the masses, Liebknecht condemned their technique. The Stewards, on the other hand, clung to their notion that in view of their political training and the history of their union movement the German workers were not prepared for incessant partial actions, and that a few mighty blows were the appropriate technique (p. 60).

The meeting compromised by appointing 11 November as the day of action. But Barth had anticipated agreement upon 4 November and had sent out corresponding instructions to his lieutenants in many parts of Germany before the meeting started. He had great difficulty in cancelling these instructions and did not succeed in all places.

The confusion was heightened by events in Kiel. The Kiel movement began on 28 October quite spontaneously and was at first unpolitical (pp. 13 and 68). For this reason, and because of Barth's cancellation, it was not supported by the local representatives of the Revolution Committee. But when these representatives saw that the movement was assuming great proportions they threw themselves into it despite the cancellation and the appointment of 11 November.

The Kiel movement then precipitated events elsewhere, including Berlin. Barth might still have waited until 11 November, but to add to his troubles two further sources of confusion opened up. For one, the twenty-six mass meetings, arranged for the

evening of 7 November by the Independents in conjunction with
the Stewards, were forbidden (p. 32). The ban interrupted direct
communication with the masses of the workers. And then, the
Independent deputy of the Reichstag, Ernst Däumig (p. 51), one
of Barth's closest collaborators, was arrested by the police at noon
on 8 November. Barth believed that this was due to a betrayal of
their plans; he advanced the date of action and called the workers
of Berlin into the streets for 9 November, with the result that the
whole organization outside Berlin was at sixes and sevens,
although, of course, 9 November became 'the day' because Berlin
was all-important.

In this situation, which was known to him, Ebert performed
his brilliant manœuvre of telling Prince Max that he would call
out the workers of Berlin on 9 November unless the Kaiser abdicated (p. 37). Actually, the Social Democrats did nothing of the
kind. To be sure, they did call out the workers, but only after the
workers were already out because Barth had called them. The
Social Democratic call came after the Party deputation had its
meeting with the Prince (p. 39). This latter manœuvre made
Ebert the recognized leader of the Revolution, at least, on
9 November. He was aided by the fact that his name was known
to everyone in Germany while few people, even among the
workers, knew of Barth whose activities had demanded the veil of
secrecy. Thus it came about that the Revolutionary Stewards
played a minor and even ridiculous role on 9 November 1918.
Barth was sitting in a back room somewhere in Berlin, at a table
covered with maps, like the commander of a great army surrounded by adjutants and lieutenants ready to carry out his orders,
and by couriers ready to convey his orders to the field officers anywhere in Germany. But no orders were given because, quite
apart from the fact that they could not be given as the organization was all mixed up, they were not necessary; the monarchy
offered no resistance.

If Ebert warned the government on 3 November of events that
were scheduled to take place on 4 November, this must have been

because his informer left the meeting of the Revolution Committee (p. 71) before the final date was decided upon. That he informed the government on 3 November, not 2 November, the day the meeting took place, was typical of the care with which he weighed every decision he made.

2

A day later General Groener arrived in Berlin. He came from General Headquarters in Spa where the Kaiser had gone at the end of October in order to be relieved of irksome discussions about his abdication (p. 10). Ever since, the cabinet had made frantic efforts to get the Kaiser back to the capital because they held that his presence there was necessary if anything at all were to be saved.

Groener had succeeded Ludendorff a week earlier. Until then he had been military governor at Kiev in the Ukraine since the beginning of 1918 when he vacated the post of Chief of the War Supply Office (Munitions Minister). As such he had issued that infuriating proclamation to the munitions workers after the strike of April 1917 (p. 59). Groener was an outstanding organizer and Germany's foremost expert on railroad matters. Later, from 1920 to 1923, he was Reich Communications Minister, and from 1928 to 1932 Reich War Minister and Secretary of the Interior.

At the beginning of November 1918 he went to Berlin at the request of Prince Max. The Prince wanted to convince the General of the hopelessness of the home situation. He hoped the General would then return to Spa to make the Kaiser face facts.

The General had permission to inform the cabinet at his own discretion that the Kaiser would come to Berlin within twenty-four hours if the cabinet so desired. But upon his arrival in the capital he found a telegram waiting for him that cancelled this permission. He went to see the cabinet. The first thing he said was: 'The Field Marshal [Hindenburg] has ordered me, concerning the question of the Kaiser's abdication, to tell you in his own words that to his mind it would be the act of a scoundrel for him

74

to desert the Kaiser. And this, gentlemen, is my feeling, too, and the feeling of every soldier with a sense of honour.' The Prince was dismayed.

Although summoned by the Prince, Groener had a purpose of his own in going to Berlin. He had just made a survey of the military situation and wanted to tell the cabinet the result: the army could hold out for another eight or ten days; if the government did not obtain an armistice by then, the generals would have to go to the enemy with the white flag. After a day in Berlin, however, Groener declared that he needed the armistice within three days; the reason was that he was finding the state of the home front worse than he had thought. As the army did not live from hand to mouth it would be difficult to see the connexion between these two things (the state of the home front and the General's revised estimate as to how long the army could hold out) had he not exclaimed: 'If the baiting of the Kaiser does not stop the fate of the army is sealed. It is melting away. The beast in the human is breaking out in the military rabble streaming back to the homeland.... The worst enemy against whom the army has to fight is the enervating influence of the homeland. It is the threat of Bolshevism.' This was Groener's old song. But it meant more now than it had when he sang it on the occasion of the April 1917 strike. It was one of the preparations for the stab-in-the-back legend, the legend that Germany's army was not defeated, or rather, that it was defeated by the German people, not the external enemy. The German people were the German army's worst enemy. The army had to be led against the people before it melted away. Therefore he needed the armistice in three days, not eight or ten.

The change in Groener's view occurred before he had a conversation with the leaders of the trade unions and the Social Democrats on the second day of his stay in Berlin. This conversation was arranged by the Prince. Legien appeared for the trade unions, Ebert and Scheidemann and four other members of the Reichstag for the Social Democrats. Ebert declared that the

Kaiser must abdicate the next day at the latest and appoint one of his sons his deputy, or the monarchy could not be saved. Groener declared that abdication was out of the question. The discussion went on and on, the Social Democrats imploring the General to save the monarchy by persuading the Kaiser to abdicate voluntarily; the monarchy would be lost if 'the street' enforced his abdication. It is piquant to note that what these leaders disdainfully called 'the street' included millions of their own followers, Social Democratic workers.

Scheidemann left the room, came back after a moment. 'Gentlemen, further discussion of the abdication is pointless, the revolution is in full swing. Hamburg...Hanover...Kiel. The present is no time for discussion. Now is the time to act.' His ruse did not work; everybody knew of course what was going on in those cities. Ebert and Legien were not to be disturbed; they continued to plead with the General. The General remained adamant. Ebert then ended the meeting by saying: 'Under the circumstances any further discussion is superfluous. Events must take their course.'

3

Groener left Berlin on 6 November. A few hours earlier General Headquarters had, with his consent, issued an order of the day: '...The Kaiser question does not exist for the army. The army stands in unswerving loyalty by its Kaiser and Supreme War Lord.' On the following day the Social Democrats put their ultimatum to the government of Prince Max (p. 33).

The grandees at General Headquarters soon began to whisper that Groener's visit to Berlin had made him uncertain. He declared: 'Whosoever believes that he must advise His Majesty to abdicate should take the responsibility in writing before the world and history.' This was sophistry. Everybody knew that the General and everybody else was talking constantly about the Kaiser question. Far from hushing up this question, the General's sophistry raised it openly. At the same time his way of raising it openly protected him from and against both the monarchy and the republic. Ebert took this sly course two days later (p. 43).

The government informed headquarters of the Social Democratic ultimatum. The Kaiser 'remained firm'.

Throughout 8 November General Headquarters asked itself whether the German workers were really so base as not to want their Kaiser any more. In their anxiety the gentlemen debated the question from every conceivable angle. They debated it so intently that it did not occur to any of them to do something. The Kaiser sent for the Crown Prince. The Crown Prince was at the headquarters of his army group; he would arrive the next morning.

In the evening, the Kaiser's military confidant, Colonel Niemann,[1] was called to the Operations Bureau of General Headquarters in the Hotel Britannique at Spa. Groener told him that the Rhine bridges were in the hands of the mutineers; the army's supplies would be exhausted in four days. Bring the fortresses to their senses by military force, suggested Niemann. Impossible, replied the General; the mutineers would not let any train pass, they would even destroy the supplies that were stored in the large cities on the Rhine. And the General asked the Colonel if he would inform the Kaiser of this. Good heavens, no, said the Colonel; this affair was so grave that it must be reported by responsible persons. Who was responsible? No one, if the duty was unpleasant.

The Colonel went to see General von Marschall (p. 78). They agreed that Groener was a sinister character. Then they went to bed, asking themselves with heavy hearts whether the German people would shake off the 'madness of rebellion'. They went to sleep with the conviction that the German people would.

[1] The political intelligence of Niemann (see Bibliography, p. 285) may be gauged by the fact that, in July 1918, he wrote a memorandum for the Kaiser in which he suggested that Germany should propitiate England by ceding the German fleet to her while, in return, England was expected to make peace and acquiesce in the realization of the German expansionist dream of the Berlin-Baghdad railroad.

4

Early next morning, 9 November, Niemann saw Groener again. The General told the Colonel that the front line troops too were showing a revolutionary spirit. Niemann asked whether the Kaiser knew of this deterioration of the situation. Good heavens, no, replied the General, 'but we have summoned a large number of front-line officers to report on the mood of the troops. The result of this investigation will be reported to His Majesty'. In Berlin, hundreds of thousands of workers were surging towards the Reichstag and the Palace.

The Kaiser and Colonel Niemann went out for a walk. The Kaiser said he considered it his sacred duty to erect a rampart against the mania of Bolshevism. He hoped the enemy, too, would realize the danger to European civilization if Germany were given over to Bolshevism. The Colonel agreed; the movement at home was only a number of unconnected putsches, he said; they could and must be crushed by force. Cautiously, as His Majesty seemed to be in a gracious mood, he added that the situation of the front-line army was rendered difficult by the spreading of rebellion to the Rhine cities. That was nothing, said the Kaiser; 'we shall master this difficulty by swift military action'. In Berlin, Ebert was having his matutinal *tête-à-tête* with the Prince.

5

The Kaiser and the Colonel returned to Villa Fraineuse, the Kaiser's quarters. They found a number of grandees waiting for His Majesty; Hindenburg and Groener; Major-General Count Friedrich von der Schulenburg, Chief of Staff of the Army Group 'German Crown Prince'; Colonel-General Hans Georg Hermann von Plessen, Adjutant-General and First Commandant of His Majesty's Military Headquarters; Major-General Baron von Marschall-Greif, Adjutant-General and Chief of His Majesty's Military Cabinet; and two mere civilians, His Excellency Paul

von Hintze, who had, however, been an admiral before he stooped
to statecraft and who was now the representative of the Foreign
Office attached to General Headquarters, and Baron von Grünau,
Acting Privy Legation Councillor and representative of the
Chancellor attached to His Majesty.

Hindenburg asked the Kaiser for leave not to report on the
military situation as was his daily duty; there were things to be
said that a Prussian officer could not say to his King and Lord.

The Kaiser motioned Groener to speak. Groener was a Würt-
temberger (Swabian), not a Prussian, the Kaiser therefore not his
king. Under the Imperial constitution the King of Prussia was
President of the German Confederation, called the German Reich,
with the title of German Emperor. Whether or not Groener was
thinking of this subtlety at that moment, his patience was at an
end; he felt that somebody had to speak out, and he did speak out.
For this, he became acceptable to the Weimar Republic while the
Reaction put him on its list of those to be hounded. At Villa
Fraineuse, on the morning of 9 November 1918, he reported
what he had seen at home. He depicted the militarily hopeless
situation of the front-line army, and he concluded that the army
was no longer reliable and a fight against the homeland impossible.

The Kaiser asked Count von der Schulenburg to state his
opinion. The count violently disagreed with the General. True, the
army as a whole could not be used for a fight against the homeland
he conceded, but there still were many units that were absolutely
reliable. They could be given several days of rest and then sent
against the rebellious Rhine cities. It would be an effective slogan
to tell them that the army supplies were being cut off by a crowd
of slackers and Jewish war profiteers.

The last sentence requires some comment. As for Jews, the only
prominent man in the whole of Germany who later that day blew
his brains out because he would not survive the cowardly end of the
monarchy was a Jew, Albert Ballin, the head of H.A.P.A.G.
(Hamburg-America Packetboat Company). The Count knew
very well that Germany could not have sustained her war effort

for any length of time without a number of prominent Jews, notably, Ballin himself, Haber, the chemist, Rathenau, the industrialist, and Melchior, the financier. These men, and many other Germans like them, Jewish or not, were just as important to the militarist state as the generals.

Schulenburg published two memoranda about the events at Spa on 9 November 1918, and his part in them. By the time he wrote the second memorandum he had regained his balance and omitted the 'Jews'. The fact remains that he, as nearly all of the gentlemen at Spa, allowed himself to be carried away by his emotions at the moment when he was faced by the most serious question of his glamorous life.[1] Ironically, when his immediate military chief, the Crown Prince, decided to write his memoirs he employed a Jewish ghost writer, the novelist Karl Rosner, in default of any literary talent of his own. The Kaiser employed a Jewish lawyer in his haggling with the German Republic when he claimed, and got, every cent the Hohenzollerns had accumulated for centuries. And the man whose labours contributed more than anyone else's to the success of the stab-in-the-back legend was a Jewish publisher and publicist, Professor Paul Nikolaus Cossmann of Munich.

To return to Spa on 9 November 1918. Groener protested against Schulenburg's views. The army was so unreliable, he contended, that the order of 'against the homeland' would lead to terrible bloodshed within the army. This must not happen, decided the Kaiser; he did not want civil war. The armistice must be concluded, and then he would lead his armies home. He knew President Wilson's notes and his own government's view of them —that the enemy would not grant an armistice without his abdication first. But he hoped that if he offered to lead his armies home, which meant of course into civil war, the Entente would see at last that he was saving Europe from Bolshevism, and would overlook the fact that he was actually saving German militarism.

[1] He became a member of the Reichstag for the reactionary wing of the German National People's Party (p. 145) later on.

Groener: 'Under its generals the army will march back quietly and in good order, but not under Your Majesty.' Four days earlier he had said exactly the opposite in Berlin (p. 75).

The Kaiser, sharply: 'Your Excellency, I demand that you give this declaration in writing. [As if this would have changed anything. But Groener himself had started this nonsense of putting things in writing.] ...Has not the army sworn loyalty to me?'

'This oath and the "Supreme War Lord" are mere ideas', said the General.

The grandees stood aghast at the man's audacity and the long suspected and now confirmed subversiveness of his views. But their superior breeding forbade them to show their contempt of this commoner's origin and his manners; they would do so later on, behind his back.

Hindenburg intervened; he respected Schulenburg's spirit of loyalty, but he agreed with Groener.

An adjutant appeared; the Chancellor, in Berlin, was on the telephone and was asking graciously to be permitted to speak to His Majesty. His Majesty did not go to the telephone. What would the Prince say? Abdication. His Majesty went out into the park after giving orders that certain reports that had come from Berlin be investigated.

6

Wahnschaffe (p. 71), in Berlin, had told Hintze, at General Headquarters, over the telephone a little earlier that rivers of blood were flowing in street fighting in the capital. Hintze tried to obtain a confirmation of this report from the War Minister in Berlin. He could not reach the War Minister and spoke to his adjutant Colonel von Berge. The Colonel said there were about thirty to forty dead so far; many regiments had gone over to the revolutionaries; the attitude of the rest was uncertain. Hintze telephoned Wahnschaffe once more and asked him how he reconciled his rivers of blood with Berge's statement (which was fairly correct, p. 16). Wahnschaffe said he had merely repeated the military reports he had received in the Chancellery.

It was quite natural that wild rumours should circulate in a situation such as existed in Berlin on 9 November 1918. But Wahnschaffe's unintentional exaggeration was used ever after to accuse the 'democratic' government of Prince Max of telling falsehoods in order to overthrow the Kaiser.

Hindenburg, Groener, and Hintze hurried into the garden to inform the Kaiser of the state of affairs in the capital. The Crown Prince had arrived meanwhile, and Count von der Schulenburg was telling him of Groener's report, his own objections, and Hindenburg's agreeing with Groener. The Kaiser was talking to the others, gesticulating vehemently. He was reproaching the 'democratic government' for having allowed an anti-monarchic feeling to develop in the people. This 'democratic government' was just over a month old, and the Kaiser blamed it for a develop-ment that had taken more than a century to mature in certain political and industrial movements and in many individual Germans, not all of whom were socialists, and whose numbers were swelled by many more who had no republican conviction but grew anti-monarchic when they began to see that Germany was losing the war into which the monarchy had led her. This 'democratic government' was frantic in its efforts to save the monarchy with the help of the Social Democratic leaders, but the Kaiser said it was weakly sailing in the wake of the same Social Democrats who, according to him, wanted 'absolute power'.

The others stood with their heads bowed as the Kaiser was talking. The Kaiser caught sight of the Crown Prince and took him aside. He told him of the revolutionary collapse of the army and the home front and of his personal intentions. To go to the front, lead his armies in an attack, be killed by a merciful bullet with the Prussian standard in his hands—what an unspeakably beautiful death! Alas, it could not be done; soldiers did not attack and die like this in a modern war (they did, of course). He could not hide in a shell-hole either, and wait for a bullet to find him; he might be mutilated and fall into the enemy's hands. What else could he do? Go back to Berlin? Did not the fate of the Tsar threaten him there? He could not expose the German people to the eternal slur of killing him, or worse, delivering him to the enemy. (He, the Crown Prince, and Ludendorff were the only members of the *élite* who fled to neutral countries later that day. Scores of other princes stayed in Germany. Not one of them was molested by anybody. They had become unimportant.) Yes, it was not easy for a Kaiser to die honourably. He was condemned to live, and he would live where he was, surrounded by his faithful lieges. The *Weltanschauung* of these lieges, like that of the Kaiser, culminated in the glorification of death in battle. Unfortunately, they did not know either how to put their *Weltanschauung* into practice. They knew only how to demand it of others, including many of their own sons. Then they went home and accepted pensions from the hated Republic that loved them.

The Kaiser and the Crown Prince rejoined the grandees. They decided that he might abdicate as Kaiser if it became absolutely necessary; but a King of Prussia did not leave his post. It was a mere trifle that as long as there was a king of Prussia he could not abdicate as Kaiser without violating the constitution he had sworn to uphold. Above all, he could not do so without destroying the Reich. But separatism was a crime only for those below the throne.

7

General Groener, who had withdrawn for a while, returned with a newcomer, Colonel Heye. The Colonel became Commander-in-Chief of the Reichswehr in 1928 (he was a General by then). He had to leave this post in 1930 because he was too democratic for the German Republic. That morning in November 1918 it was his task to interrogate thirty-nine high-ranking front-line officers who had been summoned to Spa (p. 78). They were asked two questions: could the Kaiser 'reconquer' the fatherland at the head of his troops?; and, would the troops fight with arms against the Bolshevists at home? The first question was answered positively by one officer, negatively by twenty-three officers, and fifteen were doubtful. In answer to the second question there were twelve ayes, eight noes, and nineteen doubtfuls.

The Crown Prince asserted later that this result had been improperly established. He said that these officers, who had come straight from the trenches, had had the two questions shot at them without being given a chance to shave and have a good meal. Had this been done, their outlook would not have been so pessimistic. He thus said by implication that the German Revolution of 1918 occurred because thirty-nine officers did not shave.

Heye came to report the result of the questioning of the front-line officers. He condensed it: 'If Your Majesty wishes to march with them, the troops will ask nothing better and will be delighted. But the army will fight no more, either abroad or at home.'

His Excellency von Hintze undoubtedly was quite as serious as anyone else present. But he must have had a sense of humour. He said: 'His Majesty does not stand in need of an army to take a walk. His Majesty needs an army that fights for him.'

Count von der Schulenburg opposed Heye desperately.

The Kaiser reflected for a few moments. Then he ordered Hintze to telephone to the government his decision, not of partial abdication (that is to say, abdication as German Emperor, but not as King of Prussia), but of his readiness for partial abdication if the step became quite necessary in the opinion of the government. By this, he tried even at this moment to evade the responsibility for his own fate and devolve it upon the Prince. But it was too late for any evasion; when Hintze went to the telephone Scheidemann had just proclaimed the Republic. Two hours earlier the Prince's abdication manifesto (p. 38) had appeared in the streets. Apparently no one in Berlin had had the courage to inform General Headquarters. After speaking a few words to Wahnschaffe, Hintze was interrupted by the request to listen to the report of an important development. He refused to listen; there was nothing that could be more important than His Majesty's decision. He proceeded to read it. When he finished he was told that the King of Prussia who might or might not be prepared to abdicate as German Emperor had already abdicated as both.

In countless telephone calls that morning the government had demanded the abdication. The calls were answered by Hintze, Grünau, Plessen, and Schulenburg. Each time the government were told that they must have patience, it was a matter of minutes, decisions were imminent. The first thing Hintze did on hearing of the manifesto was to protest that the government had no right to draw from his earlier telephone communications the inference that His Majesty was about to renounce the throne. Thus having looked after himself he went to tell the Kaiser that he had abdicated.

The *élite* were stunned. A *coup d'état*, and its first sentence ('The Kaiser and King has resolved to renounce the throne') a lie! Like Hintze the others who had been talking to Berlin protested that the government had no right to draw from their telephone communications the inference it did draw. The government insisted that it had this right. Time and again it was told that a decision was imminent. Could any sane person assume that this decision would be that the Kaiser would *not* abdicate?

And so the German monarchy went down amid an inane squabble of its *élite*. These men did not live in this world. They lived in a fantastically unreal world of their own dreaming, a world of long names, long titles, big words, duties for others, and a pleasantly irresponsible rule for themselves. Whatever they did or did not do had no meaning in the end. Events passed over them as if they did not exist.

X. POWER

While Scheidemann was proclaiming the Republic from a window of the Reichstag on Saturday, 9 November 1918, the German armistice commission conferred with Marshal Foch in the Forest of Compiègne. The Marshal made it clear to the German delegation that they were not there to negotiate but to receive conditions. Their decision was required by Monday, 11 November 1918. The head of the German delegation was Matthias Erzberger. He sent the terms by courier to Hindenburg. They would have to be accepted or rejected by the German government, Ebert's government. Ebert would include the Independents but the Independents did not know what they wanted; their leader, Haase, was away from Berlin.

When unrest persisted in Kiel (p. 72) the cabinet of Prince Max sent the Secretary of State, Haussmann, to that Baltic naval base on 4 November. He was accompanied by Gustav Noske, a Social Democratic Reichstag deputy. Noske persuaded the mutinous sailors to obey his orders. The government made him governor of Kiel upon his request. He reported to the government, however, that no political conclusions could be drawn from the good behaviour of the sailors; he was managing to preserve quiet in the town, but he could not prevent large numbers of sailors from leaving Kiel.

They scattered all over Germany and spread revolution wherever they appeared. Berlin and Munich were the only large cities where sailors did not figure prominently in the first outbreak of the Revolution.

On 7 November the Independents sent Haase to Kiel, too, after the government had refused their request to let him go together with Noske. Haase was to keep the Independent viewpoint before the sailors. But Noske was governor by the time Haase arrived, and he was a better political tactician in any case. Unable to achieve anything, Haase left Kiel for Hamburg on 9 November. The Independents in the capital were paralysed without him. This shows more clearly than anything else that the Independents, and especially Haase, were taken by surprise by the Revolution that they, above all others, were supposed to have 'made'; the same mishap befell them that befell the monarchy—in both cases the head was not where he should have been at the critical moment, namely, in the capital. Upon learning of events in Berlin Haase arrived back there at a late hour on 9 November.

2

Before he arrived, the Independents had started to hold a meeting in the rooms of their *Fraktion* in the Reichstag building. Liebknecht was present, and he did most of the talking. But though an irrepressible fighter he lacked the instinct for that which was practical and necessary. This had shown itself clearly earlier that afternoon when he spoke from the historic balcony of the Palace, two hours after Scheidemann had proclaimed the Republic from the Reichstag window. Scheidemann was impelled by the fear then that Liebknecht would proclaim the soviet republic. To counter him he proclaimed a Social Democratic government. He countered a blow that was not struck. Liebknecht, in his speech from the Palace, proclaimed not the soviet republic but the 'Free Socialistic Republic of Germany'. And even this he did rather inconspicuously somewhere in the middle of his speech only to forget it again and end: 'Those of you who want to see the Free Socialistic Republic of Germany [which he himself had proclaimed a few minutes earlier] raise their hands to swear.' This was nothing at all. Had he done what Scheidemann feared he would do; had he led the 'Bolshies' from the Palace to the Reichstag; had he held up Ebert as the *Imperial* Chancellor he was; and, above all, had he formed a government of his own—he might have won an initial success. But he did not even mention a government, let alone form one. How he intended to govern is a mystery in retrospect. Instead of doing anything he spent some more hours driving about in an automobile, 'like a happy child', made some more impassioned speeches, and then went to the meeting of the Independents.

Meanwhile Ebert had unofficially informed the Independents in a 'rather brusque and superior manner' that he was prepared to take them into his government that would also include representatives of the old ('bourgeois') parties. The Independent Oskar Cohn asked Ebert whether his party might present Liebknecht. He would not object to any particular person, Ebert replied coldly.

A short time after Liebknecht had joined the Independent meeting Scheidemann appeared officially to negotiate the necessary arrangements. Ledebour (p. 62) and Richard Müller, the turner, refused to work with the Social Democrats. Liebknecht went further; he demanded that all power must reside in workers' and soldiers' councils (soviets). Scheidemann was terrified, but he put on a mocking air and asked how this was to look in practice. Then he returned to his *Fraktion* to report.

The Independent meeting continued. It formulated six conditions for their entry into Ebert's government. This done, Ledebour was asked to represent the party as a minister in case the Social Democrats accepted those six conditions. Ledebour refused. Liebknecht was then asked. He consented.

3

The Social Democrats were well aware that the Independent conditions were the bare minimum of what a party that called itself socialist had to demand in a revolution. They were afraid that the rest of their followers would go over to the Independents if they did not accept this minimum. But even so they would not accept it. For a moment they suggested that the Independents form the government exclusively; they would support them. They knew that the Independents were too weak and too confused to form a government, and they used this proposal to bring pressure to bear upon them to modify their conditions. In the end, they sent a reply to the Independents rejecting four of their demands and accepting two. This reply was handed in at 8 p.m. on 9 November.

During that day Ebert had issued six proclamations: (1) to 'the citizens'; (2) to 'all authorities and civil servants'; (3) to the 'home army'; (4) to 'all the troops in Greater Berlin'; (5) and (6) 'to all'. These six proclamations were signed by 'The Reich Chancellor, Ebert'. Reich Chancellor was an Imperial title. But there was no emperor, no empire. What right had Ebert to call himself 'government'? Constitutionally none, for there was no constitution either. He had obtained his office from the monarchy as represented by Prince Max (and not even that was in conformity with the Imperial Constitution) and the monarchy no longer existed. He obviously could not convene the Reichstag. To be sure, the Reichstag would give him a majority, but this majority would contain some of the old parties, and if the workers heard what most of these people expected of the Republic they would not support the government. What right, then, had Ebert to call himself government? None but the right of revolution. But he hated revolution. What power had he to defend his position? None. The whole political, social, and economic structure of Germany was dissolving. He did not even have any force to defend his position; the home army was in full dissolution, too, and the front-line army might dissolve on its way home. By whom was his position threatened? Not by the old régime; it had died a natural death. But by the workers—if he did not give them the socialism they wanted, the workers in whose name he professed to speak, in whose interest he pretended to act.

4

The Independents formulated their six conditions under the influence of the Revolutionary Stewards, and against the opposition of those Spartacists who would not join a government that included Social Democrats. (Any Spartacists who would join, or support, the government would do so under the label of Independents; there was as yet no Spartacist Party.) When the Social Democratic reply arrived the Stewards and the Spartacists had left the Independent meeting. But Haase had appeared in the meantime and the Independents debated, with him in the chair, throughout the night. They compromised with the Social Democrats in the morning of 10 November.

This was bound to happen. The Independents had lost their *raison d'être* with the overthrow of the monarchy and the ending of the war. 'During the war they were whipped on by circumstances and the revolutionary forces in their ranks, especially the Revolutionary Stewards; the rightists among them did not dare to resist. ...After the political change the leftists within the Independent Party continued whipping, but the rightists no longer kept still.' This appraisal is correct, but it does not go to the heart of the problem. The cardinal fact was that the Independents had lost their backbone, namely, the Revolutionary Stewards. We shall see presently that the Revolution vested the political power in the workers' and soldiers' councils. These councils consisted of delegates who were elected by a specified number, usually 1000, of workers in the factories and soldiers in the barracks and hospitals. The local councils thus constituted combined to elect delegates of regional councils. The regional councils formed State councils, and finally there was a central council that covered the whole of Germany. But we must not anticipate too much here. What we must understand at the moment is that what the councils gained in democracy they lost in political ability and experience as compared with the Revolutionary Stewards. The latter were much more exclusive than the councils. They were representatives, it may be recalled, of organized workers who kept their organizations including their official trade union functionaries intact but put themselves under the leadership of the Revolutionary Stewards for political purposes. These political purposes were those of the Independents whom the Stewards and their following acknowledged as their political representation. The vesting of the political power in the councils reduced both the Stewards and the Independents to insignificance during the critical weeks of the Revolution immediately after 9 November. They very soon regained some of their lost importance, but it was too late then to save the Revolution, that is to say, it was too late to save socialism for those who wanted socialism, and it was too late to destroy militarism for those non-socialists and socialists who wanted to destroy militarism. In the meantime, the councils had their day of glory, disaster, and ridicule. They sprang up spontaneously around 9 November, unsponsored by any political organization, though once in being they formed factions that corresponded to existing political parties. They were sincere men for the most part, energetic, completely ignorant of political issues and procedure, sublimely unaware of the immensity of the power they were holding in their hands, hopelessly incapable. Crafty politicians could, and did, do with them as they liked.

5

The following was the basis of the compromise between the Majority Social Democrats and the Independents:

The cabinet consists exclusively of Social Democrats (of both persuasions) who are Commissars of the People and have equal rights.

This does not apply to Departmental Ministers who are merely technical assistants of the cabinet which alone makes policy. Each Departmental Minister is controlled by two members of the Social Democratic parties. These controllers—one Social Democrat and one Independent Social Democrat in each case—have equal rights.

The political power is in the hands of the workers' and soldiers' councils who are to be summoned forthwith to a meeting representing the entire Reich.

The question of the Constituent Assembly is not to be discussed until *after the consolidation of the order created by the Revolution.*

The last point was a bitter pill for Ebert. A day before, speaking to Prince Max, he had said he would 'consider' the question of the Constituent Assembly (p. 40). He then wanted to have the Assembly postponed because the majority of the people might vote for a republic if the elections were held immediately. But now the Republic was there Ebert suddenly wanted the Constituent Assembly at the earliest possible moment. If it were delayed, the revolutionary socialists might enforce a new social order, and the Assembly would then confirm this new order, the 'order created by the Revolution'; just as the Assembly, if elected immediately, would confirm the old and substantially still existing, though dissolving, militarist State in a new form. But Ebert had to yield for the moment; the Independents absolutely insisted that the Assembly be postponed.

The basis of the compromise stated also that the political power was vested in the workers' and soldiers' councils and that the members of the government were called People's Commissars. All this sounded very revolutionary. But Ebert agreed to the compromise, and the Council of People's Commissars was formed. It consisted of six members: Ebert, Scheidemann, and Landsberg for the Majority Socialists; Haase, Barth, and Dittmann for the Independents. Liebknecht had withdrawn when he saw the compromise.

Barth was the chairman of the Revolutionary Stewards and was now succeeded as such by Richard Müller who had also preceded him in that office (p. 64). Dittmann was the Reichstag deputy who had been sentenced to five years in a fortress for speaking at that open-air meeting in the strike of January 1918 (p. 63). He was released, along with Liebknecht and Rosa Luxemburg, on 21 October 1918.

6

Ebert agreed to become a People's Commissar, he agreed to the postponement of the Constituent Assembly, he would have agreed to anything—he had had a *tête-à-tête* early on Sunday, 10 November, before the compromise with the Independents was concluded. This *tête-à-tête* was conducted by long-distance telephone with General Groener who was at army headquarters. Ebert began the conversation by bluffing the General. He asked him, in an authoritative tone of voice, how Groener was going to treat the soldiers' councils. Nothing daunted, Groener replied innocently that the commanders had orders to put themselves on good terms with them. (Scheidemann wrote in his memoirs later that the 'Supreme Command...fully recognized and admirably hoodwinked the workers' and soldiers' councils.') The two understood each other. 'What do you expect of us?' asked Ebert. Groener said that the Field-Marshal (Hindenburg) and the officer corps expected the government to combat Bolshevism; they were placing themselves at the disposal of the government for this purpose. 'Please convey to the Field-Marshal the thanks of the government', said Ebert.

He informed his fellow-commissars of the agreement he had made with Groener about the recognition of the soldiers' councils. He did not inform them of the understanding about the combating of Bolshevism. He knew, and he wanted it to be so, that 'Bolshevism' in this case meant any kind of new State for Germany; that it meant the destruction of the power of those groups that had plunged Germany into the war. The destruction of this power would have been possible without Bolshevism.

But Ebert was not entirely happy. It was a long way from France and Belgium to Berlin. Much water would flow under the bridge before the military guarantors of his position would arrive in the capital. Liebknecht was dangerous, Barth was watchful, and the majority of the workers wanted socialism. It was small consolation that Scheidemann disparaged the workers by saying that nine-tenths of them were industrially and politically unskilled; that Scheidemann (who always told others the Social Democrats were so democratic that the leaders could not order their followers about) said of his own action of proclaiming the Republic: 'The Bolshevist wave that threatened to engulf Germany had spent its force'; merely because he made a speech. Or that Scheidemann said to Barth one of those days: 'I don't know why you are always bothering about the masses. They must do as we want, and they'll do it, too, if it is made properly palatable to them.'

7

The leaders of the Revolutionary Stewards went to the chamber of the Reichstag upon leaving the Independent meeting on the evening of Saturday, 9 November. An assembly of soldiers' councils was sitting in the chamber.

One of the six proclamations of the Imperial Chancellor, Ebert, was an 'Order to All the Troops in Greater Berlin'. It began: 'The elected representatives of all the troops in Greater Berlin have formed an Action Committee.' This was not true. When genuine soldiers' councils were elected the next day, they demanded the dissolution of the Action Committee because it had not been chosen by anyone and represented no one. It was, in fact, drummed up by Ebert and Wels. But Ebert no longer needed it the next day; for although in existence for only twenty-four hours the Action Committee had fulfilled the purpose of its creators. This purpose was to sow confusion among the soldiers; to establish a military force (a day before Ebert's *tête-à-tête* with Groener, when he did not know what Supreme Command were thinking of his government); and to 'elect' Wels commander of that force and, more permanently, commandant of Berlin. Wels was the man who had persuaded the Naumburg Rifles to join the Revolution (p. 16).

The assembly of the soldiers' councils was dominated by the short-lived Action Committee. It was incapable of doing anything

94

sensible because nobody present knew how to conduct, or to behave at, a meeting. Eventually, Barth took the chair and managed to get a resolution adopted. This resolution appeared in the Sunday newspapers. It instructed all soldiers and workers to gather in their barracks, hospitals, and factories on Sunday morning to elect delegates (councils or soviets). The details of the basis of election were given.

It was midnight by the time the resolution was adopted. The leaders of the Revolutionary Stewards tried to get in touch with as many of their sub-officers as possible in order to entreat them to dissuade the workers from electing Social Democratic councils. The right wing of the Independents did not take part in the elections in order to leave a clear field to the Social Democrats. As a result, Karl Liebknecht and Rosa Luxemburg were not elected to the councils.

Every worker read *Vorwärts* on Sunday morning. 'It had become the official gazette overnight', writes Hermann Müller[1] in his memoirs. The paper announced that the events of yesterday had united the working class, but that some small groups were making efforts to thwart the councils. The Social Democrats naturally favoured the councils (in spite of the fact that Scheidemann, for once, was slow at realizing a point, p. 88), not because they liked the soviet idea, but because the councils put the Independents and the Revolutionary Stewards as bodies out of the

---

[1] Hermann Müller was a leading right-wing Majority Socialist. He was Reich Chancellor in 1920 and again from 1928 to 1930. His memoirs are greatly concerned with proving that the Social Democrats were 'good Germans' and had nothing to do with the Revolution of 1918. Thus, he relates, for instance, that the envoy of the Naumburg Rifles (p. 15) reported at Social Democratic headquarters that the soldiers would join the Revolution. Thereupon, his memoirs continue, Wels drove to their barracks and 'made it clear to the soldiers that they had to decide whether or not they would take up arms against their own people'. Why Wels should have said this if the soldiers had already declared themselves in support of the Revolution would be a mystery if Müller were not endeavouring to convey the idea that Wels tried to make the soldiers stay in the barracks rather than fight 'against their own people', that is, those monarchists who might take to arms in defence of the monarchy.

fight for power. Said *Vorwärts*: 'Unity must not be disturbed by a few people who are embittered and whose characters are not strong enough to overcome and forget their old resentment.... The old Social Democratic Party is striving for unity with all its might and is prepared to bring sacrifices....It has no selfish goal. It is permeated by the thought that only a unanimous and united working class can get us out of the disaster into which the vanquished imperialism had pushed us.'

Jubilation reigned in the factories over the unity of the workers' movement as proclaimed by *Vorwärts*. The best the Revolutionary Stewards could obtain in many plants was the election of councils that were composed of equal numbers of Independents or Spartacists and Social Democrats. The councils were to meet the same day, Sunday, 10 November 1918.

It was obviously necessary for the Social Democrats to try to dominate the councils from which the government had consented to accept its office. In view of the possibility that the councils might not remain tractable even if they should become so for the time being, it was further necessary for the Social Democrats to replace the councils by a Constituent Assembly as the source of the government's power. It was clear that such an Assembly would acknowledge the old militaristic State as the substance of Germany's future unless a new substance were created, though not moulded in every detail, before the elections to the Assembly took place. Therefore, the Revolutionary Stewards argued, every attempt must be made to prevent the question of the Constituent Assembly from coming up at the councils' meeting. To this end they decided to propose the formation of an executive committee of the councils. For members of this committee they would suggest the most reliable Stewards and Spartacists. As they could not expect to obtain a majority for this programme by frankness, they would try to bluff the meeting by saying nothing about the functions of the proposed committee. The bluff was quite unnecessary, for Ebert, as we shall see, had no intention whatever of bringing up the question of the Constituent Assembly.

The workers' and soldiers' councils met in the Busch Circus, in the heart of Berlin, on Sunday afternoon. There were about 3000 delegates. Barth was in the chair. Ebert was the first speaker. He said the formation of the government (the understanding between Majority Socialists and Independents, p. 91) was the beginning of unity. The completion of unity would assure the victory of the Revolution. Haase spoke in the same vein. Liebknecht, who had not been elected, spoke as a guest. He violently attacked Ebert and said he was a menace to the Revolution.

Barth then proposed the election of an executive committee. He submitted a list with the names of candidates and made a speech to prove the necessity of such a committee, although the Stewards had agreed to say nothing. To be sure, he did not say what the committee's functions were to be. Just this, however, made his speech obscure. Ebert demanded the floor. He did not see the necessity for a committee, he declared; but if there was to be one it would naturally have to consist of equal numbers of Independents and Majority Socialists. Barth declared there must be no Social Democrat in the committee. Pandemonium broke loose upon this. The soldiers shouted, 'Unity! Parity!', stormed up on the platform and threatened they would establish a military dictatorship and carry on the Revolution without the political parties and the workers if there were no unity among the parties, no parity in the committee. The meeting was interrupted.

Ebert had clearly seen through Barth's bluff, though he could not have known its object (to prevent discussion of the Constituent Assembly). But the affair was so transparently fishy that he must have feared he would arouse suspicion if he did not demand parity. It is hardly likely that he was really interested in parity; the behaviour of the soldiers must have shown him what he could only hope for before the meeting started, namely, that he had nothing to fear from these councils. On the other hand, he certainly did not want a military dictatorship of the soldiers' councils.

He was quite satisfied with Hindenburg and Groener. He negotiated with the Stewards during the recess. They agreed to elect a
committee of eleven. Nine of them were to be Stewards, and two
Social Democrats.

The meeting resumed. The agreement was announced. The
soldiers raved worse than before, demanding parity. Eventually,
a committee of fourteen was elected, seven Social Democrats and
seven Independents. The latter were Revolutionary Stewards.
Suddenly the soldiers demanded they be represented on the committee, too. Fourteen of them were elected. This suited Ebert.
These soldiers were confused, quite unpolitical, and had no idea of
the struggle that was going on behind the scene between Majority
Socialists, Independents, Revolutionary Stewards and Spartacists.
Thus, the Stewards' undignified and childish attempt at making
revolution by trickery concluded with their defeat.

The new body was called the Executive Council of the
Workers' and Soldiers' Councils. It had forty members in its
final form. Thirteen were Social Democrats and thirteen Independents, each of these factions including representatives of the
soldiers of Berlin. Five others were representatives of the soldiers
of the Western Front, three of the Eastern Front, three of the navy.
And one member each represented Bavaria, Alsace-Lorraine, and
that part of the Rhineland that would shortly be occupied by the
enemy; the latter was Heinrich Schäfer (p. 15). Richard Müller,
the originator of the Revolutionary Stewards, became chairman
of the Executive Council.

The Busch meeting finally elected a provisional government;
provisional because the councils were to work out a constitution
for Germany on the basis of which a fully responsible government
would be formed. The provisional government consisted of the
six men who, on the previous day, had consented to accept their
mandate from the workers' and soldiers' councils. Ebert and
Haase were joint chairmen. Ebert was responsible for the interior
and military affairs; Haase for external affairs; Scheidemann for
finances; Dittmann for demobilization, communications, justice,

and public health; Landsberg for the press, art and literature; and Barth for social policy.

The Busch meeting ended by unanimously adopting a proclamation 'To the Working People'. It said that Germany was a *socialist* republic and that the political power resided in the workers' and soldiers' councils. The first task of the provisional government was to conclude the armistice. The following day was the deadline for the acceptance of the enemy's terms (p. 86). The proclamation then went on: 'The rapid socialization of the capitalist means of production...is possible without great dislocation. It is necessary for the building of a new economic order out of the blood-soaked ruins and in order to prevent the enslavement of the masses of the people as well as the destruction of civilization.' This programme was amateurish. But its unanimous adoption proved that the councils wanted socialism.

9

Nearly the entire Press published the proclamation of the councils which for all its defects was the basic constitutional law of the land. All classes, with the exception of the revolutionary workers, looked upon the councils as the legislative body of Germany. They knew, or thought they new, that they could not resist the councils. They resigned themselves to, or else welcomed, the fact that Germany was to be socialist.

Vorwärts did not publish the proclamation. But it published, a little later, an editorial that dealt with the situation then existing in Germany as seen by the paper's editor-in-chief, Friedrich Stampfer. The editorial said that the change in the Imperial Constitution that had come into force with the formation of Prince Max's government meant 'that a government that has not the confidence of the people must not remain in office, and that the military power is subordinate to the civilian power'. In other words, the military power was to remain unchanged, and it was to be controlled by 'the people'. But 'the people', Editor Stampfer deduced, were not holding the civilian power; only a section of the people were holding it, namely, the councils, that is to say, the workers and soldiers whom the councils represented. Therefore, the People's Commissars were not commissars of the entire people; they had to be made commissars of the entire people, and this could be done only through a Constituent Assembly.

This argument sounded very plausible. If it had meant nothing but the prevention of socialism, it would have been accepted by the majority of Germans (which majority, unlike that of the German workers, did not want socialism). But it meant more than the prevention of socialism; it meant the maintenance of the old order in the new form of a republic. 'The people' were never asked whether they wanted democratic capitalism or militaristic capitalism. They were asked whether they wanted capitalism or socialism. The majority of the nation being non-socialist they chose capitalism without knowing (because they were not told) what they were really bargaining for. Ebert could not afford to tell them, because he wanted to use militarism to defeat social change.

At that meeting between the trade union functionaries, Social Democratic leaders, and Groener (p. 76), Ebert had taken leave of the General with these words: 'We are grateful to your Excellency for this frank exchange of views, and we shall always have pleasant memories of our work with you during the war. We have reached the parting of our ways. Who knows whether we shall ever see each other again.' Several years later Groener said in public: 'I confess myself entirely to blame for not having taken up Ebert's proposal that day, for not having said at once to Ebert: "Herr Ebert, I take your word for it, we will stand by one another...." Perhaps, had I done so, the monarchy might still have been saved.' The monarchy could not be saved, but the militaristic State could be, and was, saved.

Ebert picked up the power that was lying on the ground (part of it to begin with, the rest followed soon) and restored it to those from whose hands it had fallen, the militarists and the groups they served. He alone of sixty million Germans acted that day, 9 November 1918. Whatever may have to be said about his character and his motivations (which we shall discuss in a moment), to watch in retrospect the keenness of this former leather worker's political intuition and the gigantic force of his drive must stimulate every mind that is not closed to learning by blinkers of hostility or blindness of partisanship.

XI. LEGITIMACY

Ebert was faced by a dilemma. The first proclamation he had issued on 9 November was addressed 'To the German Citizens'. It began: 'The outgoing Reich Chancellor, Prince Max of Baden, has, with the consent of all the Secretaries of State, transferred upon me the administration of the office of Reich Chancellor. I am about to form the new government in agreement with the parties and shall report to the public forthwith.' Now, the Chancellor and the Secretaries of State had no constitutional right to transfer the Chancellor's office to anyone else, nor had anyone else the right to accept this office from them. Ebert's first proclamation thus was constitutionally absurd. Of course, this happened before Scheidemann proclaimed the Republic, but after Prince Max had declared the abdication of the Kaiser. Twenty-four hours later that absurdity could no longer be maintained. Ebert became a People's Commissar and acknowledged that the political power resided in the workers' and soldiers' councils. Germany was, in fact, a soviet republic.

The government, now called the Council of People's Commissars, issued its first proclamation two days later, on 12 November 1918. It began: 'The government *that has been created by the revolution* is purely socialistic. *It sets itself the task of carrying into effect the socialistic programme.* As a beginning it proclaims with the force of law the following...' (my italics). There followed nine decrees of a mostly political character which, though laudable from any point of view except the reactionary (for instance, the special police passes that domestic servants had to carry were abolished), had nothing to do with socialism. The main point, however, is this: the workers' and soldiers' councils had, by that amateurish manifesto of Sunday (p. 99), confirmed the government. This could only mean that the councils conferred upon the government the executive power. However, with its first proclamation ('proclaims with the force of law') the government usurped the legislative power as well. But then, what should the Council of People's Commissars, that is to say, the executive branch of government, execute if the Executive Council of the Workers' and Soldiers' Councils, that is to say, the legislative branch of government, made only speeches instead of laws that could and should be executed?

As for the government's profession of socialism in its first proclamation, it certainly was sincere on the part of Haase, Dittmann and Barth. There would have to be doubts, though, about the sincerity of Ebert, Scheidemann and Landsberg if one were to judge only by their actions then as well as their actions before and after (but not by their publicly spoken words which always expressed a socialist conviction); these actions never were the actions of socialists. However, some of these doubts are dispelled if we take into consideration the revolutionary enthusiasm of the November days. For men who spent all of their lives in the socialist movement to remain unaffected by that enthusiasm would have been unmitigated cynicism, and if we can perhaps discover some measure of cynicism in the make-up of Landsberg, and traces of it in that of Scheidemann, there was none of it in Ebert. Then again it might be concluded that if men could spend all of their lives in the socialist movement without being socialists, they would have to be unmitigated cynics. This conclusion would be fallacious because Ebert, Scheidemann, and Landsberg regarded themselves as socialists, but their interpretation of socialist theory made them act in a way that looked traitorous to revolutionary doctrinaires, while it must look unintelligent, though highly effectual, to non-doctrinaires.

It is also possible that Ebert, Scheidemann and Landsberg were, on the occasion of the government's first proclamation, moved not so much by enthusiasm as by the fear that they would be swept aside if they did not once more profess socialism. We can never be certain of the motives men have at any given moment, even if they proclaim them. For instance, every time Ebert professed socialism he lied objectively because socialism could not be had without social revolution, and he did not want social revolution. Therefore, socialism never was the motive of his actions, no matter how often he professed his socialist conviction with subjective sincerity. The decisive point, thus, is that whenever he talked socialism he just talked and never let it become the motive of his actions; and when he talked it, it was either from a fleeting impulse or else because he held that circumstances demanded such talk for tactical purposes.

Of course, German history was not changed because Ebert, Scheidemann, and Landsberg did not want social revolution. It was not changed at all. It had arrived at a cross-roads, one of which led deviously back to the old State while the other led straight on to social revolution (either socialist or democratic-capitalist). German history, or rather the German nation, had arrived at that cross-roads and stood faltering, waiting for leadership. This leadership could have come from Ebert or from Liebknecht. Liebknecht, as we have seen and shall see in more detail, failed hopelessly. Had he been a leader he would have taken the road ahead. But both roads were open to any leader. Ebert chose the road back. That he chose it deliberately is shown by his actions at every turn, except those turns where his actions were guided by the needs of the moment (e.g. p. 92), or where the force of events overwhelmed him (e.g. pp. 169 and 171). Why he chose the road back is a psychological problem that cannot be solved, not even if we assume that he was sincere in his interpretation of socialist theory. This (Reformist) interpretation culminated in the belief that a social change in Germany at that time could only be reactionary, because any progressive change required that capitalist evolution ran its full course before capitalism could change to socialism; it had not done so, according to Reformist interpretation, and therefore change had to be prevented. Now, no matter how sincere Ebert was in holding these beliefs, his interpretation did not demand and (if the thought had ever occurred to its originators) would have rejected the use of violence by one group of socialist leaders and their followers against the leaders and followers of another group of socialists who held a different interpretation of the same Marxian theory.

Ebert could take the road back only because the masses that followed him, followed him blindly. Being what they were (see especially p. 160), their leaders could have led them into socialism or democratic capitalism just as they did lead them back to the old State.

In so far as the government's first proclamation was not socialist talk, it was anti-revolutionary (in every sense) action. It said: 'All elections to public bodies are in the future to be carried out according to the equal, secret, direct, and universal suffrage on the basis of the proportional electoral system for all male and female persons who are at least twenty years of age. *This franchise applies also to the Constituent Assembly concerning which a detailed statement will be made*' (my italics).

The manifesto of the workers' and soldiers' councils (the one that was not published by *Vorwärts*) was two days old. It contained not a word about a Constituent Assembly. To be sure, the majority of delegates at the Busch meeting on Sunday afternoon were politically unskilled and undisciplined, but if Ebert had brought up the subject of the Constituent Assembly then they would have realized its meaning, namely, the question whether or not Germany was to be militaristic. Though not synonymous with socialism, non-militarism did mean socialism to the otherwise confused Busch meeting, while a Constituent Assembly to be convened soon meant no socialism to them. They could see nothing but black or white, and this was due to the propaganda of the Revolutionary Stewards and their allies. The failure of these men to realize this effect of their own propaganda, and their consequent engineering of the bluff to prevent discussion of the Constituent Assembly (p. 97), were a remarkable example of political denseness. They failed to see, too, that Ebert appraised the effect of their propaganda correctly. Because he did appraise it correctly he said nothing of a Constituent Assembly at the Busch Circus. He had to be careful anyway because the compromise on which the government rested (p. 91) was quite fresh in everybody's mind on Sunday afternoon; it had been laid down only that morning. And it stipulated that the question of the Constituent Assembly was not to be discussed until *after the consolidation of the order created by the Revolution.*

But Ebert discussed this question two days later, in the first proclamation of the new government. And this created his dilemma. The councils, the source of the political power he had acknowledged, wanted socialism. He 'hated social revolution like sin' (p. 33). By conjuring up an *early* Constituent Assembly, this bulwark against any (including democratic-capitalist) social change, he divested the councils of political power, if only in anticipation. At the same time he shattered any basis of legitimacy. For if the councils were divested of political power, the government was divested of its legitimacy; it had no legitimation other than the mandate of the councils. There can be no government with an anticipatory legitimation unless it be a dictatorship. And indeed, Ebert, Imperial Chancellor for twenty-four hours, a People's Commissar for the next forty-eight, became a member of a dictatorial government.

This dictatorial government had no force whatever behind it; and on what else could a dictatorial government rest for any length of time? There were no reliable soldiers in the capital. The Spartacists, by comparison, would have had behind them the force of the majority of the workers—if their leaders had succeeded in enlightening the workers about the issues at stake. However, these leaders, with the exception of Rosa Luxemburg perhaps, were hardly less confused than their following. Worse than that, they were incompetent to the point of criminal folly. It took no particular acumen to realize this fact. Ebert, a politician of unsurpassed astuteness and energy, did more than merely realize it. He set in motion a train of legalistic dodges that were as tragic in their consequences as they are instructive to view in retrospect. He did so under the very eyes of a great nation whose politically conscious if uneducated and slow-thinking masses he was deceiving. He did so under the very eyes of the whole world. He ought not, however, to be given all the credit for the Social Democratic stratagems of 1918–19. It is likely that many of them were thought up by his Social Democratic co-Commissar, Otto Landsberg, a lawyer. It is significant that Landsberg was one of the few prominent Germans of that time who never wrote a line of memoirs.[1]

2

Shortly after their proclamation about the Constituent Assembly (p. 105), or perhaps simultaneously with it, the Council of People's Commissars issued a decree as follows: 'The Federal Council (*Bundesrat*) is empowered to exercise also in future the administrative functions incumbent on it according to the laws and decrees of the Reich.' This edict was a masterpiece of casuistry. The last few words implied that it was new future laws the Federal Council was to administer. But there was no law that constituted the Federal Council itself, or rather, there was only one such law, namely, the old Imperial Constitution.

Under that Constitution the members of the Federal Council were appointed by the rulers of the Federal States. If they had been elected by the people, the *Bundesrat* would superficially have resembled the United States Senate. The same would have been true if they had been appointed by elected representatives of the people, which constitutional practice is commonly pursued in the United States in certain circumstances. But there were two fundamental differences. The first of them was that the Members of the *Bundesrat* did not vote as individuals but were instructed by their

[1] Landsberg (born in 1862) fell into political oblivion long before Hitler came to power. For a time he was German ambassador in Brussels. After the advent of the Nazis he went into exile in Belgium. At the end of the Second World War he was found to be living in Baaren (Utrecht), Holland.

governments. And secondly, the German Federal States did not have an equal number of representatives in the *Bundesrat*. The whole body had fifty-eight members of whom no more than seventeen were Prussian. But Prussia had the power of veto in Reich constitutional matters in that a proposed change of the Reich Constitution was considered rejected if more than fourteen votes were cast against it in the Federal Council, the upper house of the two-house Imperial German Parliament (the lower house being the Reichstag). Beyond this, Prussia had a preponderance in all matters because she found it always easy to obtain a majority in the *Bundesrat* with the help of some of the smaller Federal States that were dependent on her in many ways. Considering that Prussia comprised three-fifths of the population of the Reich, this state of affairs was natural, but it was intolerable in the long run; a representative body that is not based on proportionality cannot last if the number of its component parts is relatively small and one of these parts is as preponderant as Prussia was in Germany. The trouble with Prussia was not that she was politically dominant in the Reich, but that she was numerically and economically preponderant while her political and social structures were trailing decades behind her economic and population development.

Now, the rulers of the Federal States had disappeared in November 1918, but the People's Commissars appeared willing to have in the Republic a law-making body that was not elected and could not, for the time being, be appointed by elected representatives of the people because such representatives had not yet been elected themselves. That the Independent People's Commissars signed the decree continuing the Federal Council reveals their bewilderment. But the Social Democratic Commissars had several good reasons for wanting to maintain the *Bundesrat*.

The most obvious reason was of course that the Federal Council perpetuated the Prussian right of veto in constitutional matters. However, only the administrative functions of the *Bundesrat* were to be continued for the time being, and in this sphere the Reichstag had, on 4 August 1914, given the *Bundesrat* extraordinary powers in economic affairs as well as financial affairs. Throughout the war the *Bundesrat* occupied a central position in the regulation and control of Germany's economic life. These extraordinary powers of the *Bundesrat* were not revoked in the Revolution. Instead, the *Bundesrat* was 'to exercise also in the future the administrative functions incumbent on it according to the laws and decrees of the Reich'. If, then, the workers' and soldiers' councils should misguide themselves into enacting socialistic laws, these laws would have to be administered by the *Bundesrat*, or else the *Bundesrat* could thwart their execution if they were to be carried out by some other agency. In any case, confusion would be heaped upon confusion, and this was what Ebert and his friends wanted. They wanted to create a multiplicity of competencies and play with all of them by setting them against each other. They achieved what they wanted.

However, this particular success was not wholly due to their brilliant inspiration. It was also due to the incompetency of the Executive Council of the Workers' and Soldiers' Councils. A day earlier, 11 November 1918 (the day between the Sunday meeting in the Busch Circus and the Tuesday proclamation about the Federal Council), the Executive Council had published the following decree: 'All the authorities of the Countries [*Länder*, as the Federal States were called after the Revolution], of the Reich, and of the Military continue to operate. All orders of these authorities are made in the name of the Executive Council of the Workers' and Soldiers' Councils.... All further orders and regulations will be issued immediately by the competent civilian and military authorities.' What the Executive Council meant to express by this decree was, of course, that there was no other power in Germany but theirs. But in their ignorance of the fundamental facts of political life they did not realize that they were writing, with a recklessness that almost surpasses belief, a *carte blanche* such as has seldom been written.

The Social Democratic People's Commissars must have been

amazed when the Executive Council issued this decree; it was infinitely more than they could have dared to expect. The decree said in simple words that the entire administrative and military apparatus of the seemingly dead militaristic State, an apparatus wholly manned by Conservatives, reactionaries, and their satellites, was to continue to function unchanged. Ebert acted quickly. He implemented this decree by giving substance to the form it set up. It was not his fault that if the Executive Council for once made a law instead of talking, it established executive agencies without making any laws that these agencies were to execute. The substance Ebert poured into the form was the laws and decrees of the Empire. Cautiously, he wrapped it in that ambiguous proclamation about the Federal Council. Cautiously, he revived only the administrative functions of the *Bundesrat*, not its legislative functions. Even the Executive Council of the Workers' and Soldiers' Council might have awakened from its political slumber if its legislative prerogative had been encroached upon openly. Of course, all the government needed was that administrative function in order to forestall socialism, if the Executive Council should at any time take its socialistic protestations seriously. But Ebert and his friends did not make plans for the day; they worked with undiminished vigour each day. They made plans for the morrow.

Through no initiative of theirs, but through a brilliant follow-up, the old State had been brought back to life at one stroke, or two strokes if you will. No general election, no Constituent Assembly, nothing at all except a social revolution (democratic capitalist or socialist) could get around this fact. The militaristic State had come back to life, then. It was shaky, it could not stand on its own feet as yet, Hindenburg and Groener and their cadres were still far away. But the thing was living.

The Executive Council was blissfully unaware that by its decree about the authorities of Imperial Germany it had formally abdicated the power it never wielded in reality. Five days later, on 16 November 1918, it debated a motion by the Independent member Däumig (p. 73), that meant in effect the elimination of the middle and upper classes including their reactionary wings from the political life of Germany, the very wings whose power the Council itself had confirmed by that decree. To be more precise, it had confirmed the power of the upper middle class (the large industrial, commercial, and financial interests) and the aristocracy. The lower middle class was at that time overwhelmingly democratic and anti-militaristic though rather inarticulate; it was represented by the comparatively small progressive Liberal Party under its brilliant leader, von Payer, and by the majority of the Catholic Centre Party which had to live down a disagreeable recent past but was rapidly growing progressive under the leadership of the equally brilliant Erzberger and several others like him.

Däumig's motion was also to do away with the impossible situation that the workers' and soldiers' councils represented, not the entire Reich, but only Berlin. The motion said in its most important points: 'The endeavour of the bourgeoisie [these revolutionaries never distinguished between the progressive bourgeoisie on the one hand, and the conservative and reactionary bourgeoisie on the other] to convene a Constituent Assembly as soon as possible is designed to rob the workers of the fruits of the revolution.... By combining all workers' and soldiers' councils of Germany a central council...must be formed. It must deliberate a new constitution conforming to the principles of proletarian democracy.' The motion was defeated by 12 votes to 10. It was then changed, and carried, to the effect that the proposed central council 'shall draft a new constitution conforming to the principles of proletarian democracy. This constitution is to be submitted to a Constituent Assembly convened by...the central council.' Thus the Executive Council changed a motion that condemned a Constituent Assembly to one that demanded it. It retreated step by step.

The incident nevertheless emphasized a development that, though not dangerous to Ebert and his friends, was unpleasant to them. The Executive Council was growing radical in that non-partisan members (for the Council's composition see p. 98) frequently voted with the Independents who could in almost every case rely on obtaining compromises based on motions of theirs. Of course, the Executive Council remained ineffectual. But it needed watching. A grave difficulty, though again no real danger, would have arisen if the Executive Council had carried the original Independent motion with its demand that the constitution to be drafted by the Executive Council was to be submitted for approval to a central council of the workers' and soldiers' councils to be created by the same resolution. Instead, the compromise demanded that the draft constitution of the Executive Council was to be submitted to the Constituent Assembly that Ebert wanted (although it was to be convened by the central council; in other words, the field of disagreement had narrowed down). The vote was close, but the Executive Council, for ever grappling with revolutionary theories and social theories in general, had at last produced something that was realistic. As against this achievement, however, the Council was clearly incapable of drafting a constitution; it lacked everything this task required—men, ideas, and all hope of agreement. None the less, it was worth Ebert's while to show the Council his appreciation of their having agreed to the Constituent Assembly.

Consequently, an agreement was signed between the government and the Executive Council of the Workers' and Soldiers' Councils on 22 November 1918. It spoke of a new *constitutional* order. What the Executive Council wanted, and Germany needed, was of course a new *social* order. They made things easy for the old State and its defenders at every point.

The Revolution has created a new constitutional order. For the initial period of transition the new legal state finds its expression in the

following agreement between the Executive Council of the Workers'
and Soldiers' Councils and the Council of People's Commissars:

1. The political power resides in the Workers' and Soldiers' Councils
of the German Socialist Republic. It is their task to maintain and build
up the achievements of the Revolution and to hold down counter-
revolution.

2. The Berlin Executive Council exercises the functions of the
Workers' and Soldiers' Councils of the German Republic in agreement
with the Workers' and Soldiers' Councils of Greater Berlin until an
assembly of delegates of the Workers' and Soldiers' Councils elects an
executive council for the German Republic.

3. The investiture of the Council of People's Commissars by the
Workers' and Soldiers' Councils of Greater Berlin signifies the transfer
of the executive power of the Republic.

4. The appointment and dismissal of the policy-making cabinet of
the Republic...is the prerogative of the Central Executive Council
which also has the right of control.

5. The Executive Council must be consulted before Departmental
Ministers are appointed by the cabinet.

A Reich assembly of delegates of the Workers' and Soldiers' Councils
will be convened as soon as possible. The date will be proclaimed.

This agreement, for what it was worth, declared in unequivocal
terms that Germany was a republic of councils (soviets). Yet it did
no harm for the Social Democratic People's Commissars to sign;
not only because it dealt merely with questions of political
organization, but also because they knew that what real power
there was at the time was in the hands of the administrative and
military State apparatus, not in the hands of the Executive
Council. And the State apparatus was in Ebert's hands through his
agreement with Groener (p. 93) as well as through the Executive
Council's decrees about the continuance of the authorities of the
old State (p. 109).

4

However, there was an immediate issue that was really menacing
the government's position. The leaders of the Executive Council,
for once, realized this issue as clearly as Ebert and his friends. If

they succeeded in establishing an armed revolutionary force (which they had the right to do) the Revolution might still be saved. To be sure, vast quantities of arms were in the hands of the revolutionary workers. But these workers did not command an organized military force. They had not used their arms so far because no one was openly resisting socialism. But the old militaristic groups were waiting. They were waiting for Ebert to disarm the revolutionary workers. Ebert was not yet in a position to do so, but he knew that with the administrative and military apparatus of the old State in his hands things were bound to take almost any course he wanted them to take, provided he was not thwarted by an organized revolutionary military force created before his own military force under the command of Hindenburg and Groener arrived in the capital. Time was what he needed more than anything else.

At the second meeting of the Executive Council Däumig moved that a Red Guard be formed. He demanded that the Executive Council have at its disposal a force of at least 2000 politically and industrially organized men for the protection of the Revolution. So precarious was all power in Germany at that time that a loyal force of 2000 men would have sufficed to establish the authority of anyone who had such a force at his disposal.

The Social Democratic leaders had anticipated such a move; and had taken preventive counter-measures. They had told the soldiers' councils that the Executive Council would sooner or later regard them as superfluous and that they would lose their jobs if a revolutionary force were established. The soldiers' councils met to discuss Däumig's motion.

It was quite natural that many individual soldiers of the German army were demoralized through the war. It was equally natural that a number of shady elements found their way into many of the councils. Ebert's most effective agitator among the soldiers was Lieutenant Colin Ross.[1] As a soldiers' representative Ross was a

[1] Ross became one of Hitler's foremost geopoliticians. A world traveller of renown whose books were translated into many languages and read in many

prominent member of the Executive Council. He succeeded in rousing the soldiers to such a pitch of fury over Däumig's motion that the Executive Council had to drop it; the attitude of the soldiers threatened, unintentionally, to bring about a military counter-revolution. Ebert had won another battle.

5

The paralysing and discrediting of the workers' and soldiers' councils took various other forms, too. For instance, the old civilian and military authorities sent all kinds of people who had all kinds of petitions, requests, complaints, and demands to the Executive Council telling them that their affairs could be settled by this body only. On certain days the building of the Prussian Diet where the Executive Council was quartered was besieged by thousands of persons who had business that was no concern whatever of the Council's. They went away cursing the body which was the source of political power and, as they saw it, unable to do anything. This game of persecuting the Executive Council had a special reason in so far as it was played by the administrative government departments. They wanted to prove by it to the people at large and to the People's Commissars, in which latter case they succeeded, that they would be foolish to attempt any interference with the permanent gentlemen of the bureaucracy. It was a demonstration of their indispensableness and their might. The right of control of the departments, which was a prerogative of the Executive Council (pp. 91 and 113), was never exercised. It was sabotaged out of existence by the *Geheimräte* (privy councillors, heads of sections in the departments) while it was still in embryo.

Money topics are always a favourite means of slander among

countries, he was a high-class spy between the two wars, cordially accepted everywhere in certain social and political circles. Hardly a non-European country was spared his visits and clandestine activities. He committed suicide in 1946.

political hypocrites. Early in December 1918, the Reich Finance Minister, Schiffer, formerly a National Liberal, then a Democrat, made a speech at the Berlin Chamber of Commerce. He said, among other things, that 'the sums that have been taken from the Treasury for higher soldiers' pay, for new emoluments of all kinds, and for expenses connected with present conditions, exceed a billion' (i.e. marks; at that time a billion marks was equivalent to $125 millions). The soldiers' councils were not mentioned in Schiffer's speech. On the next day, *Vorwärts* quoted a 'reliable source' to the effect that 'the workers' and soldiers' councils have spent 800 million marks in the first two weeks of their existence'. The general Press took up *Vorwärts* report and asserted that the figure of 800 millions was decidedly too low; 1800 million marks had been spent by the councils. These writers knew of course that they were speaking, and that Schiffer had spoken, of the entire cost of the demobilization of the army. The money spent for this purpose certainly approached the billion mark then, but it had nothing to do with the workers' and soldiers' councils.

In fact, the Executive Council, which was none the less only one council of many, never received much more than 619,943·70 marks (roughly $75,000). This money had a curious origin. A professional swindler by the name of Ettisch had managed to be made commander of the Imperial Palace in Berlin on 9 November 1918. A few days later, a registered packet addressed to the Keeper of the Kaiser's Privy Purse and containing an amount in Swiss franc notes arrived in the Palace. Ettisch put the money in his pocket, but the Independent deputy, Vogtherr, somehow learned of the letter and forced Ettisch to give up his loot. It was turned over to the treasurer of the Executive Council to be used by that body. The treasurer sold the Swiss francs for the amount named above. A few unimportant additions were made later. For instance, when Colin Ross was ousted in December, he was found to be in possession of 24,000 marks said to have come from reactionary circles. The amount was confiscated and turned over to the Executive Council. In the second half of December,

Müller, the chairman of this council, laid a detailed cash report before the Reich meeting of the workers' and soldiers' councils (p. 159). The Press ridiculed him for making 'an accounting house of the parliament of the revolution'.

The Executive Council was boycotted by the entire Press: by the general and Social Democratic Press because they held it was revolutionary; by the revolutionary Press because they held it was 'bourgeois'. When the Council tried to compel the Press to publish its announcements, the government objected on the grounds that this was a violation of the freedom of the Press, and the Council acquiesced without realizing that it was clearly its, and not the government's, prerogative to decide in such fundamental constitutional matters.

Otherwise, Ebert and his Social Democratic colleagues in the government were as wary as their Independent colleagues were obtuse. When the government addressed themselves to the workers, they signed their proclamations and decrees as 'The Council of People's Commissars' of the 'German Socialist Republic'. When they addressed themselves to the 'German People', they signed as 'The Reich Government of the German Republic'. For the rest, Ebert, Scheidemann, and Landsberg (like the Conservatives and reactionaries) continued waiting. They knew what was brewing. They were the brewers.

While they waited they won another important victory in the matter of the Constituent Assembly.

XII. PARTICULARISM

On 25 November 1918, a Reich conference of the governments of the Countries (*Länder*, formerly Federal States) met in Berlin. This conference took the place of a meeting of the *Bundesrat* (Federal Council). We have seen (p. 107) that the members of the old *Bundesrat* were appointed by the rulers of the Federal States, and that a new *Bundesrat* had not yet been constituted. But the members of the *Bundesrat* were instructed by their governments, and consequently a meeting of these governments was in essence the same thing as a meeting of the *Bundesrat*.

The conference dealt with two main points: National (Constituent) Assembly, and armistice negotiations. Only the former interests us at the moment.

The largest German country after Prussia was Bavaria. The Bavarians at large, and the people of some of the other Free States (the words, *Länder*, Free States, and Republics were interchangeable), too, had a traditional antagonism against Prussia and against the Reich in general. This feeling was strong in the upper classes. It was less strong but more crude in the lower classes where it was mostly the reflexion of a well-calculated propaganda that sprang from interest rather than conviction. For instance, Rupprecht (p. 13), the last Crown Prince of Bavaria, wrote in a letter to his father in 1916: 'I do not deplore the growth of particularist tendencies in Bavaria if only the government is able to control them....' Particularism is what Americans call States' Rights, that is to say, the sovereign rights of the sovereign States which form a federal union under a sovereign federal government. 'Particularist tendencies' in Germany meant the strengthening of existing States' rights.

Rupprecht went on: 'The governments of the Federal States are progressively eliminated by the parties of the Left.' This referred to another tradition in Germany, the demand for a centralized (unitary) State, that is to say, a State such as, for instance, England, in which all governmental authority is vested in one organization. The demand for a unitary German State went back to 1806 when the impact of Napoleon dissolved formally what had existed for centuries past in name only, the Holy Roman Empire. The centralizing tradition was closely bound up with anti-Prussian feeling in many parts of the Reich because Prussia was the only possible leader in any German scheme, and centralization under Prussian leadership was regarded by many non-Prussian Germans as tantamount to their subjugation.

It is profitable to discuss this subject by looking at the interests which opposed and those which favoured unification and, later, centralization. But first we must explain these terms a little further.

Between 1806 and 1871 many Germans were in favour of unification in the form of a federation of the various German States. In 1871, Bismarck brought about such a unification, excluding Austria, in the form of the federal German Reich. The opposite of unification is separatism. Before 1871, separatism meant opposition to unification; after 1871, it meant secession from the Reich. Although there were some Germans who, before 1871, desired unification in the form of a centralized rather than a federal State, centralization became an important problem only in the Federal Union, that is to say, after 1871. From that year until 1918 centralization meant the expropriation of the multitude of princes, and after 1918 it meant the abolition of the multitude of *Länder* governments (which was achieved by Hitler). Just as separatism or secession is the opposite of unification, so particularism is the opposite of centralization. We have seen (p. 10) that at the end of the First World War particularism went so far as to degenerate into separatism in Bavaria (and also in other parts of the Reich, p. 227 n.).

In the German Reich, that is to say, after 1871, the interests
which favoured and those which opposed centralization formed a
grotesque pattern of conflict.

2

There were, first, the Prussian Junkers, the ruling clique in the
Kingdom of Prussia, some of whom never went to court because
it was customary to bow to the king and they felt they were just as
good as the Hohenzollerns and would not bow. That the Prussia
they dominated should dominate the world by means of the
military might of all Germany was often said to be their dream.
But they maintained their rule in Prussia only through an anti-
quated three-class suffrage in which votes were not counted but
weighed according to the class in which a voter found himself on
the basis of property and income. The effect of this suffrage was
that in 1912 the Social Democrats, who in spite of incongruous
delineations (p. 17) had 110 members out of 397 in the Reichstag,
had only 10 members out of 443 in the Prussian Diet, when
Prussia's population comprised three-fifths of that of the Reich.
Various Prussian rulers had promised their people a reform of this
suffrage. The last Kaiser made a determined effort in this direction
in 1917. He was supported by a majority in the Reichstag. He
wanted this reform not because he liked it but because he, like
anyone else, was well aware that the demand for reform of the
Prussian suffrage was the foremost political demand in all the
great strike movements during the First World War. But the
Junker majority in the Prussian Diet thwarted the 1917 attempt at
reform as it had thwarted every previous one. They pigeon-holed
the Reform Bill until the Prussian House of Lords finally passed it
on 24 October 1918. By that time defeat in war, and revolution
were at Germany's door-step, and it was of course too late.[1]

---

[1] The Lords' unintelligent procedure was faithfully copied, in January 1933,
by the Prussian Diet in which the Social Democrats were the largest *Fraktion*,
under the leadership of the Prime Minister, Otto Braun (p. 62). The Republican Prussian Constitution of 1919 said that it could be changed by a simple

The end of the three-class suffrage would have meant the end of Junker rule in Prussia. By the same token, the Junkers had to oppose centralization because few, if any, of the other Federal States would have tolerated the extension of the Prussian three-class suffrage to their countries. Many of these countries (especially in the south and south-west of Germany, such as, for instance, Bavaria, Württemberg, Baden, Hesse) elected their Lower Houses by universal and secret suffrage. They knew no privileges such as certain classes had in Prussia, and consequently their dynasties were not as unpopular as the Hohenzollerns were with many Prussians, notwithstanding the fact that in the question of the suffrage some of the Hohenzollerns including the last Emperor were captives of the Junkers. While there was no hope, then, of extending reaction to non-Prussian Germany, there was every prospect that some of the democratic forms of the south could not be kept out of Prussia. Thus, much as they would have liked to dominate a centralized Germany the Junkers could not afford to entertain any idea of centralization. However, the influence they did exercise upon the whole of Germany by way of dominating Prussia and Prussia dominating the *Bundesrat* was by no means small.

3

There were, secondly, the National Liberals, the political spokesmen of large-scale finance, industry, and commerce. Unless the Social Democrats became a government party, the National Liberals were sure of being an indispensable part of any majority. Their economic interests demanded a government that would protect them on the seas and in the colonies, in other words, a strong central government. Thus, the National Liberals and the

majority vote of the Diet. With Nazi victory looming as a distinct possibility in the next elections, the Prussian Diet, a few weeks before Hitler came to power, changed the Constitution by simple majority vote to the effect that future constitutional changes required a two-thirds majority. This procedure was as ludicrous as the belated passing of the Reform Bill in October 1918.

interests they represented were the natural German jingoes, the natural advocates of military adventures and overseas expansion. But they needed the Conservatives and the reactionaries of whom the Junkers formed part. They needed them, and especially the Junkers, because the latters' names (as long as their family traditions), their acquaintance with the glamour of courts, and their inborn gift of domineering, the result of centuries of practice in insolence mixed with condescension, were necessary ingredients of the psychology of militarism (see Chapter xxi below).

Just as the Junkers needed the three-class suffrage, so the National Liberals needed the Junkers and thus, indirectly, the three-class suffrage too. In all important questions of the military and naval budgets these two parties could count on each other. And the National Liberals could afford to be vociferous champions of centralization because they knew that the Junkers would prevent it if and when the situation should become critical. But Pan-Germanism, which went together with the National Liberal propaganda for centralization, was almost as effective for their purposes as centralization would have been, and the profession of centralization on the part of the National Liberals receded into the background as Pan-Germanism grew in intensity.

4

Thirdly, there were the Social Democrats. For a long time they were republicans as a body. As republicans they naturally had to favour centralization. Bebel (p. 23) once said in private to a Frenchman: 'It was easy for you Frenchmen to bring about your revolution. You had only one head to cut off. But we should have to cut off twenty-five.'

However, the trend of Social Democratic development in the years before the First World War was bound to weaken their desire for centralization. If, for instance, the Bavarian Social Democrats were able to obtain concessions from their government which the Prussian Social Democrats could not obtain from theirs, the Bavarians would of necessity become unwilling to risk their local chances by running up against the stone-wall of Prussian reaction in order to try to help their Prussian friends. On the other hand, no other German country had as concentrated a working population as Prussia, and this fact made the Social Democrats in those other countries automatically more prone to Reformism than their Prussian counterparts who could afford to be more intransigent. Thus, Reformism in the non-Prussian Federal States not only weakened the Social Democratic determination to centralize Germany; it actually strengthened particularism by drawing the non-Prussian Social Democrats into the particularist net. In this development mitigating circumstances may be seen for the change of Ebert, Scheidemann, Landsberg and their likes from republicanism to 'republican leanings', a change that was above all conditioned by their characters, however. Stubborn centralism on their part would have alienated their non-Prussian friends still more from the general aims of their common party than social, political, and economic conditions in most non-Prussian Federal States did in any case. The most important point was that the south and south-west German Social Democrats did not want to get rid of their local monarchs; they hoped they would become government parties in their respective Federal States some day. And centralism and republicanism were bound up with one another. Thus, little was left by 1914 of the original vigour of the Social Democratic demand for centralization. The little that was left was formally buried by the deeds of the Revolution of 1918, as we shall see presently.

5

But first we must look at the attitude of the Catholic Centre Party toward centralization. This attitude, too, changed remarkably from the turn of the century onwards. Until then, the Centre had been predominantly particularist. But the view gained ground rapidly that the odious power of the Junkers could only be overcome by centralization. This view put the Centre between two fires and kept it perpetually split. For if the power of Prussia was overcome by centralization, the special religious and educational rights that Catholics enjoyed in certain other parts of Germany were seemingly menaced, too. However, Pope Leo XIII seems to have favoured the centralizers among the members of the Centre. Their view was constantly put before him by such men as Groeber (p. 29) and Hertling (p. 2), and others who thought like them. The opposition to centralization in the Centre took the view that Pope Leo XIII was weakened by age and ill-health at that time (he died in 1903).[1] The centralization course was uncompromisingly pursued by Erzberger. But he kept clear of the National Liberal jingo rocks that his party colleague, Hertling, used as a jumping-board. In fact, it was Erzberger more than anyone else who was responsible for Hertling's fall because he realized that Hertling and many other members of the Centre confused democratic centralization and Pan-German centralization. Erzberger could truly say of his own early speeches in the Reichstag: 'Such tones had not been heard from the Centre of the House for a long time. They were accustomed to hearing such things from the Social Democratic side only.' It was clear that only a democratically centralized Germany could end the power of Prussia, and that no individual and no group needed any special rights in a democracy.

We must now return to the meeting of the *Länder* governments in November 1918.

---

[1] Back in 1887, when nobody could say that Pope Leo XIII was weakened by age and illness, the diehard wing of the Centre opposed his will by different means. In that year, the Reichstag debated a certain bill that the Pope wished to be supported by the Centre Party. He had his Secretary of State, Cardinal Jacobini, send a note to this effect to the leaders of the diehard wing that was in control of the Party then. The leadership suppressed this note, and the Centre Party voted against the bill in the Reichstag, which was dissolved on account of this vote. The Pope publicly rebuked the Centre Party. The new Reichstag passed the bill with a huge majority including the Centre.

6

The Revolution put Social Democrats and trade union functionaries in the leading political positions in the Free States just as it did in the Reich. Their newly won glory weighed more heavily with these men than anything else. They had not suddenly become ministers to give up their glory for an 'idea'. If this idea were realized, if Germany became centralized, there would be no Free States governments. Furthermore, if the workers' and soldiers' councils, especially the former, remained the source of political power they were bound sooner or later to hit upon the idea of centralization for the reason advanced by Bavaria's Prime Minister, the Independent Kurt Eisner (p. 257): there were some *Länder* that could not become socialist if they retained any degree of political and economic autonomy because they were predominantly agricultural and little developed industrially.

Thus, it was easy enough for Ebert to persuade the governments of the Free States to accept the idea of a Constituent Assembly as opposed to that of a councils' constitution. In fact, they not only agreed to the principle of the Constituent Assembly; they welcomed the 'intention of the Reich government to carry out the preparations for the National Assembly with the utmost speed'.

The Constituent Assembly was thus assured, at least on paper. When it was elected, a little later, it had a majority, composed of members of various parties, in favour of centralization. However, this majority did not attempt to press its view upon the raucous federalist minority; with most of the members of the majority, unitarianism was a conviction rather than a policy. Only the Spartacists were vigorous in pursuing it.

Though the Constituent Assembly was assured on paper, then, there were still other obstacles that had to be removed to clear the road back to the old State, the State in which militaristic Prussia dominated Germany and particularists were happy to gain petty honours and distinctions.

XIII. DIPLOMACY

Every night at eleven o'clock Ebert closeted himself in his office to have a prolonged long-distance telephone conversation with Groener. For painfully long weeks the General had scant consolation to offer; he was not, just then, in a position to send troops the government could use. The soldiers of the old army had only one desire, they wanted to get home. Thus, the government was still unable to 'legalize' its position with bayonets. At the same time, it was chafing under the legitimacy bestowed upon it by the workers' and soldiers' councils, and it was constitutionally suspended in mid-air because it had repudiated the competency of these councils by reinstating the *Bundesrat*. Moreover, the heavily armed revolutionary workers might oppose the Constituent Assembly by force although the confusion (not the sanity) of their leaders made such an insane course doubtful.

The Government—this meant four of the six People's Commissars: Ebert, Scheidemann, Landsberg, and Dittmann. The latter, an Independent, had lost his bearings. Of the other two Independents, Haase never knew what he wanted anyway, and Barth had no grasp of political realities, no understanding of political, social and economic theory and development, and no personality. But he possessed an extreme quick-wittedness that made up for some of his shortcomings, and an ungovernable temper. He opposed the others constantly.

To make sure there would be a National Assembly soon, to devise other legalistic means that provided a new form for the unchanged substance of the old State, to discredit the Executive Council—all these things and many others were necessary from the viewpoint of Ebert and his friends. However, they concerned the near future, not the immediate future. As for the near future, the bayonets would take care of it. But the immediate future was threatened by ominous rumblings that came from 'below', from the workers. These rumblings had to be muffled. There was no military force available to muffle them. Therefore, the People's Commissars roused the patriotism of the public. They began a few days after the outbreak of the Revolution and were assisted by the general Press and *Vorwärts*. Naturally, this was done in the sphere of foreign policy. Foreign policy chiefly meant three things at that time: the armistice negotiations; American food supplies for starving Germany; and the Polish question.

On Friday, 8 November 1918, Erzberger sent a courier with the armistice terms to Hindenburg (p. 86). Two days later, he received a reply by wireless telegraphy urging him to try to get certain points mitigated. But if he could not obtain this mitigation he was to accept the terms as they stood. This code message was, later the same day, followed by an open telegram authorizing him to accept the enemy's terms unchanged. The telegram was signed by the 'Reich Chancellor'. Actually, it was sent by Hindenburg who could not get in touch with the government because communications with Berlin were interrupted. He simply usurped the name of the Chancellor.

The German armistice commission consisted, apart from Erzberger, of the former German ambassador in Sofia, Count von Oberndorff, representing the German Foreign office; Major-General von Winterfeldt, representing the Army; and Naval Captain Vanselow, representing the Navy. They were embarrassed by the 'Chancellor's' open telegram. For the last forty-eight hours, since they had been handed the terms, they had tried to obtain modifications, and now they were empowered by an open telegram the enemy was bound to see, to accept without modifications.[1]

---

[1] Our account is based on Erzberger's memoirs. A more detailed account which differs in various points from that of Erzberger is documented from other sources by Professor Rudin (see Bibliography, p. 285). It is hardly likely that the exact details will ever be established. The existing differences do not, however, affect the overall picture.

Their first conversation with Marshal Foch and a number of other French and British officers had taken place on Friday afternoon, 8 November. The Germans were emphatic then that the Allied terms would deliver Germany to Bolshevism. They were disappointed to see that their argument did not impress the gentlemen of the opposite side. These gentlemen openly declared their belief that the Germans were trying to lay a trap for the allies.

The Bolshevism argument became known in Germany, however, and during the following weeks and months it was incessantly employed by the Reich government, the general Press, and *Vorwärts*. The inventiveness with which it was varied was great.

2

One of the results that Erzberger had achieved at Compiègne was the clause that the 'Allied and Associated Powers contemplate supplying Germany with foodstuffs during the period of the Armistice'. Suddenly, *Vorwärts* wrote that the contemplated food supplies were being detained in Rotterdam and Copenhagen because the American government wanted to wait and see 'whether Germany would fulfil the guarantee that the United States regarded as prerequisite, namely, a democratic constitution and orderly distribution'. In point of fact, neither the United States government nor the Allied and Associated Powers ever made an outright utterance on the question of Germany's future form of government although it was of course understood that they expected democracy in Germany.

Vorwärts' story, however, was not invented; only its treatment was fictitious. Immediately after the signing of the armistice on 11 November 1918, Ebert sent the following cable to the United States government: 'The German government requests the President of the United States to inform the Reich Chancellor by wireless whether he may count on the American government sending foodstuffs to Germany without delay *provided public order in Germany is maintained and a just distribution of the foodstuffs guaran-*

128

teed' (my italics). There was no such stipulation in the clause of the armistice agreement. But in his reply to Ebert's cable the United States Secretary of State, Lansing, repeated the phrase of the guarantee. This was merely the usual confirmation of a communication received. No foodstuffs for Germany were detained anywhere. This part of *Vorwärts'* report was a pure invention to serve the same purpose as Ebert's suggestion of the guarantee to Lansing; it was to induce the Allies to interfere with Germany's internal affairs in accordance with Ebert's designs. Ebert's cable was published by the whole German Press the day it was dispatched. But when the Press of the Independents and Spartacists probed into the story as given by *Vorwärts*, Ebert declared that neither he nor any other German authority had sent that cable.

A short time after this incident *Vorwärts* carried a report from Washington: Secretary Lansing had said in the Senate (*sic!*) that the United States would send foodstuffs to Germany only after the elections to the Constituent Assembly. Immediately, Reuter's telegraph agency circulated a denial of the report; the Secretary had not made this statement.

A little later again *Vorwärts* printed an 'order by the British Admiralty to the German Fleet'. It said that ships with red flags would be sunk without warning; ships without officers (this meant ships with sailors' councils) would be treated according to martial law; and if a sailor were caught disseminating Bolshevist propaganda the entire crew of his ship would be shot. Again Reuter's agency circulated a denial; every word of *Vorwärts'* story was an invention.

3

In this boom of 'diplomatic' activity Constantin Fehrenbach could not contain himself. Fehrenbach, a deputy of the Centre Party, was the Speaker of the Reichstag. As such he had the right to convene the House at his discretion. But Ebert could not afford to have the Reichstag convene (p. 89). On the other hand, he could not formally dissolve it because he had reinstated the Federal Council; he could not formally abolish one of the two houses of parliament when he retained the other. It was quite logical that Fehrenbach should summon the Reichstag when Ebert decreed the continuance of the Federal Council. But the government protested, and the Reichstag did not assemble. Fehrenbach, however, was not to be daunted. Four weeks later, when the foodstuff diplomacy was at its height, he once more announced that he would convene the Reichstag. The reason he gave was that the armistice would lapse shortly (it was of course extended), and that the Entente was demanding a session because it did not recognize the new German government. This assertion was pure nonsense; the Entente was negotiating with the new German government all the time. Fehrenbach's assertion made *Vorwärts* very indignant, and the paper wrote innocently: 'It is conceivable that the Entente takes Herr Fehrenbach's letter as a hint, as an encouragement to interfere with the internal affairs of the Reich in favour of the bourgeois parties.... Herr Fehrenbach of the Centre cannot evade the charge that he and his bourgeois wire-pullers have committed an act of national degradation by indirectly asking the Entente to interfere with our internal affairs.'

The government, too, was indignant. It declared that the Reichstag *and the Federal Council* had ceased to exist in consequence of the political change that had taken place. What, then, about the decree concerning the continuance of the *Bundesrat*? The answer is simple. This decree had been issued four weeks earlier. Many things had changed since then; above all, the Constituent Assembly was assured and, as we shall see, the first bayonets had arrived. The statement that the Reichstag had ceased to exist (no such statement had been made when Fehrenbach tried to convene the Reichstag the first time) in consequence of the political change was merely a political view uttered by the government; it was not a formal dissolution and abolition with the force of law. The old Reichstag was finally disposed of in a peculiar fashion. In February 1919 the government decreed that the payment of indemnities to the deputies had ceased as from 9 November 1918. This decree naturally implied the formal abolition which had not been proclaimed. It is interesting to note that this happened on the eve of the meeting of the National Assembly. In other words, Ebert and his friends kept the Reichstag alive if dormant as long as appeared necessary so that they could use it as a *deus ex machina* should it suit them to do so.

4

Kurt Eisner, the Independent Prime Minister of Bavaria, violently attacked the Foreign Secretary, Solf,[1] and Erzberger at the conference of the Free States governments. He said that their activities were causing great harm to Germany, and that the negotiations with the Allies must not be conducted by men who had been high functionaries of the old régime. Solf and Erzberger must go. Ebert and Landsberg rejected Eisner's accusations as far as Erzberger was concerned. They defended Solf with less ardour, but they did not drop him. Eisner thereupon walked out of the conference, returned to Munich, and broke off Bavaria's relations with the Foreign Office of the Reich; he would not deal with the Office as it was constituted then. Immediately after the outbreak of the Revolution he had made use of one of the privileges that Bavaria seems to have exacted as her price for joining the German Reich in 1871, the privilege of having a certain number of diplomatic representations abroad.[2] Eisner appointed a Bavarian

[1] Dr Wilhelm Solf hailed from a family of wealthy mine-owners. In the German Empire he had a distinguished career in the Colonial Service, being at one time Governor of Samoa. Prince Max made him Foreign Secretary. Ebert kept him on in this capacity until he was succeeded by Brockdorff-Rantzau in January 1919. From 1920 until his retirement in 1928 he was German ambassador to Japan. Helping many political and Jewish victims of Nazism to leave Germany he died as an active foe of Hitler in Berlin on 2 June 1936, aged 73.

[2] I say that Bavaria *seems* to have exacted a price for her joining because German historians are split into two schools of thought as to who blackmailed whom into what when the German Reich was founded at Versailles in January 1871. While the granting of the privilege of maintaining diplomatic representa-

ambassador to Switzerland, the pacifist, Professor Friedrich Wilhelm Foerster. Professor Foerster had lived in Switzerland during the war and conducted propaganda against nationalist and imperialist Germany. He was a glowing idealist, with as much understanding of social and political forces as the glowing idealist Eisner. While democratic people in the Entente countries who had a good deal of such understanding were afraid of their own militarists (p. 9), Eisner and Foerster believed that Clemenceau and Lloyd George were the 'greatest of idealists'. Incongruously they linked these names with that of President Wilson.

The day before the conference of the Free States governments began, Eisner published a number of documents from the secret archives of the Bavarian Foreign Office. These documents were supposed to prove that Germany alone was guilty of bringing about the war of 1914. Eisner believed that the Entente would be lenient if the Germans cried *nostra culpa*. He was instigated to do this by the Bavarian ambassador in Berlin, Muckle, who in turn was advised by the publicist Maximilian Harden, once an indiscriminate admirer of Bismarck and Nietzsche, and then a radical socialist. The advice Muckle gave Eisner was that he urge the Reich government to publish all secret German documents relating to the outbreak of the war. These documents would prove Germany's exclusive guilt, and the guilty men should be tried by a special court. If the Reich government refused, the German South should threaten to secede. The Reich government did refuse. The Social Democrats had throughout the war maintained that

tions abroad seems to indicate that Bavaria was indeed in a position to exact a price for her joining the Reich, there are German historians who hold that Bismarck clubbed Bavaria into submission with certain documents which had come into his possession and which, if they were genuine and had been published, would have aroused revulsion against the Bavarian crown during the popular upsurge of German patriotism in 1871. These documents are said to have formed part of Napoleon III's private political correspondence captured by the Prussians at the Castle of Cerçay outside Paris. They are alleged to have contained letters which showed that Bavaria and several other South German States had tried to conclude a military alliance with France against Prussia in 1865/66 and in 1870.

they were supporting the war because Germany had been attacked. They could not suddenly declare that Germany was the aggressor. It is another indication of the *naïveté* of the people around Eisner that they expected the Social Democrats to do so. The Eisner faction was of course right in contending that only a radical change of German foreign policy could secure future peace. But they believed that the clamour of a few idealists was enough to bring about such a change. They did not realize that the foreign policy of a State is bound up with that State's social substance. This substance did not change in Germany after 1918, although its form changed. Consequently, Germany's foreign policy could not change.

But Eisner's attacks on Solf had an effect; the Reich government informed Solf that they would be pleased if he resigned. In reply, the entire staff of the Foreign Office declared that they would go on strike if Solf were forced out of office. Most of the gentlemen of the foreign service and the diplomatic service were of the Junker class and many of them came from high industrial and financial circles. Their threat was an open declaration of war against the Revolution.[1] Ebert, however, was no revolutionary either. He persuaded the gentlemen that Solf's withdrawal was better than a complete change in the Foreign Office; and a complete change might be enforced if they were stubborn. At last, they acquiesced in Solf's resignation.

---

[1] When the fifteen victims of the fighting in the streets of Berlin (p. 16) were buried, 'the red flag was hoisted for two hours over the dignified building of the Foreign Office, during which time all the officials left the place on a protest strike'. Count Bernstorff, who relates this incident in his memoirs, relates also the following story: 'All of us who lived through that time were involved in daily conflicts of spirit and conscience. The Soviets at that time sent out a great many wireless messages addressed to Haase, the People's Commissar, and these were read in the Foreign Office. One of them made a great impression on my mind. It ran as follows: "If you wish to make the revolution complete, you must get rid of all the old officials. If they remain, the revolution will fail."' This, of course, applied to a democratic-capitalist revolution as well as to a socialist one.

5

Then there was the question of Germany's relations with Russia and Poland. The Busch meeting of the workers' and soldiers' councils had demanded, in a final resolution (p. 99) which was drafted by Haase, that diplomatic relations with Russia be resumed forthwith. Delighted by this resolution, the Russians dispatched an ambassador. He was arrested by the German authorities in a White Russian village and confined there. The reason was that Radek[1] demanded that he and a number of his friends also be admitted and allowed to make Bolshevist propaganda in the camps in which British and French prisoners of war and civilian internees were kept. While there were no declarations to the effect that the Entente would frown upon friendly German relations with Russia, it certainly would have looked upon Bolshevist propaganda among its imprisoned nationals as a most unfriendly act. The Russians, of course, regarded the last-minute German refusal of their ambassador as a despicable German attempt to curry favour with the Allies.

However, the resumption of diplomatic relations between Germany and Russia always remained a possibility, provided the Russians abandoned unreasonable conditions. It was regarded as undesirable by those Germans who were to the right of the Independents. They constantly tried to forestall it. For instance, one morning in December 1918, the three Social Democratic members brought a document to a meeting of the Council of People's Commissars which said in part that 'the admission of a Russian ambassador would be taken by the Entente as a confirmation of Radek's wireless message, i.e. as a confirmation of a Russo-German offensive alliance. Its immediate consequence would therefore be the cancellation of the armistice.' This document was an alleged

[1] The Russian revolutionary, Karl Radek, who twenty years later became a star victim of the great Russian purge, played an important role in both his country and Germany where he had spent the ten years preceding 1918 as a 'guest' in the revolutionary workers' movement.

dispatch of the German ambassador in the Hague. The three Social
Democratic People's Commissars also brought a copy of Radek's
alleged wireless message. These two documents were all that has
been learned about the affair. In his wireless message Radek was
supposed to have announced the common fight of Germany and
Russia against 'the capitalist Entente'. This idea was actually
entertained by the Russian government at that time, but they
knew that its execution was quite impossible then in view of the
war-weariness of all ordinary Germans including those who
sympathized with the Russian goal of world revolution. Of such
sympathizers there were few even among the rank and file of the
Spartacists then, and these few, like all of their revolutionary
friends, were more interested in the German revolution than in
Russia. They realized the difficulties of their revolution clearly,
more clearly than the brilliant but eccentric Radek, who was a
disciple and intimate of the brilliant but eccentric Trotsky.

Radek did use the phrase about the common fight, though,
but not in a wireless message. He used it in a pamphlet that was
openly circulating in Germany and in which he called upon the
German government to conclude a secret alliance with the Soviet
Republic and secretly to hand over to the latter the arms the
German soldiers were throwing away in the occupied territories,
'*for every day of the existence of the Russian Soviet Republic means a
strengthening of the German Socialist Republic, means the maintenance
of a force combined with which the German Republic will have to fight
against a world of capitalist enemies tomorrow*' (italics in original).
It is possible that somebody in the Foreign Office (but hardly the
honest Foreign Secretary, Dr Solf) faked the two documents and
duped the Social Democratic Peoples' Commissars with them.
Strangely, they never asked why *they* should have been given the
dispatch from the German ambassador in the Hague when their
Independent colleague, Haase, presided over the Foreign Office to
which such dispatches would be addressed. On the other hand,
Solf's two political controllers (pp. 91 and 113) were the Social
Democrat David, and the Independent Kautsky. And Kautsky,

who might have objected to a falsification, did not take much interest in current affairs; he was burrowing diligently in the archives of the Foreign Office to find out whether Germany had not really started the war, after all.[1]

The attempt of the German armistice commission at Compiègne to make Germany acceptable as an Allied partner against Russia had failed (p. 128). The Radek affair was another such attempt. Like the first, it evoked no response. If, then, the Germans at large could not profitably be worked up against Russia by way of the Entente, there still was Poland. No one could say that the new Polish government acted democratically, or intelligently, towards Germany. But the German government was no better. When Barth proposed to his colleagues of the Council of People's Commissars that steps be taken to get on friendly terms with the neighbouring countries in the East, Landsberg exclaimed: 'What shall become of our national honour if we run after every Polack people in the East?' It was grist for his mill that the Poles broke off diplomatic relations with Germany on 15 December 1918. They gave the preposterous reason that the German authorities in the East were making common cause with the Bolshevists.

On 12 November 1918 Barth persuaded his colleagues to issue orders to the military for the immediate evacuation of all territories in the East occupied by German troops. A few days later, the government received information from Supreme Army Command under General Groener that the Poles were forcibly preventing the repatriation of the German soldiers. Actually, Groener had issued a secret order to the Army Command East: rapid evacuation was not in the national and economic interest of Germany; the armistice conditions did not demand it; the soldiers were to be told that anyone who left his post made himself liable to punishment and the loss of demobilization benefits.

---

[1] He came up with one of the most useful, because most honest, compilations of secret documents relating to the outbreak of war in 1914. An edition in English came out in New York (1924), *Outbreak of the World War, German Documents Collected by Karl Kautsky.*

Article XII of the armistice agreement of 11 November read in part: 'All German troops who are at the moment in territories that belonged to Russia before the war must retire behind...the German frontiers as at 1 August 1914, as soon as the Allies deem this appropriate in consideration of the internal conditions in these territories.' This clause was interpreted by the local and central German military authorities as obliging them to protect these territories from the Bolshevists.

Groener's order soon became known to the German government, and Barth demanded that the General be dismissed for insubordination, treason, and promoting war against Poland. His five colleagues voted him down, and Groener stayed.

6

A few weeks later, towards the end of December 1918, a meeting of the six People's Commissars was attended by a number of gentlemen of the Foreign Office, of the War Ministry, and of Army Command East. One of the officials of the Foreign Office reported that a Polish ultimatum had been received; it demanded 10,000 rifles and 500 machine-guns for the fight against the Bolshevists, and the surrender of German-occupied Wilna with all the war material in the city; the time limit was 24 hours. The two Departments and Army Command East insisted that Germany comply with the Polish demands because the territories in question could not protect themselves from the Bolshevists otherwise. Ebert and Scheidemann held the same view. But the three Independent People's Commissars objected; they wanted peace with all nations, and especially they would not agree to any action against socialist Russia. Haase, moreover, contended that Russia was stronger than most people believed, and a war against her would end in military disaster. The meeting adjourned without result, Ebert, Scheidemann, and the others declaring that they declined all responsibility for anything that might happen in the East if the Polish ultimatum were rejected.

The meeting was resumed the following day. The three Social Democratic People's Commissars did not appear, but Erzberger and the Soldiers' Council East were there. Erzberger supported the Independents against the interference of the Foreign Office with affairs of the armistice commission (which was under the direct jurisdiction of the cabinet, not the Foreign Office). He held that compliance with the Polish demands would violate the armistice agreement. This silenced the gentlemen of the Foreign Office. But the gentlemen of the War Ministry and Army Command East were not satisfied. They demanded that August Winnig be given authority to consummate a preliminary agreement he had concluded with the British officer commanding in Riga.

Winnig was a Social Democrat who had just become Reich Commissar for the East. The Bolshevists were marching on Riga which had a large German population that was violently persecuted by the new Latvian government. Outwardly, it was Winnig's endeavour to repatriate these Germans, but below the surface he did all he could to thwart the Bolshevists who regarded Latvia as Russian territory. A British auxiliary cruiser and a torpedo-boat appeared at Riga at the height of the trouble. They had a handful of soldiers on board who were to supervise the fulfilment of the armistice conditions by Germany. A young British colonel went to see Winnig, interpreted Article XII of the armistice agreement to the effect that Germany was obliged to protect the Baltic countries by military force, and demanded that the Germans hold Riga and all territory not yet occupied by the Bolshevists. He also hinted that the Germans ought to reconquer those parts of the Baltic countries that the Reds had occupied.

All this was impossible. The German soldiers wanted to go home, and the German army was in full dissolution in the East as everywhere else. Winnig had maintained himself until then only because he had the support of the Latvian middle and upper classes (the latter including the notorious German 'Baltic barons') who used him and the German army, as far as it could be used, against the Bolshevists. As soon as the Russian advance stopped for a while, these Latvians 'spit in the Germans' faces', according to Winnig's memoirs. But they made friends again quickly when the Bolshevists resumed their advance.

Winnig and the English colonel laid plans for collaborating against the Bolshevists with the help of a German volunteer corps to be raised from among the German soldiers still in Latvia. (This corps used the swastika as its emblem and became the terror of all Germany a little later, until the Reich government managed to dissolve it. It went underground to form the nucleus of the first German reactionary force and to commit countless political murders.) As a beginning, the Englishman marched seventy of his soldiers with a few machine-guns through the town. He was instantly rebuked by London.

To complicate matters, Winnig's alliance with the anti-German Latvian middle and upper classes (the latter with the limited exception of the Baltic barons who were anti-German only because they believed that Germany was socialist) was directed not merely against the Russian Bolshevists, but also against the Latvian workers and peasants, many of whom were Bolshevists, too, and constantly rebelled against the Latvian government. One might think that Winnig, the 'socialist', would have leaned on these Latvian workers rather than on the other Latvian classes. But he was another of those socialists who hated social revolution like sin; and not only social revolution that would establish socialism, but also social revolution that would eradicate German militarism.[1]

He tells the following delightful story in his memoirs: 'In the land question the Latvian socialists upheld the most radical viewpoint—they demanded complete expropriation. I invited some of their leaders and discussed the whole question with them.... One of them referred to Marx and said that Marx had postulated the expropriation of the expropriators, and they would not budge

---

[1] August Winnig (born in 1878), once an international socialist, became a rabid nationalist and reactionary between the two world wars. After the Second World War he published pseudo-religious writings warning the world of the 'demoniacal' forces at work among men.

from this postulate. I told him that we were discussing politics, not literature.' Disgusted, Winnig returned to the Latvian land-owners who 'spat in his face' because he was a German.

7

After discussing the doings of Winnig and the British colonel, the three Independent People's Commissars, supported by Erzberger and the Soldiers' Council East, made a decision; any person who ordered or carried out any operation against Russia would be prosecuted for common murder. This ought to have settled the affair. But the gentlemen of the Foreign Office, the War Ministry, and Army Command East came back the following day. Ebert opened the meeting by saying that he had come to discuss an affair still more important than that of the previous two days. He called upon a representative of the Foreign Office to make a statement. This gentleman reported that Paderewski[1] had made his triumphal entry into Posen yesterday, 26 December 1918. (Posen was the capital of a Polish province that belonged to Germany (Prussia) until the First World War.) The houses, he went on to say, were decorated with French, British, American and Polish flags. The German officers in Posen made patriotic speeches to their troops; the German troops tore down the British and French flags. Two British officers went to see the German commander to protest. They were told that the troops were out of hand, would not obey the German authorities, and could not, therefore, be stopped. After all, the chief of staff of the German commander said, Posen was German territory, and English and French flags could not be tolerated there. Heavy street fighting between German and Polish troops ensued. So much for the report of the gentleman of the Foreign Office. (The street fighting lasted for two days and con-tinued sporadically for another two weeks until the German officers were disarmed and the German soldiers, who had in the

---

[1] Paderewski, the great pianist, was the first President of the new Polish Republic.

meantime begun to fraternize with the Polish soldiers to the dismay of the officers of both sides, were deported.)

The report of the gentleman of the Foreign Office was followed by an impassioned speech by Landsberg. He declared that the disgrace could only be wiped out by blood, and he implored the Independent People's Commissars to declare war against Poland.[1] Ebert and Scheidemann supported him. But the declaration of war was rejected by three votes against three.

Naturally, these deliberations did not become known to the German public at the time. But the frame of mind of the military, the diplomatists, and the Social Democratic People's Commissars, this frame of mind that made them demand an alliance with Poland against Russia one day, and war against Poland the next day; this frame of mind that did anything to whip up the normal but temporarily dormant warlike instincts of their friends, especially the aristocracy; this frame of mind communicated itself to other groups and classes by other means. It communicated itself to them through the general Press, through *Vorwärts*, and through many public speeches of Ebert, Scheidemann, Landsberg, and their faithful lieutenants. The Pan-Germans themselves were lying low at that time; the question whether or not Germany was going to be socialist was not yet definitely decided, at least not openly. But it soon was decided openly, and then their 'patriotism' burst forth with explosive vigour.

[1] This account is largely but not exclusively based on Barth's memoirs. His story was attacked from many quarters, especially the Social Democrats, who called it fiction. It is significant, however, that its truth was denied only by partisans of the men concerned, not by these men themselves. They did not deny it, though they did not confirm it either. It deserves credence for three reasons. First, it tallies with Winnig's account of events wherever the memoirs of these two men cover the same ground; and there was no love lost between Barth and Winnig. Secondly, it is supported by the characters of the men concerned. This holds good especially of Landsberg (p. 107) who as a budding jurist served at a German court of justice in the village of Ostrowo close to the German-Polish Russian border, in the 1890's. There, he contracted a strong hatred of the Poles for the intolerable anti-Semitism of the administration in Russian Poland —an emotion quite understandable in a man who was Jewish. Thirdly, Barth was the last man to have the imagination to invent the story; some of the details may be embellished and exaggerated but, again, not invented by him.

XIV. 'BÜRGER'

The political leaders of the *Bürger*[1] and the aristocracy saw with amazement that the supposedly international socialist government was encouraging a type of nationalism that concerned itself with nebulous national wrongs instead of doing what everybody expected it to do, namely, introducing socialism. And these leaders, who had given up their cause for lost on 9 November 1918, took heart. Three of their parties were re-formed out of their debris before that fateful month was over. A fourth party continued unchanged.

The first of them to reappear on the scene was a Radical Liberal Party. On 16 November, the old Progressive Liberal Party published a proclamation proposing the formation of 'a great democratic party for the united Reich'. This proclamation demanded a 'new social and economic policy'. It accepted the socialization of such branches of industry as had grown into 'monopoly'. The crown lands (of which there were many, especially in Prussia) were to be parcelled up, and the large estates (of which there were many, especially in Prussia) were to be curbed in order to strengthen and increase the peasantry. The system of taxation was to be democratized, and the rights of workers, employees, and civil servants to be guaranteed by law.

The Progressive Liberals invited the National Liberals to join

---

[1] The German word *Bürger* means citizen or citizens, not, however, in the sense of national or nationals, which in German is *Staatsbürger* (citizen of a State) or *Staatsangehöriger* (member of a State, plur. *Staatsangehörige*). But *Bürger* also means bourgeois as distinguished from workers and aristocrats. This is the meaning the word has in this chapter. It is free of the connotation which the word *bourgeois* has in English, in French, and also in German. Therefore, I prefer the use of the word *Bürger* here.

them in the new party. The right wing of the latter, however, refused. The new party constituted itself, on 20 November 1918, as the German Democratic Party. Von Payer, the chairman of the Progressive People's Party, became its head, but its most influential leader was Karl Friedrich von Siemens of the great electrical concern. He turned a Democrat only in order to prevent the Democrats from moving too far to the left, that is to say, from becoming too democratic (they were of course opposed to socialism). When any danger to the old German State was past, Siemens resigned his Reichstag seat after an ugly put-up quarrel in 1924.

2

The remaining National Liberals and some right-wing Progressive Liberals formed another organization on 23 November 1918: the German People's Party, which was to be right of Centre just as the Democrats were left of Centre. But this new party could not find a satisfactory platform, and on 4 December decided to join the Democrats lock, stock and barrel. The Democrats, however, imposed special conditions on any person who had been prominent in the demand for annexations and in the policy that brought the United States of America into the war against Germany, and who had, moreover, taken up a stand against universal suffrage before the Revolution. These conditions were specially designed to keep Stresemann out. Stresemann took the hint and generously declared that he would refrain from becoming a Democrat in order not to embarrass the new party.

On 15 December those Liberals who had first formed the German People's Party and then joined the Democrats held another meeting as though nothing had happened. They decided they would continue as an independent organization under the name of German People's Party. Stresemann became their leader. Their vacillation regarding their ideas and aims became a deliberate ambiguity in their programme. In the party's first proclamation of 18 December 1918, prominence was given to the demand that

'State and war loans, savings deposits and bank deposits' must be safeguarded, which was of course impossible. Church and State were not to be separated, and the 'present government, which rests solely upon the fact that there was a revolution, must establish quiet and order'.

But less than a year later, things looked different. In a new programmatic declaration the People's Party then advocated that a new empire be established, that Church and State be separated, that socialization be rejected (as if anyone wanted it but the Communists who had just been hopelessly crushed, as we shall see), but that industry must be 'furthered' by the State. A prominent German of that time called these and similar demands with regard to industry, the private enjoyment of profits and the socialization of losses. Especially, the new manifesto of the People's Party went on, the Reich government was emphatically to support the reconstruction of the German merchant marine (which belonged to private interests). The railroads were to be transferred to the ownership of the Reich, a demand that must not be taken as a concession to socialism; the railroads belonged, with unimportant exceptions, to the *Länder*. Thus, the National Liberals remembered once more their centralizing tradition (p. 122) in a case that, significantly, benefited the interests they represented. They were less enthusiastic, and joined in the newly coined cry of 'Bolshevist', when Erzberger, then Reich Finance Minister, carried through, with singular determination, circumspection, and efficiency, another centralizing measure a little later: a Reich income and corporation tax system.

The German People's Party manifesto of October 1919 marked the transition of this party from floundering in the storms of revolution to the unswerving political championship of large-scale interests in industry and finance, the interests which, because of the psychological make-up of their managers, provided the economic backbone of German militarism.

3

A number of conservative groups constituted themselves the German National People's Party[1] on 22 November 1918. Their programme declared that they would co-operate with any form of State if Germany *returned* from the dictatorship of one class (which she did not have, of course) to parliamentary government (which she never had except for six weeks before the collapse of November 1918, and which the Conservatives had always opposed), the only government possible after 'recent events' (they would not print or pronounce the word 'revolution'). A week earlier the leader of their agricultural Junker wing, Baron von Heydebrand und der Lasa, the 'uncrowned king of Prussia', had issued a proclamation to the effect that his followers were to support the government of Ebert because it was working for the 'maintenance of quiet, order, and the security of life and private property'. Private property meant to Heydebrand the latifundia of the Junkers, but for once it did not mean quite the same thing to Ebert; the latifundia were shorn of certain privileges they enjoyed, but otherwise they were left alone.[2]

The German National People's Party at least did not disdain openly to show its demagoguery from the start. In time it fell entirely under the influence of Alfred Hugenberg,[3] a Pan-German industrialist, publisher, and financier. Its Junker wing, then under Count von Westarp, declined as a consequence of the economic

[1] It is interesting to note that the two leading parties of the Right, which most certainly stood for certain privileges of certain groups, were the only ones that called themselves 'people's parties'.

[2] When the Social Democrat, Albert Grzesinski, became Prussian Minister of the Interior in 1926, he listed as one of his 'main tasks...the abolition of Junker privileges in Prussia'.

[3] Alfred Hugenberg, who started his career in the Prussian civil service, rose to be chairman of the board of Krupp's which post he held until Germany's collapse in 1918. He was elected to the National Assembly for the Conservatives, and was so reactionary that he split his party in 1928. Hitler made him his first minister for economic affairs but dropped him in June 1933. He died in March 1951, aged 87.

development of Germany after the Revolution. But the party as a whole, though no longer dominated by the Junkers, upheld their ideology.

4

The Catholic Centre Party remained unchanged with respect to principles and organization. Its attitude was that 'war and peace aims had nothing to do with the ideals of the Centre Party and that they would settle themselves once peace was concluded'. The ideals of the party were 'a policy of conciliation in a Christian, i.e. eminently social, spirit'. The Party denounced socialism in a declaration of 30 December 1918, and demanded that the federal character of the Reich be fully maintained. This latter plank contradicted the former centralizing tendencies of the Centre's left wing. This wing gained the ascendancy in the Revolution to such an extent that it repelled the aristocratic right wing, which disappeared from the party's ranks, for the time being. The Centre became a thoroughly liberal-democratic party. However, the uncertain attitude of the Social Democrats made it appear risky to the Centre to agree to centralization; that would of necessity have meant the separation of Church and State since there were three large Christian denominations in the Reich: the Lutheran Church, the Reformed Church and the Catholics. Only in a federal Reich could the Catholics maintain any influence upon the governments of those *Länder* in which they formed the majority of the people, notably in Bavaria. When it became clear that the Social Democrats did not press for centralization either, the Centre gave up its intransigent attitude towards that party and formed coalition governments with it in the Reich as well as in many *Länder*. By that time, however, the policy and the actions of the Social Democrats in the Revolution had prevented any democratic change of the substance of the German State.

During and immediately after the Revolution the most influential leaders of the Centre were the radical Erzberger, and the still more radical Josef Wirth who became Reich Chancellor in 1921 and who coined the famous and correct, but inflammatory words, 'The enemy is on the right.' The revolution being what it was, however, it was inescapable that within a few years the aristocratic wing of the Centre, most conspicuously represented by the notorious von Papen, should gain the upper hand. It was a futile gesture that the party tried to force Papen to resign his seat in the Prussian Diet in 1925 because he contributed in that year to the overthrow of a Prussian government dominated by the Centre. Far from resigning the gentleman managed at that time, through share-holdings, to become the policy-making head of *Germania*, the central Reich Press organ of the party.

Even this development was not enough for the then private citizen, Max of Baden. More than a year later, in September 1926, he wrote to Count Bernstorff: 'The problem seems to me to be to split the Catholics, so as to induce a section of the Centre, which would not be disposed to co-operate with Wirth's proletarian party, to join the middle bloc.' By the middle bloc he meant a bloc extending from the Papen wing of the Centre to the extreme right. The left wing of the Centre was of course too weak by itself to bring about that democratic-capitalist revolution which would have eradicated German militarism without changing the substance of the German State to socialism. It was too weak even in conjunction with the Democrats who pursued the same aim (though, naturally, there were other points on which these two parties did not agree). But while too weak in this positive sense, the left wing of the Centre Party was strong enough (especially as it had the support of the politically thinking, well-organized Catholic youth) in the negative sense of forestalling the 'middle bloc' which Prince Max, and many Germans who thought like him, had in mind. If, then, the Prince spoke of splitting the Centre, he either did not consider carefully what he wrote, or else he was thinking of aims that he dared not express even in a private correspondence. Hitler realized these aims later on, and not only with regard to the left wing of the Centre, but to the whole of the Centre.

The four *Bürger* parties we have discussed were not all, but they were the most important. Two of them were progressive, namely, the German Democrats and the Centre, the latter with the qualifications we saw a moment ago. Two others, the German People's Party and the German National People's Party, were reactionary. They were politically reactionary because they wanted to re-establish the monarchy. They were economically and socially reactionary because they wanted to maintain the economic and social substance of the militaristic empire. They, and the circles they represented, were in control of this substance, and they also controlled the apparatus of the State, because it had been left to them by way of their own people, the old bureaucracy and the generals, through the decree of the Executive Council (p. 109).

But they did not hold the political power. The political power, and the apparatus of the old State, was nominally in the hands of Ebert. However, Ebert had no economic and social power behind him to support his political power. All he had was the promise of military support through his agreement with Groener (p. 93). This agreement was not known to any but the parties concerned. But though not known it was easy to surmise, because the generals were keeping quiet, at least for the time being. Whether he wanted to or not, whether he knew it or not, Ebert was a captive of the generals. Whether he wanted to or not, whether he knew it or not, whether or not he foresaw its consequences, he had deliberately brought himself into that position.

In these circumstances it was logical that the reactionaries should try to make their possession of the State complete by adding the political power to the economic and social power that was already theirs. The first step they had to take was to make sure that Germany remained a *Bürger* State; that is to say, they had to make sure that there would be early elections to the national assembly and that these elections would take place before the revolution established a new social order that was either democratic-capitalist or socialist. The National Assembly was not yet definitely assured in fact, though it was assured on paper. The reactionaries could not afford to lose any time because the revolutionary workers might change the substance of the State before the elections took place. (The chances of a democratic-capitalist change were not great, as we have seen.) On the other hand, the reactionaries did not command any force to attack the revolutionary workers. Moreover, if they had such a force they could not use it because such an attack would have united the working class, revolutionary workers and non-revolutionary workers.

By the same token the generals could not attack the revolutionists with whatever forces they had at their disposal or could build up. These facts and arguments made the problem and the task of the reactionaries easy: they had to manœuvre Ebert into ordering the generals to use military force against the revolutionists. If this manœuvre were successful, it would crush the Revolution; it would perpetuate the deep split in the working class; it would discredit the Social Democrats in the eyes of large numbers of Germans without making Communists of them; and it would, thus, make Germany safe for the generals and the men behind them.

This chain of events started in the streets of Berlin on 6 December 1918, the day that marked the dawn of reaction.

XV. DAWN

A troop of soldiers appeared in the Wilhelmstrasse and made a demonstration in support of Ebert in front of the Reich Chancellery on the afternoon of 6 December 1918. There was nothing unusual in such demonstrations; they took place frequently and for the most diversified of reasons. When made by soldiers they had usually been ordered by commanders of units who hoped for promotion or other advantages for themselves.

The units of the old army, with the exception of many front-line units (p. 178), had elected commanders and officers from among the soldiers' councils. These commanders were responsible to the regional military commands which in turn were politically responsible to the regional soldiers' councils and militarily responsible to the Supreme Command in the hands of Hindenburg and Groener. The Supreme Command was responsible to the War Minister, the War Minister to the Council of People's Commissars, and this Council, at least nominally, to the Executive Council of the Workers' and Soldiers' Councils. General von Scheüch was War Minister. He had held the same post in the cabinet of Prince Max.

2

Although there was nothing unusual in soldiers' demonstrations in favour of Ebert, the demonstration of 6 December had a special purpose. Its leader was a sergeant by the name of Spiero who was commander of the Franzer Regiment of the Guards. Spiero proclaimed Ebert President of the German Republic, which meant of course that he proclaimed him dictator. Ebert was surprised and said he would have to discuss the matter with his friends. The demonstrators withdrew, disappointed.

A member of a soldiers' council, Gräber, had learned of the impending undertaking and, knowing that it was reactionary, had gone to the Chancellery the previous day to inform Ebert. But the People's Commissars were holding a meeting then, and Gräber deposed his information with Moser and Brecht, the secretaries of Ebert and Landsberg. The two secretaries made a protocol of Gräber's deposition. When the affair was investigated later, Ebert and Landsberg said they had no foreknowledge of it. The secretaries were questioned, but it did not become clear whether or not they had shown the protocol to their chiefs. All that was established beyond doubt was that the protocol had mysteriously disappeared. This was unfortunate, for as Ebert and Landsberg said they knew nothing of the affair in advance they could not have initialed the protocol, which they would have done had they seen it. And the absence of their initials from the document would have supported their words and quelled all insinuations. But the document had disappeared.

3

Simultaneously with Spiero's proclamation, another troop of soldiers occupied the building of the Prussian Diet, the quarters of the Executive Council of the Workers' and Soldiers' Councils, and declared this Council arrested. Barth chanced to arrive at the Diet at that moment. He explained to the soldiers that they must have been misled by somebody, and they withdrew.

Again at the same time, three processions of Spartacists were marching through various parts of Berlin. They had obtained permission for their demonstrations on condition that they were unarmed. But soldiers suddenly opened fire on one of these demonstrations. Sixteen of the Spartacists were killed, another twelve seriously wounded. According to the first official report, the casualties were caused by a machine-gun that a nervous soldier fired for a few seconds until his comrades pulled his hand from the trigger. The nervous soldier said later that the demonstrators had fired two pistol shots at the troops. This was not proved. A revolver was found on the pavement. That it had been planted by the soldiers was not proved, either.

4

Although there were large numbers of soldiers in Berlin, and although they were generally speaking loyal to the Social Democrats, they were not wholly reliable for the purpose of crushing by force the Spartacists and those workers who, though not Spartacists, were watching the progress of the Revolution, prepared to fight if and when counter-revolution should arise. None of them was subtle enough to detect the cold counter-revolution that was in full swing at that time.

Many of the new troop commanders were old-time professional non-commissioned officers. These men could not see any prospect for themselves in civilian life, and they were an easily malleable material for anyone who promised them a future. Otto Wels was constantly at loggerheads with them. As commandant of Berlin (pp. 16 and 94) he was the highest military authority in the capital, but subordinate to the General Command for the Province of Brandenburg which, as a regional command, was directly responsible to the Supreme Command. In the second half of November, Wels had organized a troop of volunteers to which he gave the name of 'Republican Soldiers' Wehr' (*Wehr* means defence force). He had no money at his disposal in the beginning because the Republican Soldiers' Wehr did not figure in the budget of the War Ministry, and the government refused to ask the Reichsbank for an advance for fear of creating a precedent by encroaching on property relations. As the volunteers demanded immediate payment of wages, Wels would never have succeeded in organizing this first government troop had not a foreigner turned up one day who had some business at the *Kommandantur.*

This foreigner learned of Wels's difficulties and offered him a fairly large amount of money on the grounds that all businessmen were interested in the maintenance of quiet and order in Berlin. Wels would not accept money from 'capitalist' sources, but he left it to his deputy's discretion to take the money 'unofficially' and to use it to pay the soldiers. This deputy, Lieutenant Anton Fischer (p. 185), took the hint and the money. Word of this transaction conveniently leaked out into certain circles, and from thereon the *Kommandantur* was inundated with money and offers of money.

Wels and the Republican Soldiers' Wehr were independent of any of the soldiers' councils of Berlin. These councils feared that their existence was threatened by the Republican Soldiers' Wehr, and they agitated for the formation of a garrison soldiers' council with jurisdiction over the Republican Soldiers' Wehr as well as all other units in Berlin. On 3 December, the Association of Professional Non-Commissioned Officers held a meeting to discuss ways of protecting their interests. No one had any idea how this could and should be done. Adroitly, the chairman of the meeting, who was a creature of Fischer and Wels, turned the discussion in another direction. He asked those present who sympathized with 'Spartacus' to leave, and then told the meeting that Spartacus was contemplating a counter-revolution in the next few days, and that it was imperative that this action be crushed. The meeting decided upon the necessary measures. Wels and Fischer were present. Wels made a violent final speech against the Spartacists. In conclusion, the meeting was asked to preserve absolute secrecy. Thus, the attention of the participants was successfully diverted from their grievance against the Republican Soldiers' Wehr. The chairman of this meeting was the same man who, three days later, led the troops that shot up the Spartacist procession (p. 151).

When this shooting was investigated, the office of the commandant, Wels, declared that the order to shoot had been given by the General Command for the Province of Brandenburg. (In the first place, the shooting had been put down to a nervous soldier.) But the war minister, General von Scheüch, protested that the troops had acted upon orders received from the office of the commandant, Wels. There the matter rested.

The soldiers who did the shooting wore black badges with a red border and a red heart. Their watchword was 'Red Heart'. Many of the soldiers who proclaimed Ebert President wore like badges. The badge was worn, too, by the members of an organization called 'Soldiers' Reception, Association of German Women'. This organization had been formed by a certain Marten with the approval of Wels. Marten's domicile was searched after the shooting, against the protest of Wels's deputy, Fischer. The search had been ordered by the Executive Council, and was carried out by the police, which was in the hands of the radical Independent, Eichhorn.

The investigation established that the order to arrest the Executive Council had been given by Marten. He was connected in this venture with Count Matuschka and Baron Rochus von Rheinbaben, both of the Foreign Office. They disappeared the same day. Rheinbaben, however, returned soon.[1] Both he and Matuschka were in turn connected with Count Wolf Metternich of whom we shall hear more presently. Metternich again was connected with Alfons Sack,[2] and the law student Günter Axhausen. These two jurists had formed an organization called 'Students' Guard'. The Students' Guard was to 'protect' the

[1] He became a member of the Reichstag for Stresemann's party. When Stresemann was Reich Chancellor for a few months in 1923, he made Rheinbaben the permanent head of the Chancellery.

[2] Sack became one of Germany's leading corporation lawyers in the Weimar Republic. The Nazis appointed him official counsel for one of the defendants in the Reichstag fire trial.

government. Its formation had been approved by Wels, by the War Minister, by the Foreign Office, and by the General Command of the Berlin garrison under the direction of those elected non-commissioned officer commanders. The approval of the Foreign Office had been given by Baron von Stumm.[1]

The arms of the Students' Guard were supplied by the War Ministry. The ministry was represented in this transaction by a Captain Lorenz who acted for a section chief in the ministry, General von Wrisberg (p. 36). Lorenz was connected with Colin Ross and with Moser, the secretary of Ebert and co-author of that missing protocol. Although the investigation of Moser never established whether or not he had informed Ebert in advance of the affair of 6 December 1918, it became clear that he had so informed the permanent head of the Reich Chancellery, Privy Councillor Simons,[2] who was formerly one of the most trusted confidants of Prince Max.

The investigation established further that the idea of the putsch had come from the Students' Guard. The intention was to eliminate the Executive Council of the Workers' and Soldiers' Councils, the source of political power, and simultaneously to proclaim Ebert dictator. The reasoning of the putschists was logical: there could be no dictator as long as the Executive Council existed, and there had to be a dictator once the Executive Council was eliminated at that time. If, moreover, shooting occurred in the streets as a token of threatening chaos, success was certain.

[1] Wilhelm von Stumm, a member of one of the families of great iron and coal industrialists, was permanent head of the Foreign Office under the last Kaiser, in the Weimar Republic, and under Hitler. His official longevity is a significant indication of the fact that the substance of the German State and consequently its foreign policy was the same in all of these three shapes. It is remarkable, too, that three German régimes regarded him as indispensable in their conduct of foreign affairs although he wretchedly misjudged the attitudes of both England and Russia before the outbreak of war in 1914.

[2] Simons became President of the Supreme Court (Chief Justice) of the Weimar Republic. As such he was, according to the Weimar Constitution, acting Reich President in 1925 from the death of Ebert until the inauguration of Hindenburg.

Ebert could not have acted otherwise than he did had he known of the plan; he would have had to play for time until he received information that the Executive Council had been eliminated.

But the well-conceived plan was frustrated, chiefly through the astuteness of Barth in preventing the arrest of the Executive Council (p. 151). His action showed great presence of mind, especially as he had no idea of what was going on.

How Marten, who was not a soldier, should have come to give orders to the military was not explained. The fact was simply stated by the government on large red posters on 7 December. Marten was arrested by an agent of Eichhorn (p. 154), Weg-mann. Wegmann delivered his prisoner to Wels's *Kommandantur* which immediately released him 'by mistake'. He vanished.

6

Though it miscarried, the putsch showed that reaction was ready to strike. It was entrenched in the three most important political departments of the Reich and, by way of Stumm, Marten, Sack, and several others, in heavy industry. The administrative apparatus of the old State, as was to be expected, became the fountain-head of reaction. But Ebert and his friends went on talking about counter-revolution from the impotent Spartacists. They went on 'saving the State'. As late as 1922 Ebert made a speech at a meeting of Social Democratic workers in the town of Dessau in which he said: 'It is our task to save the State and mould it in the interests of the working people.'

Eichhorn's police arrested a number of other persons involved in the three adventures of 6 December 1918. They were ordered to do so by the Executive Council of the Workers' and Soldiers' Councils. But the Social Democratic People's Commissars pro-tested that this was an interference with the executive power which the Executive Council had conferred upon the government by the agreement of 22 November (p. 113). The prisoners had to be released. Barth then demanded in the Council of People's

Commissars the arrest of Stumm, Simons, and Lorenz. His five colleagues voted him down. But upon his insistence the Council of People's Commissars appointed a commission of three jurists to investigate the affair. The commission found that no one was guilty of any offence. Its three members had many special reasons for believing that they would oblige Ebert, Scheidemann, and Landsberg by not finding any guilt. Neither did they find the missing protocol. Nor did they find out, in spite of repeated and 'thorough' questionings of Moser and Brecht, whether or not these two men informed Ebert of the coming of the putsch.

7

The impotence of the workers' and soldiers' councils, the source of political power, increased with every day that passed. This applied particularly to the Executive Council of Greater Berlin. Ridicule contributed its share to this body's demise. In the middle of November it held a meeting that was unmitigated tragicomedy. The subject of the meeting was the question of the Constituent Assembly. Richard Müller, the Council's chairman, declared: 'We do not want a democratic republic, but a proletarian republic; we will not give up power; if this government does not act as the Executive Council wants, we have the right to throw it out of office.' The leaders of the Social Democrats confused force and power. The leaders of the revolutionary workers confused right and power. Müller crowned his bluster by exclaiming: 'The road to the national assembly leads across my dead body.' Ridicule is no respecter of accidents of appearance. The pose Müller struck was the more ridiculous as he looked like the incarnation of a small-time book-keeper. It earned him the sobriquet of *Leichenmüller* ('Corpse Müller'). Within a very short time this sobriquet was all that was remembered of the existence of the Executive Council of the Workers' and Soldiers' Councils.

In the latter part of its life, which was altogether a few short weeks, this Council was persecuted with especial viciousness by the Social Democratic leaders, who no longer needed it for their purpose, by their Press, by the general Press, and by the government bureaucracy; for it had become predominantly Independent in spirit though not in numbers (p. 112). Its impotence was made absolute by the Reich Congress of Workers' and Soldiers' Councils that was convened by virtue of the agreement of 22 November (p. 113). This congress, the 'parliament of the revolution', met in Berlin on 16 December 1918, and lasted five days.

XVI. COUNCILS

I

There were 500 delegates. The Social Democrats had a great majority with 299 votes. Of the others, 101 were Independents and 25 Democrats, while 75 delegates did not state their political allegiance. The latter 100 votes were usually cast for the Social Democrats.

Karl Liebknecht and Rosa Luxemburg had not been elected again (p. 95). This fact, and the great majority of the Social Democrats in the Reich Workers' and Soldiers' Council, has often been regarded as proof that the German workers in general wanted neither revolution nor socialism. But there were other facts that showed this conclusion to be incorrect.

A typical instance was the preamble of a resolution that was proposed by a delegation of soldiers' councils which invaded the Congress. This preamble began: 'We are at the disposal of the present government, i.e. *the government which, according to its programme, pursues as its final goal the socialist republic*' (my italics). This goal was not, of course, pursued by the government, but the point was that the masses of the Social Democratic workers and soldiers, who wanted socialism, were led to believe that the government, too, wanted socialism. They could therefore not understand the Spartacists.

The Social Democrats and the trade unions had well-knit organizations and an enormous Press. These institutions worked for the government. They persuaded the workers at large that nothing was to be feared from the Junkers and the other militarists because the government was in the hands of workers. And this government, they proclaimed, was threatened by the Spartacists.

The institutions of the Social Democratic Party and the trade unions, such as assembly halls all over Germany, publishing houses, libraries, co-operative societies, and many more, had become vested interests. The officers of the workers' political and industrial organizations had, in the course of five decades or so, become administrators and beneficiaries of these vested interests. A revolution involved risks (it might not succeed) and the workers' institutions might be threatened by failure. A revolution involved risks for the individual worker, too; he might have to fight for socialism. The German workers abhorred this idea. To the extent of not wanting to fight a civil war there existed indeed in the rank and file a predisposition towards being betrayed.

To be sure, the rank and file armed themselves in the summer of 1918. However, they did so not for the sake of social revolution but in an attempt to demolish the old German State and thus participate in a task in which a large part of the civilized world was engaged at that time. Of course, they believed that success in this task would bring socialism to Germany. Except for this one instance, however, the majority of German workers, though socialists, were not revolutionary. But if, as the Social Democratic leaders had told them since Bernstein's return from England (p. 20), socialism could be had without fighting for, what more could the individual socialist worker of the rank and file wish for? Who would want revolution if its fruits could be had without it? Was it not best to sit back and let the leaders do as they saw fit? Thus it is to be explained that when the socialist workers for once freed themselves of their evolutionary passivity and became revolutionary, they lacked the training to do the right thing because the right thing was not staring them in the face.

As socialists the rank and file had done the right thing in the latter stages of the war. The gulf between the State and themselves was glaringly visible then. The workers reacted by using the organization of the trade unions, by pushing aside the official functionaries and replacing them by the Revolutionary Stewards. There was nothing glaring, however, about the cold counter-revolution that was in full swing when the Reich Congress of the

Workers' and Soldiers' Councils met in December 1918. The great majority of these delegates went to Berlin in the firm belief that socialism was assured and that it was imperilled by the Spartacists for reasons incomprehensible to ordinary people (while most of the Spartacists did not know what they wanted either). Huge red posters, put up by a government agency, covered the walls of Berlin. They screamed in huge black letters: 'Socialism is on the march', 'Socialization is here'. And how could ordinary people believe anything else after reading the Social Democratic and trade union Press?

2

There were two main points on the agenda of the Congress: the choice between a republic of councils and a national assembly, that is to say, the question of socialism or militaristic capitalism (here again democratic capitalism was not in the running), and the question of socialization. The Social Democratic leaders naturally wanted the National Assembly. They argued that if it were elected immediately, the majority of the people would vote for them, and this would provide a basis for socialism. They were sincere in saying that they wanted a majority, but they were too intelligent to believe that they would get one.

At the last general (Reichstag) elections (1912), 14·4 million people had been entitled to vote. Of these, 4·3 millions voted for the Social Democrats. In the election to a National Assembly, 36·8 million people would be entitled to vote. The difference of 22·4 millions was accounted for by the proposed lowering of the age limit from 25 to 20 years, and by the proposed extension of the suffrage to women. The point, then, was that 22·4 million people who were entirely without political experience, and mostly without any political knowledge, would decide a question of the greatest importance to the whole world. Hard-headed politicians of the Ebert-Scheidemann type could not possibly have believed that they would obtain a majority, especially in view of the female vote which, as everyone knew, would benefit the old, and particularly the reactionary, parties. The whole procedure carried democracy *ad absurdum*.

Ebert unintentionally highlighted this absurdity when he exclaimed at the Reich Congress of the Workers' and Soldiers' Councils that the victorious proletariat would first establish political class equality and then economic equality (whatever the latter was supposed to mean). Now, political class equality was assured. There had just been a revolution to this effect. Nobody dreamed that there could be a class suffrage, that there could be anything but universal suffrage in Germany. But the problem was what the nation was to decide by its vote. In any fully developed political democracy, at any time, the nation decides periodically which party or parties are to form the government *in the State as it is*. Until 1918, though with certain qualifications since 1917, this question had been decided in Germany by the Kaiser. After 1918, it was, according to the wish of Ebert and his friends, to be decided by the people. Only reactionaries could object to this wish. The fault of the Eberts, their historical guilt, was not that they insisted on the National Assembly, that is to say, on political democracy. Their guilt was that they used political democracy merely to have a politically ignorant majority decide whether they or somebody else was to form the government *in the State as it was*. Certainly, this was a political revolution, a political change as compared with conditions in the Empire. But just as certainly this change did not affect the substance of the State.

The substance of a State cannot be changed by a vote. It can be changed only by power, whether the power be exercised by men who were given it democratically, or by men who usurped it by violence. But Ebert, as we have seen (see p. 40), and many people like him, before and after, in Germany and elsewhere, cherished the belief that the use of power was undemocratic in itself. Yet seldom in history did a situation exist like the one that existed in Germany in 1918, a situation in which power could be used, and the substance of a repulsive State be changed, without any violence; a situation in which political democracy could have been established in a short time after appropriate social and economic measures had been taken to demolish the militaristic substance of the State. To be sure, this political democracy would still have been precarious in view of the political ignorance of the masses of Germans. But it would have had a chance to live and develop.

Of course, the militaristic substance of the German State could not be demolished by making a pact with the military and using them supposedly against the impossible Spartacists, but in fact against the very democracy the pact was allegedly to serve. If Ebert had been a socialist he would have changed the substance of the State by socialist measures. Non-socialist economic and social measures, such as would have been supported by the Democrats and the Centre (and by the Spartacists had they had any sense), would have had the same effect of breaking militarism. As things were, Ebert and his friends did not make any attempt either to break militarism or to take the wind out of the sails of the Spartacists by economic and social measures that would have achieved both results at the same time. Rather, as is usual with little men who have power and do not know what to do with it, yet are afraid of losing it, they became violent. All they could think of was to take the wind out of the sails of the Spartacists by shooting holes into those sails with machine-gun, mortar and cannon, and then burning them with flame-throwers, all of it with the obliging help of the military who must have thought that Ebert was born under their lucky star. Whether the guilty men were consciously or unconsciously guilty is a question of minor importance. It may be said, however, that there is much evidence (notably their indecent haste in issuing writs for the election of the National Assembly) that points to a conscious guilt.

3

The Congress naturally adopted the National Assembly, by 450 votes to 50. The election date was set for 19 January 1919.

The question of socialization was debated next. The Independent, Rudolf Hilferding,[1] was the main speaker. His address was very learned and without any practical implications. In the debate, however, Democrats, Social Democrats, and Independents alike demanded the socialization of coal-mining, the iron and steel industry, the potash industry, the oil industry, and a number of other branches. An Independent (subsequently a Communist), Koenen,[2] doubted that the Social Democrats really wanted socialization. He moved, as a test: 'The government is instructed to begin *immediately* with the socialization of the mining industry.' This motion was, surprisingly, expanded by the Social Democratic leaders. They moved: 'The Congress of Workers' and Soldiers' Councils instructs the government to begin *forthwith* with the socialization of all industries ripe for this process.' As the latter motion went beyond that of the Independents it was obvious that the Social Democratic leaders attached a special meaning to the word 'forthwith'. They must have chosen this word because it appeared to them capable of a wider interpretation than the word 'immediately' (used by Koenen). In the end, both motions were combined and carried by the Congress. 'Forthwith', however, won the day.

[1] Hilferding, who was an Austrian physician, became an important Marxian theorist. After the Revolution of 1918 he was naturalized in Germany. When Stresemann was Chancellor, in 1923, he made Hilferding his Secretary of Finance. When Hitler came to power in 1933 Hilferding fled to France. When the Nazis overran most of France, Marshal Pétain's Vichy government handed Hilferding over to them. As he was a Jew they treated him with especial brutality and he 'committed suicide' in La Santé prison in Paris in February 1941 at the age of 64.

[2] Wilhelm Koenen (born in 1886) organized, together with Max Hoelz, the great Central German Communist uprising of 1923. Hoelz called him 'Barricade Bill without a barricade' because he managed to extricate himself before the uprising started. He was a member of the Reichstag when Hitler came to power, and fled to England. Most of his political friends who fled to Russia were liquidated there, including Max Hoelz. After World War II he returned to Germany and became prominent in his home district in Saxony (Russian Zone). But fate caught up with him. In January 1953 his party superiors began to persecute him until he was arrested in April 1953. He was soon released, however, and given a non-political post.

The two main points on the agenda were thus decided according to the wishes of the Social Democratic leaders. Only two further points of the long agenda may be mentioned here. At one stage of the Congress, the Independents moved that there be no elections to Free States parliaments; that the boundaries of the Free States ought to disappear altogether and a Greater German Republic be founded; and that the final settlement of the problem of federalism versus centralization ought to be left to the National Assembly. This motion was very vague, and the movers hardly recognized the importance of the issue. Of course, the motion was voted down after a short debate.

The Bavarians opposed centralization with particular vehemence. One of their strongest, and least reasonable, arguments was that a centralized Germany would fall under the domination of Berlin because the Berliners were more alert than all other Germans. They spoke of the 'Berliners' as if they were a 'race', and as if their 'racial' characteristics outweighed all other distinctions between individual Berliners and groups of Berliners. Their argument may best be stated in the words the philosophical inspirer of the Eisner government, Professor F. W. Foerster (p. 132), wrote at that time: 'This type of humanity [the Berliners], composed of Prussian precision and energy, Jewish intelligence and tenacity, and Slav suppleness and keenness, will dominate always and everywhere where a central régime is established.'

4

But the Congress adopted another motion that was of the utmost significance. Just as Germany's militarism was condemned abroad, so it was in Germany itself by many people. The latter, for the most part, confusedly regarded the army as it was then constituted as the typical expression of Prussianism, or of militarism, or of the old State, or of the Junkers and their industrial and financial allies, in any case, of all the evil they thought had been overcome by the Revolution. But Hindenburg and Groener were still there. The soldiers and workers did not object to these two men in particular; they thought that the generals could be dangerous only if the army as a whole remained as it had been. They did not see what was behind the army: the old State. They set out to change the army.

A soldiers' motion (the beginning of its preamble is given on p. 159) was adopted unanimously. It became known as the Hamburg Points because its chief promoter was the Social Democratic delegate Peter Martin Lampel[1] of Hamburg. Its main points were as follows:

1. The supreme command of the army and navy is exercised by the People's Commissars under the control of the Executive Council.
2. As a symbol of the destruction of militarism... the removal of all insignia of rank is decreed and the wearing of arms off duty is forbidden.
3. The soldiers' councils are responsible for the reliability of the troop units and the maintenance of discipline. There are no superiors off duty.
4. The soldiers elect their leaders. Former officers who enjoy the confidence of their units may be elected.
5. The abolition of the conscript army and the creation of a people's army is to be accelerated.

It was easy to see that no army could exist on such a basis. But this was not the decisive point. The decisive point was that militarism as an institution could outwardly be recognized by the existence of the army. There is no reason to doubt that if the social, economic, and political issues of which the army was but one expression had been as easily recognizable as the military issue, the Congress would have attempted to deal with them in the same vigorous if ineffective fashion. But apart from being much less visible to the politically untrained and mistrained, these other issues were deliberately obscured by the Social Democratic leaders.

---

[1] Lampel (born in 1894) became a successful playwright in the Weimar Republic. He spent the years of the Hitler régime in exile, mostly the United States. Having returned to Germany in 1949 he lives in Hamburg and continues his success as a writer. He has developed pro-Russian leanings in his thinking about Germany's future.

The tactics of these leaders were illustrated by an incident that took place in connexion with the vote on the Hamburg Points. We have seen a number of instances of the constant friction between the People's Commissars and the Executive Council regarding their spheres of competency. Now, when the text of the soldiers' motion was distributed among the delegates before the vote, the text of another, Social Democratic, motion was distributed with it. By this second motion, both the executive and the *legislative* power (which latter was the prerogative of the councils) were transferred to the government. The Independents protested against such shock tactics, as the second motion had not been debated, but the Social Democratic chairman of the Congress ignored their protests, and the motion was passed without debate. Of course, it would have been adopted in any case, but the Social Democrats shunned a debate, for obvious reasons.

5

The Hamburg Points did not come from within the Congress; they were carried into the Congress from outside (p. 159). Spartacists and other workers were ceaselessly demonstrating in the streets while the Congress sat. True, the (Prussian) provinces and the Free States were quiet, but there was an undercurrent of social revolution noticeable in many places. The unanimous adoption of the Hamburg Points proved this fact beyond doubt. Was the basis for socialism (so skilfully evaded by that indiarubber resolution of the Congress, p. 164) to be established before the National Assembly met? Before the bayonets arrived? Was everything to be spoiled at the eleventh hour?

Profoundly perturbed by the Hamburg Points, Ebert hurried to his office at the close of the day's session. How would the Supreme Command take the soldiers' motion and its unanimous passage by the Congress? He telephoned by private line to General Groener who was at army headquarters in Kassel.

XVII. OFFICERS

———◦✕◦———

I

It was certain by the end of November 1918 that the first returning front-line soldiers would arrive in Berlin shortly. These
troops had not been affected by the revolutionary spirit as long as
they were fighting, but they succumbed to it as soon as they
reached Germany, and some of them even in former enemy territory. Certain quarters, however, hoped they could keep intact a
number of units sufficient to put down the Revolution. Starting
out from this hope, Colonel von Haeften[1] submitted a set of suggestions to Supreme Command which he represented as liaison
officer attached to the Council of People's Commissars. Supreme
Command thoroughly discussed his suggestions and adopted a
corresponding plan, the gist of which was that the old Reichstag
would be convened to draft a new constitution to be confirmed by
a national assembly; the workers' and soldiers' councils would be
abolished and the power of the officers restored; and the civilian
population would be forced to surrender all the arms in their
possession.

Supreme Command sent a confidant, Major von Harbou, who
had once been Ludendorff's right-hand man, to Ebert to submit
their plan to him. Harbou arrived in Berlin just in time to witness
the events of 6 December (see chapter xv). He and his superiors
realized that these events made the immediate execution of their
plan, and much of the plan itself, impossible; if the workers were
to be disarmed in the midst of the excitement caused by the
killings of that day, endless bloodshed would result. Supreme
Command realized, moreover, that the Reichstag could not be

———

[1] Haeften was an intimate of Niemann's whose witless scheme to end the
war he had supported (p. 77n.).

convened at all in the circumstances. Therefore, they modified their plan and accordingly informed Harbou, who submitted this modified plan to Ebert.

According to the terms of the revised plan nine divisions of front-line soldiers were to be drawn into places west, south, and east of Berlin. Between 10 and 21 December they would march into the capital, disarm the population, clear the barracks of 'unreliable elements', restore the power of the officers, that is, abolish the soldiers' councils, and establish units of volunteers. Such volunteer units were necessary because the bulk of the front-line soldiers would have to be demobilized. In this one point the 'right of revolution' was effective; no one could be kept in the army against his will although conscription was not formally abolished until August 1920. On the other hand, any soldier who could not find work had the right, according to a law made by Prince Max's government shortly before its demise, to stay in barracks for four months after his return from the front. Large numbers of soldiers made use of this right.

2

Ebert told Harbou that he did not doubt the officer's word of honour that they had no ulterior motives and wanted nothing but the restoration of quiet and order; but he had misgivings about the course and the outcome of the proposed undertaking. His sudden balking was not easy to understand. Perhaps he feared for his own position if the military obtained the enormous power that would fall to them if the action succeeded; perhaps he shrank from bloodshed among the workers at this last moment when things were really becoming serious. The latter alternative must appear doubtful, however, in view of the fact that he did not shrink a short time later. Harbou (who ought to know, as he had the conversation with him) reported to Supreme Command his notion that Ebert did not want to be burdened with the responsibility for the action and would rather be confronted with a *fait accompli*. Perhaps, then, Ebert realized the true motive of the military and the reactionaries which was to use him, the outstanding representative of the political power, as a front for their designs (p. 149). If they started the operation without his express consent though with his tacit approval, he could disavow them and their action at any time he liked, should such a disavowal appear advisable to him.

Harbou further reported to Supreme Command that he had impressed upon Ebert the necessity of acting before Christmas; the troops would have to be discharged by the holidays, and Supreme Command would have no force at their disposal afterwards. Upon this, Ebert dismissed the Major with some meaningless phrases which Harbou took as a confirmation that Ebert agreed with Supreme Command on the goal to be reached but was not sure that the means were appropriate. Harbou concluded his report by expressing his opinion that the moment had come for Supreme Command to launch a strong drive.

3

On 8 December, Barth learned that a transport of front-line soldiers, named General Command of General Lequis, had arrived at a western suburb of Berlin. Harbou was Lequis's Chief of Staff, and the unit was under the direction of Lieutenant-General Hoffmann. No one connected with the events of those days ever set eyes on General Lequis, and many people believed he was a fictitious person. With his usual impetuousness Barth thundered at a meeting of the People's Commissars that treachery was being committed. Ebert replied that Lequis's soldiers were staying in Berlin only a couple of days to be discharged. Barth travelled to Wannsee (half an hour by train from Berlin) where the unit was stationed. He had a conversation with their commanding officer, Captain Pabst, who readily answered all the questions Barth put to him. Barth gained the impression that the troops had been called to Berlin by Ebert and Landsberg for sinister purposes, and that the affair had been deliberately concealed from the Independent People's Commissars.

Barth returned to Berlin. For once Ebert was afraid of him and yielded. The plan was thwarted. To save what could be saved, Harbou tried to win over the War Minister, General von Scheüch. The minister knew nothing of the intended action; neither the government nor Supreme Command had informed him. He refused his support as he held that there was no prospect of success. Desperately, Harbou telephoned Groener to tell him of the turn of events. Groener sent a secret order to Lequis: Lequis was to take instructions solely from Supreme Command. For the moment, these instructions were that he was to act according to his own discretion and that any orders coming from the government or the war ministry were to be disregarded if they deviated from the original plan that had been 'agreed' upon by Supreme Command and Ebert.

The troops marched into Berlin two days later with the usual military ceremonial amid the enthusiasm of the non-working-class population. But they did not disarm the workers. Rather, they were said to be disbanded according to the promise Ebert had given Barth. The news that troops were coming had spread like wildfire through the capital on 8 December. It caused intense excitement among the workers who responded by a wave of strikes and demonstrations. So great was the excitement that the People's Commissars felt impelled to pass a law on 12 December by which a People's Wehr was to be created that was independent of the army, and directly responsible to the Council of People's Commissars. It was to elect its own leaders, and its members were to pledge themselves to the *socialist-democratic Republic*.

Another three days later, the People's Commissars issued a decree that all arms in private possession were to be surrendered. This course had always been open. But the military were bent on using violence, and the Social Democrats in the government though not yet giving them a completely free hand were not resisting them either. For the time being, however, the military and the reactionaries behind them were frustrated.

4

There matters stood when the Reich Congress of Workers' and Soldiers' Councils adopted the Hamburg Points. Groener had already learned of them when Ebert got in touch with him (p. 167); Harbou had telephoned. Groener told Ebert that the Field Marshal (Hindenburg) did not recognize the decision of the Congress and would fight against it with all the means at his disposal. Groener added that the same applied to himself. Ebert pleaded; they must try to remove that 'unpleasant resolution' by clever manœuvring. Groener declared that he had assembled all the officers of General Headquarters before Ebert called him; they had adopted the same attitude as Hindenburg and he; and their decision was final. Ebert said it was his intention to attempt a mediation between Supreme Command and the Councils; would Groener come to Berlin on 20 December? Groener said he would.

But to disabuse Ebert's mind should he believe that Supreme Command were prepared to compromise, Hindenburg issued an order of the day to all army commanders a few hours later. It said that Hindenburg did not recognize the resolution of the Congress; that he acknowledged nothing but the agreement made with Ebert on 10 November (p. 93); and that the officers would continue in service only if the government honoured its pledge.

Ebert certainly recognized Hindenburg's order, which became known to him a few days later (p. 174), for what it was, namely, an open declaration of war by Supreme Command against the Republic. Nothing but the Republic could be meant, for nobody could seriously maintain that the Reich Congress that had adopted the Hamburg Points was Bolshevist. But at this stage Ebert was no longer able to resist Supreme Command even if he had wanted to, unless he were prepared to resign and support a revolutionary socialist government. But this would have meant chaos, as there were no revolutionary leaders capable of governing, and civil war, which would have been started by Hindenburg.

On 20 December, Barth was informed that there was to be a

meeting in the evening, a meeting of the People's Commissars and the Central Council. The Central Council of the Workers' and Soldiers' Councils had been elected by the Reich Congress as its executive according to the terms of the agreement of 22 November (p. 112). It may be recalled that until this body was constituted the Executive Council of the Workers' and Soldiers' Councils of Greater Berlin had exercised the functions of the Workers' and Soldiers' Councils of the German Republic, according to that same agreement. The Executive Council continued in existence after the election of the Central Council, but its sphere of competency was confined to Greater Berlin. As the overwhelming majority of the Reich Congress was Social Democratic, the Independents had refused to be represented in the Central Council, and this body was thus entirely Social Democratic.

Leaving his office in the Chancellery to go to the meeting, Barth had to pass through a certain hall. He found that a session was in progress there with Landsberg in the chair. He sat down and stayed until the end, Landsberg's presence making him think that the other meeting would be later. Eventually, he asked Landsberg when it was to be and was told that it had been going on for a long time. It may or may not have been Landsberg's and Ebert's intention to keep Barth away. In any case, when Barth and Landsberg arrived at the meeting Barth was looking for, they found only Ebert and Scheidemann and several members of the Central Council. Neither Haase nor Dittmann, the two other Independent Peoples' Commissars, was there. But Groener was present, to the surprise of Barth. Groener was accompanied by Major von Schleicher who began his amazing performance of political intrigue at that time, a performance in the course of which he became Reich Chancellor for two months (immediately preceding Hitler) and was eventually murdered in the purge of 30 June 1934.

Groener was just summing up what had transpired at the meeting so far. 'Gentlemen, I thank you for your far-going spirit of accommodation.... We are agreed, then, that everything remains as it is in the army at the front and the army of the East.' Barth exploded. He shouted that Groener must resign if he did not like the Hamburg Points. But if he did not resign and acted against the Points, he was guilty of treason and the Socialist Republic would know how to get rid of him.

Haase and Dittmann had arrived by then. They took sides with Barth. The representatives of the Central Council who otherwise were completely under the influence of their Social Democratic leaders began to waver, and the government decided in favour of Barth; regulations for the putting into effect of the Hamburg Points were to be issued immediately, and the Points were to be presented to the soldiers as a Christmas gift from the Republic.

On the following day, Haase brought Hindenburg's order (p. 172) to a session of the government. Even Landsberg did not like it, but he pleaded good faith on the part of Hindenburg. Ebert, however, said there was nothing wrong with the order; it was natural that things must remain as they were until the government regulations about the Hamburg Points were issued. Barth roared that Supreme Command must be deposed, arrested, and tried for treason. But he stood alone.

The three Independents then moved that the Central Council be convened to debate the matter. The motion was lost by three votes against three. Ebert, Scheidemann, and Landsberg were not sure of their own Central Council because some of its members had wavered the day before. It was the old story: this issue was (or seemed to be) understandable to everyone; therefore, even the Central Council might become dangerous; and therefore, the Social Democratic People's Commissars would not have it convene to debate the issue.

Nothing was done for a few days about the regulations concerning the Hamburg Points. And then, before anything was done about them, things suddenly took a turn that became disastrous to the Revolution.

It began with the sailors.

XVIII. SAILORS

The Revolution tossed a small number of sailors to Berlin. They decided, on 11 November 1918, to form a unit to maintain order in the capital. As they preferred the Independents to the Social Democrats, they marched to police headquarters and put themselves at the disposal of Police President Eichhorn. Eichhorn could not use them, but he assigned them quarters in the barracks of the Alexander Regiment of the Guards. The number of sailors had swelled to about 600 by the time they began to set out for the barracks, a few minutes walking distance from police headquarters. On their way, a soldier asked them where they were going. They told him, and thereupon he offered to take them to the *Marstall* (Imperial stables, opposite the Palace) instead; everything was prepared there for the reception of a unit, he explained. They followed him to the Marstall, and found that his information was correct. The arrangements, they were told, had been made in connexion with the *Kommandantur* and its head, Wels.

The sailors were received at the Marstall by a Count Wolf Metternich. They elected a council of which Metternich became a member, and assumed the name of 'People's Marine Division'. Metternich had large amounts of money at his disposal which were probably contributed by financial and industrial circles. But he was wealthy in his own right, and he regaled the sailors well.

The elected commander of the People's Marine Division was a sailor by the name of Vitschorek. He was soon shot down by a naval captain, Brettschneider, who in return was lynched by the sailors. A Berlin metal-worker, a confused individual called Tost, was then elected commander, but he left the Division a few days later to become a member of the Central Navy Council (p. 177).

175

Metternich, who declared that he had renounced his aristocratic title and officer's commission, was then elected commander and thus reached his immediate goal.

As the sailors seemed reliable, the government asked Noske on 12 November to send another 2000 of them to Berlin. The government were also impressed by the good behaviour of the sailors in Kiel (p. 86) which continued although most of them had Independent leanings and Noske's militaristic bent of mind was well known to them. However, railroad traffic between Kiel and Berlin was interrupted at that time, and only 600 sailors were sent to the capital, not from Kiel but from Cuxhaven. They became part of the People's Marine Division. This body was 3250 strong by the middle of December, but no more than 1800 of them were active as there was a lack of clothing and other necessaries. Only a comparatively small number were really sailors; the personnel files of the Division showed that three-fourths of the men had joined up because they could not find work after being discharged from the army.

The Palace opposite the Marstall had been occupied on 9 November by a dubious crowd of soldiers who were under the command of the crook Ettisch (p. 116). These men stole many articles of great value, and destroyed many others. Six days later, Metternich asked the sailors to occupy the Palace and turn out the soldiers. The sailors demanded an order from the government. Metternich procured the order within twenty minutes; it was signed by Ebert. The close connexion between Metternich and Ebert greatly perturbed the sailors later. Metternich was also a personal friend of the Kaiser's, and many people believed he had the childish notion of restoring the Palace to him. The Palace had become the national property of Prussia[1] through the Revolution, but the Hohenzollerns were paid a compensation.

The sailors occupied the Palace and lodged the arrested soldier plunderers in the city prison, notifying the *Kommandantur*. In the general confusion prevailing in those days the prisoners were

[1] Situated in the Russian sector of Berlin, the Palace was razed to the ground after World War II.

released shortly afterwards. There is no evidence to the effect that the release was deliberate, but one of its consequences was that the sailors were charged with the pilfering and destruction in the Palace.

The Marine Division stayed on in the Marstall and kept merely a guard in the Palace. They further guarded a number of other important buildings in Berlin, among them the Chancellery, the seat of the government; the Kaiser Friedrich Museum which contained treasures of incalculable value; the Reichsbank; the Prussian Diet, the seat of the Executive Council of the Workers' and Soldiers' Councils. Nothing was ever taken from these and other buildings while they were guarded by the sailors.

When Metternich was ousted as a consequence of the putsch of 6 December (p. 150), the relations between the sailors and the *Kommandantur* grew cool because the Marine Division, indirectly established by Wels, had become a competitor of Wels' Republican Soldiers' Wehr. Wels was now pleased that the sailors were being maligned because of the thefts in the Palace. He stopped payment of their wages and demanded that the Division be disbanded. The reason he gave was that the sailors had increased their numbers by secret enlistments (which was not true, as Wels must have known by the pay-lists). The general Press and *Vorwärts* also demanded the dissolution of the Division.

2

A Central Council of the Navy functioned in the Navy Department which like all other government departments was located in Berlin. It had been elected at Wilhelmshaven by a great meeting of sailors' councils. On 9 December, it published a 'Political Programme of the Central Council of the Navy'. It demanded that ten specific measures be taken 'in accordance with the Erfurt Programme'. Nearly all of these measures concerned points that were constantly being reiterated by the government, but there was also the demand for 'a socialist-republican army and navy (people's Wehr)'.

Three days later, the government published a law establishing a people's Wehr. This law was made for two reasons in addition to the one stated before (p. 171). It was to sugar the pill of the contemplated decree ruling the surrender of all arms in private possession, and to appease the Navy Council. At the same time, the Navy Council, agitated by the arrival of Lequis's troops, unanimously adopted the following resolution: 'To maintain quiet and order we stand as a security force at the disposal of the Ebert-Haase government, the government that has for its programme the socialistic republic.' Indeed, the government had never declared that it was following any other programme. The Navy Council, like anyone with inside knowledge at that time, knew that there were serious differences of opinion within the government over the putsch of 6 December. Many people expected the government to break up. Therefore the resolution of the Navy Council went on to say that if the government were to break up, the sailors would be united behind Haase and would defend his ideas by force of arms if necessary.

Shortly after this resolution was adopted, the advisers of Lequis's troops appeared on the scene. Lequis's troops, supposed to have been disbanded (p. 170), had no soldiers' councils, only advisers, that is to say, ordinary soldiers whose function was to apprise the officers of the wishes and complaints of the troops. Such advisers were a feature of many returning front-line units; unlike the soldiers' councils they had no powers whatever. It is possible that Lequis's advisers had learned of the sailors' resolution. In any case, they issued a declaration demanding the withdrawal of the Marine Division whose existence they considered to be a disparagement of the returning front-line soldiers. This declaration alarmed the soldiers' councils of Berlin who otherwise stood by Ebert and his friends. They protested: 'The comrades of the navy have been the first promoters and protectors of the Revolution. Their presence in Berlin is absolutely necessary.' They demanded, further, that the Marine Division be increased to 8000 men.

Ebert was thus faced not only by the unruly Marine Division

but also by the prospect of losing the allegiance of the soldiers of Berlin. (The number of officer-commanded returned front-line soldiers was still small.) If earlier in the month, December 1918, he had been reluctant to let Supreme Command have their way (p. 169), he now threw himself unreservedly into their arms.

3

On 13 December, the Marine Division concluded an agreement with the Prussian Ministry of Finance which administered all Prussian State property and thus the Palace. Under this agreement the ministry was to provide additional space for the Division in the Marstall not later than 20 December, whereupon the sailors were to evacuate the Palace and hand over the keys to authorized representatives of the ministry. At the same time, the Reich government made different arrangements about the same matter with the Central Council of the Navy.

To end this confusion, the Reich government issued an over-riding order to the *Kommandantur* that the sailors were to be paid their arrears (Wels had stopped payment of their wages, p. 177) after evacuating the Palace and delivering the keys to the *Kommandantur*, that is, to Wels. The order said, further, that from 1 January 1919, payment would be made for 600 sailors only. The sailors, thus faced with what almost amounted to dissolution of their division, went to the government to discuss the matter with Ebert. An understanding was reached covering the main points. A further discussion was to take place after Christmas. The sailors then evacuated the Palace (on 23 December).

Most people are easily excitable and more or less unreasonable in turbulent times like those. The sailors disliked Wels and did not want to negotiate with him. Consequently, one of their leaders, the former naval lieutenant, Dorrenbach, and a few other sailors childishly took the keys to Barth. Barth telephoned Wels and told him the matter was settled, he had the keys. But Wels was equally childish and insisted that the sailors bring the keys to him or at least take them to Ebert who was responsible for military affairs. This childish behaviour on both sides had terrible consequences.

The sailors with the keys looked for Ebert but could not find him. They talked the matter over with their comrades who were on guard duty in the Chancellery, and resolved to blockade the building and cut its telephone connexions. This was another immature decision, but it had at least a reason that made sense from the point of view of the sailors. Dorrenbach and his companions knew that several of Lequis's regiments, now stationed at Potsdam, had been ordered that morning to be ready to go to Berlin. This order may or may not have been given in the hope that the quarrel with the sailors would not be settled. Moreover, it was now two days before Christmas, and Supreme Command had told Ebert that they would not be able to do anything after Christmas (p. 170). As they could not find Ebert, Dorrenbach and his friends feared that the soldiers would be called to the capital. To prevent this they cut off the central telephone switchboard of the Chancellery (they ought to have known that there were many direct outside lines in the building).

Leaving the guards at their posts they returned to the Marstall and reported to their comrades what had happened. Angrily, the sailors decided to demonstrate in front of the *Kommandantur*, which was only a few minutes distant from the Marstall. Suddenly, as they were marching there, an armoured car of the *Kommandantur* drove up and opened fire on the tumultuous crowd of sailors who returned the fire. Three sailors and one soldier were killed, several others wounded. Wels suddenly was prepared to pay out the money although the sailors had come without the keys of the Palace. But the sailors were now wild with anger. They declared it was not a question of money but of their honour and revenge for their dead. They took Wels, Anton Fischer (p. 153), and Bongard, the administrative director of the *Kommandantur*, as hostages of the Marstall.

4

While this was happening Barth was informed of the coming of Lequis's troops; the chairman of the Potsdam soldiers' council, Klawunde, telephoned and told him. Once again, Barth violently accused Ebert of treachery. Ebert promised him that the order to Lequis would be cancelled and that no troops would come to Berlin. Late in the evening, however, some thousand soldiers, heavily armed, appeared at the Chancellery and occupied it (the sailors' blockade had been lifted a short while after it began). Learning of the arrival of the soldiers, the sailors marched to the Chancellery and it looked as though a battle would develop. Amidst tremendous excitement, however, Barth made a suggestion that was adopted: the soldiers marched away to one side, the sailors to the other. Nearly everybody else went home, too.

At eight o'clock the next morning, 24 December, Berlin was shaken by the roar of cannon. Lequis's troops were shelling the Palace and the Marstall. Barth, who knew nothing of Wels's detention by the sailors, hurried to Unter den Linden. In the University he found Captain Pabst, the commander of the troops. Pabst said he would be very grateful to Barth if he stopped the bloodshed. 'You know that I am a soldier through and through, but that I, a German, must shoot upon Germans revolts me.'[1] Barth hurried to the Chancellery; no one was there. He telephoned to the War Ministry and spoke to Harbou. Harbou told him that the soldiers were acting upon orders from the government, and the attack could be stopped only by a resolution of the Council of People's Commissars (it had been started, of course, without such a resolution). But Barth could not find any of his five colleagues. He hurried to the *Kommandantur*.

[1] A little over a year later, when Pabst was one of the prime moving forces behind the reactionary Kapp putsch, he no longer found it revolting to shoot upon Germans. But then his orders did not come from a former leather-worker; they came from former Imperial generals.

5

Ebert, Scheidemann, and Landsberg had stayed behind in the Chancellery after the turmoil of the previous evening. In the dead of night, Groener, informed by Harbou, telephoned Ebert furiously demanding an explanation of what the government meant by yielding to the sailors. Ebert replied that he sympathized with Groener; he realized that the yielding must have a disastrous effect upon the army, especially the officers, but a bloodbath *at this moment* would be still more disastrous. Groener collected himself and declared that Hindenburg and he insisted on the dissolution of the People's Marine Division, and they would take steps to carry it out.

Ebert discussed the situation with Scheidemann and Landsberg, and they telephoned to the Marstall asking whether Wels had been released (Fischer and Bongard had already been set free, p. 185). The answer was No. Somewhat later, at half past two in the morning of 24 December, the commander of the sailors, Radtke, Metternich's successor, telephoned Ebert and told him, according to Ebert's account, that not only was Wels still there but the mood of the sailors was such that he, Radtke, feared for Wels's life. Ebert thereupon telephoned to the War Minister, General von Scheüch, and asked him to come to the Chancellery. When Scheüch arrived, Ebert told him of Wels's plight and ordered him to arrange for his liberation through Lequis's troops. But Scheüch's order was superfluous; Lequis had already made the necessary arrangements, either upon his own initiative or upon orders from Groener.

It was true that Radtke had told Ebert he feared for Wels's life, though he did not say that he feared for it from the sailors. Also, when Ebert recounted this conversation he failed to remember that Radtke had added: if Wels were released at that moment. To explain the meaning of this qualification it is necessary to refer to the Republican Security Wehr. We have heard that there was constant friction and jealousy between the soldiers' councils of

Berlin, Wels's Republican Soldiers' Wehr, and the People's Marine Division; each of these bodies wanted to garrison the capital exclusively, and each feared that the others were undermining its existence. There was a fourth troop in Berlin, the Republican Security Wehr of the Independent Police President, Eichhorn, about 3000 men. We shall hear a good deal of this troop, its status and character, as we proceed. Here it is necessary to know that a number of Eichhorn's men, who were most undisciplined at that time, went to the Marstall upon learning of the capture of the three heads of the *Kommandantur*. They meant to shoot them and began by maltreating them, but the sailors rescued the prisoners from the Eichhorn men and locked them up in a room of the Marstall. Most of them had come to their senses and wanted to release Wels, but they feared that if they released him at once the Eichhorn men would kill him. They knew, however, that the Eichhorn men would leave the Marstall at three o'clock, and they decided to postpone Wels's release until then. This was what Radtke told Ebert at half past two, and it was the reason why he said that he feared for Wels's life *if Wels were released at that moment*. The Eichhorn men left the Marstall at three o'clock, and the sailors told Wels that he was free to go. Wels thereupon telephoned Ebert and told him that he was free to go but that he was suffering from shock and would stay to sleep in the Marstall until later in the morning. In spite of this, Ebert and Scheidemann and Landsberg did nothing to stop the military operation against the sailors which did not begin until five hours later.

6

The shelling and fighting went on until ten o'clock when the sailors asked for a half-hour truce in order to remove the women and children living in the Marstall (families of old Imperial servants). Meanwhile, Ebert, Scheidemann, and Landsberg, and Barth's party colleagues Haase and Dittman, had turned up at the Chancellery. Barth was still at the *Kommandantur*. Ebert was impatient to receive news from the 'battle front', but Barth arrived before news came. Ebert told him that he had no idea of what was going on. Barth roared that Ebert was either a liar or a bloodthirsty rogue. But Haase declared that he believed Ebert; he would not believe that the man was lying in such a grave matter. Ebert, under pressure from the Independents, telephoned Scheüch to stop the fighting.

This order was as unnecessary as the order to begin the battle had been. For tens of thousands of workers and women had edged in among the soldiers during the truce, paralysing them. Moreover, a great number of soldiers, men of Lequis's troop, threw away their arms in disgust upon being told by their sailor 'enemies' what it was all about. When word of this development reached the Chancellery, Ebert went deathly pale and Barth gloated.

Nine sailors had been killed and many more wounded. Also killed were twenty of their worker-partisans and more than another forty of them wounded. The low figure of casualties was due to the fact that the Marstall was a huge complex of buildings of massive stone that could not be reduced by the light field cannon the attackers used (although it was badly damaged) and which gave the sailors ample scope to hide and protect themselves.

A number of Eichhorn's incorrigibles were again in evidence during the truce. They arrested many of Lequis's officers for 'disturbing the peace' of the city and took some thirty of them to police headquarters. The embarrassed Eichhorn sent a few of his confidants to the private addresses of the captured officers and friends of theirs to fetch civilian clothes for them, and quietly let the prisoners go.

The result of the battle was an agreement along the lines of the agreement between the sailors and the Prussian Ministry of Finance (p. 179). Moreover, the Lequis division was to be withdrawn from Berlin, and the sailors were pledged not to participate in any further action against the government; differences were to be settled by negotiation between the competent authorities of both sides.

Wels appeared at the Chancellery. Scheidemann was the first to see him. 'He looked like a ghost. His face was ashy-gray and wrinkled; his eyes, which had looked death in the face, were sunken.' Scheidemann hurried to Ebert to break the glad tidings of Wels's return. Ebert said: 'Yes, what are we to do with him? He's finished with; he'll see this himself. He's no longer any good to us.'

Wels was deposed as commandant of Berlin. His deputy, Lieutenant Anton Fischer, succeeded him. Fischer was one of those strange characters that are thrown up by any revolution. In the course of following many callings he had forgotten his former ambitions and his once sheltered past; he had started out in life as a Franciscan friar. In the Revolution he obtained large amounts of money from various reactionary and foreign sources and used it to maintain an extensive 'intelligence service', employing scores of low type vigilantes who differed from him in everything but character. He often distorted his 'intelligence' when he thought this would help his career. Otherwise, he suffered from the delusion that he was indispensable to the Revolution and that his merits were not appropriately recognized.

While a prisoner in the Marstall he persuaded his captors, the sailors, that Wels was no good and he, Fischer, would be a better commandant. The sailors got in touch with the soldiers' councils who agreed that Fischer was preferable to Wels. They all got in touch with Ebert, and Ebert agreed, too; he was not in a position to object. Fischer was taken to the Palace where the leaders of the sailors and of the soldiers' councils congratulated him on his appointment. He accepted on condition that Wels and Bongard be released immediately. Bongard was released, but Wels had to be kept because of the Eichhorn men. Fischer returned to the *Kommandantur* to take over, by a sudden lapse of memory forgetting about Wels.

When Ebert told Wels that he was deposed, Wels rushed to the *Kommandantur* and made a scene with Fischer, accusing him of having engineered his capture to get him out of the way so that he could become commandant himself. But Wels was not finished; Ebert changed his mind. Wels became chairman of the Social Democratic Party in 1920 when Ebert, being Reich President and 'above party', had to give up that post. The indubitable political honesty of Wels, which was coupled with severe intellectual limitations, made him just the right tool in the hands of leaders of the Ebert-Landsberg type; the right tool to pull the wool over the eyes of the Social Democratic workers and try to stop the mass exodus of rank-and-filers to the Communists. Wels died in penury in Paris on 18 September 1939.

7

On the evening of 24 December 1918, the day of the battle of the Marstall, a Colonel Reinhard appeared in the *Kommandantur*, an out-and-out reactionary. He declared that he had been appointed commandant by the War Minister, General von Scheüch. Fischer summoned his new friends, the soldiers' councils, and they booed Reinhard out of the place. He never came back. Actually he had been sent by Ebert who was smarting because Fischer had been forced on him by the soldiers' councils and the sailors. Of course, a Fischer was not the proper person to be commandant of Berlin. But a Reinhard was not the proper person either.

Ebert declared after the battle of the Marstall that he had not given the order to attack the building. Scheüch declared that he had received the order from Ebert. Ebert declared that he had merely given the order to liberate Wels (who he knew was free). Scheüch declared obligingly and with sombre sarcasm: 'I never received the order to break brutally, by military force, the resistance of the sailors and to uphold the authority of the government.' Thereupon he resigned. General von Lequis was replaced by General von Lüttwitz who became one of the chief driving forces of the Kapp putsch a little over a year later.

On the face of it, it was of course senseless to try to liberate a prisoner by shelling the building in which he was kept. But Ebert did give the order. Why? Probably because he overestimated the strength of the military and underestimated the revolutionary spirit of the workers of Berlin.

8

The three Social Democratic People's Commissars issued an explanation to their party. It contained this passage: 'The 24th of December has cost us an enormous amount in national property and national reputation. Another such day, and *Germany will lose the rank of a State with which other States negotiate and conclude peace*' (my italics). But the Entente did not do Ebert the favour.

The veiled appeal to the Entente was of course made because the battle of the Marstall ended with a clear defeat of the military. What made this defeat particularly dangerous for Ebert, Scheidemann, and Landsberg was not so much its military aspect as its political aspect: the force split when many of its members realized that they were being used for counter-revolutionary purposes.

The general press and *Vorwärts*, having no intimate knowledge of the government's military straits, blamed the government for being weak. Landsberg, who ought to have had this inside knowledge, exclaimed upon learning of the agreement that ended the battle of the Marstall: 'What is the idea? One does not negotiate with rebels, one beats them to their knees.' Friedrich Stampfer wrote in the same vein, but more cautiously phrased, in *Vorwärts*. The leading Democratic paper, *Berliner Tageblatt*, wrote in reply to Stampfer: 'The sailors have rightly seen a victory all along the line in this result [of the battle of the Marstall]. The Ebert-Haase government has capitulated; it sways rudderless from one conception to another. The editor-in-chief of *Vorwärts*, Friedrich Stampfer, writes very brave articles, but the government he serves does not act as he writes. And what use is the energy of words and printed fortitude?'

The People's Commissars held a heated session on 27 December. Three main items were on the agenda: the battle of the Marstall, the problem of socialization, and the regulations about the Hamburg Points.

In discussing the first topic Barth made a statement that was as simple as it was irrefutable, a condemnation of Ebert's order to 'liberate' Wels. He said that if Ebert had informed him of Wels's detention he would have gone to the Marstall and told the sailors to release the prisoner. Considering the friendly relations between Barth and the sailors there can be no doubt that this would have solved the conflict peacefully.

In connexion with the last topic (the Hamburg Points) the Independents demanded light on certain dark machinations which Supreme Command was carrying out in the East (as the Independents believed with the approval of their Social Democratic colleagues) and which were directed against Russia and Poland.

Ebert, Scheidemann, and Landsberg on the one hand, and Barth, Haase and Dittmann on the other, violently disagreed on all three subjects. The Independent Commissars formulated eight questions and submitted them to the Central Council of the Workers' and Soldiers' Councils. The questions concerned the attitude of the Social Democratic People's Commissars towards recent events. The replies of the entirely Social Democratic Council did not satisfy the Independents although the Council took the exchange as an opportunity to show its helpless confusion by once more instructing the government to put the Hamburg Points into effect.

The three Independent People's Commissars resigned. A few days later, their party friends resigned from the Prussian government which like the Council of People's Commissars had been composed of Social Democrats and Independents. A few months later, Haase said in a speech at the Independent Party Congress on 3 March 1919, that 'on 24 December, after the attack on Marstall and Palace, when Ebert, Scheidemann, and Landsberg were completely broken, we Independents could have taken over the government by ourselves.... We would have swept with us the masses who were following us....' Why did they not do it? Because, as

Haase put it, his party had committed the grave blunder of refusing to be represented in the Central Council (p. 173), and this entirely Social Democratic Council 'could have thrown us out at any minute'. How could it have done this if the masses had been swept along by the Independents? We see here another example of a man who abhorred the use of power even for his most cherished ends. Of course, his decision not to use it was wise, though for a different reason; for if he might have eliminated Ebert and the Central Council for a time, he could not have eliminated Hindenburg who was on the march for good.

The Central Council and the remaining three People's Commissars tried to fill the vacancies in the government. Only three Social Democratic candidates of the required calibre were available. One of them, Paul Löbe, refused, the two others accepted. Of the latter, Rudolf Wissell disappointed his friends; he remained insignificant in office. The other was Gustav Noske, governor of Kiel.

With the resignation of the Independents vanished the last possibility of mediation between the Social Democrats and the steadily growing Spartacists. An immense restlessness seized the workers of Berlin. The air was charged with conflict. It was clear that a violent eruption was inevitable. Indeed, a week later, two months after 9 November, the events began to take place that shattered the Revolution. Yet these very events might have offered a certain chance to the revolutionaries. This chance, however, did not come near materializing owing to the breakdown of Liebknecht at the critical point.

XIX. COMMUNISTS

A revolution must find leaders after it has begun. If the objective chances of success are hopeless, even the best of leaders cannot produce victory. If the objective chances of success are good (as they were in Germany in November 1918), even the worst of leaders might still produce victory. But if those who grasp the leadership fail to promote the revolution and at the same time those who want to promote the revolution fail to grasp the leadership (both of which happened in Germany in November 1918), even the best chances of success are not good enough.

However, the incredible happened in Germany; those who put themselves at the head of the Revolution let the reins drop from their hands. But just as he failed to seize the reins on 9 November 1918, so Liebknecht failed once more in January 1919; failed finally then, and paid with his life for his failure.

On the day of the battle of the Marstall (24 December 1918), the executive committee of the Independent Social Democratic Party received an ultimatum from the executive committee of the Spartacus League. The League was still an organization within the Independent organization. The Revolutionary Stewards, too, were still with the Independents, but they were so as individual members; as such they formed the left wing of the Independent Party under the leadership of Ledebour. Their social and political attitude differed little from that of the Spartacists, that is to say, of those Spartacists who were genuine socialist revolutionaries; but their tactical views differed widely.

The ultimatum demanded a party convention not later than the end of December. As it was impossible to call a convention in so short a time, the meaning of the ultimatum was obvious to all concerned: the Spartacists were going to form a party of their own.

They held a conference beginning on 30 December 1918. Their leaders, Karl Liebknecht and Rosa Luxemburg, realized the significance of the large majority with which the Reich Congress of the Workers' and Soldiers' Councils had adopted the National Assembly. They consequently proposed that the Spartacists take part in the elections to this Assembly. But putschist influences had gained the upper hand among the Spartacists. Their exponent was Otto Rühle (p. 47). He demanded that the followers of the League be called upon to place every obstacle in the way of the elections to the National Assembly. Rosa Luxemburg tried to convince the conference that the attitude of 'machine-guns versus national assembly' was hopeless. But Rühle's motion was carried by 62 votes to 23. With difficulty, Liebknecht and Luxemburg managed to persuade the conference not to declare itself entirely and fundamentally anti-parliamentarian. This was of great importance, but in view of that vote this importance had a bearing only in the more distant future.

The Spartacus League constituted itself as a separate political party and adopted the name of 'Communist Party of Germany (Spartacus League)'. The 'Spartacus League' was dropped from the name some time later.

2

The new party had no more than about a thousand members at the beginning and its influence in the plants was negligible, although it had a large and steadily growing influence elsewhere. To gain more adherents in the plants the Communists were eager to absorb the Revolutionary Stewards, whose fortunes were reviving after the slump of 9 November (which had been caused by the formation of the workers' and soldiers' councils) as many workers came to realize their mistake in believing in the Social-Democratic-proclaimed unity of the workers' movement (p. 96). But their fortunes were reviving only to lead them and their Independent friends into the disastrous venture of 5 January (see the following chapter). More than that, they put themselves in this venture under the command of Liebknecht, though they had just rejected fusion with his Communists because they saw the danger of those putschist influences among the Communists and demanded that they be curbed. Naturally, the putschist majority of the Communists would not admit that they were putschist. The Stewards demanded, further, that if they were to join the Communist Party, this party must participate in the elections to the national assembly. This condition, too, was turned down, and the Stewards decided to stay with the Independents.

The refusal of the Revolutionary Stewards and the fatal vote at the Communist conference were heavy blows to Liebknecht and Luxemburg. There was nothing left them but the support of a motley and largely contemptible crowd (apart from their industrially unorganized, largely intellectual, and numerically small following) that was not to be depended upon for any serious undertaking. Outstanding among these supporters was the 'Union of Soldiers on Furlough and Deserters' which had grown out of the deserters who made common cause with the British Secret Service during the war (p. 67). They always were, at that time, in the wake of Liebknecht in his propaganda activity which otherwise constituted a really superhuman effort.

This activity took place mainly in the streets and at public meetings where Liebknecht tried to drive the masses on by speeches and leaflets. The Revolutionary Stewards agreed that the street ought to be used to drive forward the Revolution. But they were suspicious of the Deserters' Union and of those among the hangers-on of Liebknecht who believed in individual action for the sake of action and not any ends to be achieved by it. The Stewards' suspicions were justified. In the hideous civil war that broke out a few days later, the committee of the Union accepted payment from the government in return for which they pledged themselves to keep their members quiet.

3

On 12 November 1918, the Independent Social Democratic Party had issued a proclamation that contained the following dazzlingly imbecile paragraph: 'The revolutionary people has made short shrift with the representatives of the old régime, the generals and the bureaucrats. It has broken the rule of the Junker caste in the administration, the power of the officers in the army, the rule of the capitalist clique in public life, and has grasped the sovereign power.'

Two days earlier the Spartacists, too, had issued a proclamation. It demanded *inter alia* that all military posts of command be taken over by 'men who have the confidence of the workers' and soldiers' councils'. This postulate was in accordance with the programme of the Spartacists (revised on 14 December 1918) which said in part: 'In the bourgeois revolutions, bloodshed, terror and murder were indispensable weapons in the hands of the rising classes. The proletarian revolution does not stand in need of terror to achieve its aims; it hates and despises murder. It does not stand in need of such weapons because it fights against institutions, not individuals, and because it does not enter the arena with naïve illusions whose disappointment it would have to avenge by blood. [As if these words did not reflect a naïve illusion themselves; as if any anti-militarist German revolution could have fought, for instance, against the Foreign Office without also fighting against Stumm, Rheinbaben and their likes. Of course, Liebknecht was right in distinguishing between fight and murder.] It is not the desperate attempt of a minority to model the world according to its own ideal; it is the action of the millions of the people who are called upon to fulfil the mission of history and to transform historical necessity into reality.'

This programme, then, held in essence that the majority of the people in highly developed industrial countries were proletarians or proletarianized petty bourgeois, and that socialism was *objectively* their interest, their goal, and their historical mission. But

Liebknecht and Luxemburg realized that this was not so *subjectively*. This fact was proved by the great majority with which the Reich Congress of Workers' and Soldiers' Councils accepted the National Assembly, that is, the militaristic State in the form of a democratic republic (and this form could not last long in this State, or course). We have seen that this majority wanted socialism, but they relied on the mere fact that the greater part of the people were proletarians and members of classes that had the same interests as the proletarians; and they believed that there would naturally be a socialist majority in the elections to the National Assembly. They did not see that this objective basis existed in other countries as well as in Germany, and that it was combined there with universal suffrage and other democratic forms; and yet these countries were not socialist. They did see, however, that the democracy of those other countries precluded militarism, but they remained blind to the fact that the political democracy just established in Germany could not by its mere existence eradicate militarism. Of course, they thought that socialism would do this job, but they did not see again that there would be no socialism. Their thinking moved in a pitiful circle.

The Communist leaders, and also the putschists among them, realized all these things, and they realized also, with illogical bitterness, that the Social Democratic workers did not understand them. One of the causes of this non-comprehension was the less theoretical than palpable fact that the Communists consisted of a few intellectual leaders, a mere handful of organized workers, and a host of undisciplined rowdies. The arguments of the first were too esoteric to be understood by the great mass of Social Democratic workers, and the behaviour of the last was repellent to them, accustomed as they were to strict discipline in everything they did.

When it came to discussing the seemingly obvious problem of the army, the Social Democratic Workers' and Soldiers' Councils, and the Social Democratic workers at large, did what they thought the Revolution demanded of them. But this was the only obvious problem. In all other points the Social Democratic workers, and

also some of their leaders who were sincere if blind, could not dis-
tinguish between the objective prerequisites and the subjective
prerequisites of social revolution. They believed that the former
automatically conditioned the latter if only political democracy
were introduced. They believed this because they had no experience of full universal suffrage and because they did not see
through their leaders.[1] The thought that social revolution to eradicate militarism did not necessarily mean socialist revolution was
quite beyond them. They did not realize that nothing was being
done to change the substance of the militarist State. But had the
attempt been made to change this substance to a progressive and democratic capitalist State, they would have regarded this attempt as
reactionary counter-revolution and would have fought against it.

The example of the Hamburg Points showed that it would have
been possible to create the subjective prerequisites of socialist
revolution among the Social Democratic workers. Rosa Luxemburg summed up the situation and the immediate task in her speech
at the conference of the Spartacists on 31 December 1918 as follows. It was necessary for the Communists to conserve and concentrate the revolutionary will and strength that were still present
in all the workers though latent in the Social Democratic workers.
This task was to be carried out while the government (as it was
bound to, in her opinion, in a relatively short time) was losing the
last vestige of good-will and reputation it had with any worker.
The means to accomplish this task were mainly industrial. Furthermore, it was necessary to take corresponding steps among the
appropriate section of the agricultural population with whom

[1] We are not concerned here with an evaluation of the Marxian proposition
that a majority of proletarians and proletarianized petty bourgeois in a nation
means objectively that the coming of socialism is inevitable. Of course, this
proposition was accepted by the Social Democrats, the Independents, the
Revolutionary Stewards, and the Spartacist-Communists. Many of their
arguments and actions sprang from it. Many of them appear wrong to us in the
light of this proposition. In the light of any other proposition, all of them must
appear wrong to us. But the latter kind of argument would contribute nothing
to our understanding of the German Revolution of 1918.

'unfortunately not even the beginning of a beginning had been made'. To paraphrase her analysis, from a revolutionary socialist viewpoint the well-understood task of the Communists would have been to seize the reins of political education and propaganda. Liebknecht, too, recognized this. Had he been consistent (Rosa Luxemburg was) they might have overcome the anarchist resistance in their own ranks as well as the confused hesitancy in the ranks of the Social Democratic workers. All this would have been the more easy as the events of the battle of the Marstall had revealed the military impotence of the government.

Conversely, it would have been folly on the part of the Communists to risk disaster by staking in a rash enterprise that revolutionary will and strength which was consciously bent on socialist revolution; that is to say, that will and strength which existed not even in their own ranks at large but as yet only in a small part of their own ranks. Such a gamble would change into antagonism the bewilderment with which the Social Democratic workers looked upon the Communists. And just as a rash enterprise on the part of reaction would have united the working class (Communists, Social Democrats, and Independents, p. 149), so a rash enterprise on the part of the Communists would unite the upper and middle classes, that is, progressive, conservative, and reactionary bourgeois, and aristocrats. It would be grist for the mills of reaction.

Precisely this came to pass. For instead of concentrating on revolutionary-socialist indoctrination and biding his time, instead of making the Revolution the 'action of the millions of the people' as the Spartacist Programme said, Liebknecht suddenly lost his head. He became a putschist, a terrorist, he became the leader of a 'desperate attempt of a minority to model the world according to its own ideal' (p. 193). He tried to seize the reins of government that were trailing on the ground after the battle of the Marstall, tried to seize them at the wrong moment. And, as he should have foreseen, he not only broke the back of socialist revolution but made impossible any change whatever in the substance of the German State.

XX. FRATRICIDE

When the Independents resigned from the Prussian government, on 3 January 1919, it was clear that their party comrade Eichhorn would not be able to maintain himself in office as police president of Berlin. He belonged at that time to the left wing of the Independents, the wing to which the Revolutionary Stewards belonged, too. The police was under the jurisdiction of the State, not the municipalities. It is important to understand this point clearly. The police president of Berlin, for instance, was a servant of the Prussian Ministry of the Interior.

On 9 November 1918, Eichhorn happened to be at Independent headquarters in Berlin when a number of workers and soldiers appeared. They declared they were coming from 'Police Presidium' (as it is called there), which had been occupied by the revolutionaries, and they wanted an Independent to become police president. Another deputation of workers and soldiers went to Social Democratic headquarters with the same request at about the same time. A new police president was needed not only because there was a revolution but also because the nerves of the Royal Prussian president, Baron von Oppen, had collapsed when a crowd invaded his office. Eichhorn, the highest party functionary present, went with the men and declared himself police president. He was, a little later, confirmed in this office by the Executive Council of the Workers' and Soldiers' Councils.

The Social Democrats had many reasons for hating Eichhorn, apart from his party allegiance. The most important among these reasons was that he was supposed to have helped the sailors in the battle of the Marstall; which he did not (p. 183). And, then, there was the important political reason that he opposed the National

Assembly. A further potent cause for hating him had been added recently. Huge demonstrations of workers took place in Berlin the day after the battle of the Marstall. During one of them a number of workers occupied the building of *Vorwärts*, declaring they were restoring to the workers their rightful property (p. 50). The government had no means at its disposal to dislodge the invaders, but the Revolutionary Stewards, seeing the criminally putschist character of the action with which no workers' organization was connected, mediated and prevailed upon the invaders to leave the place. This was merely the first in a series of occupations of the *Vorwärts* building. While in possession of it on this first occasion, the invaders had found a considerable store of arms there and had notified Eichhorn of their find. Eichhorn confiscated the store, which included an armoured car and twenty-one machine-guns, and had it taken to police headquarters because he held that such articles did not form part of the stock-in-trade of an editorial office. The Social Democratic leaders hated him the more for this.

The truly humorous touches he sometimes imparted to his actions should not, however, obscure the fact that he was anything but a desirable character. Past fifty at the time of the Revolution, he resembled Richard Müller ('Corpse Müller') in insignificance, though not details, of looks. Intellectually he was insignificant, too. Politically he turned his coat many times in the course of his career between radicalism and 'respectability', according to where he saw an advantage (usually a monetary advantage) for himself, though his whole career was within the workers' movement. The best that can be said of him is that he made up by strong elbows and a certain kind of nimbleness for what he lacked in brains; and he knew how to use his elbows. For instance, the Social Democrats wanted their friend, Eugen Ernst, to become police president of Berlin. Eichhorn beat him to the punch, by crafty manipulation and timing as well as by 'muscling' his way into office.

2

Vorwärts was leading in the clamour for the surrender of arms in private possession. This surrender (p. 171) made hardly any progress, least of all in Berlin where the operation had been entrusted to Wels. He simply could not carry it out; his Republican Soldiers' Wehr was too small and too unreliable for the purpose. He had a better control over it, though, than Eichhorn had in the beginning over his force, the Republican Security Wehr. This force included a good many serious-minded revolutionaries, but also many shady elements. They were so insubordinate that Eichhorn appealed to Wels for help early in December, when his own men wanted to arrest him because they held that he of all people was pampering the old police officers. Wels's deputy, Anton Fischer, who was an effective orator, persuaded Eichhorn's men to keep quiet. This incident was another consequence of the confused propaganda of the Social Democrats; instead of educating their followers as to the meaning of militarism they had incited them against the officers, with the result that no competent military force could be established by the Revolution, because there can be no military force without trained officers.

Naturally, that Eichhorn had to appeal to the military for help against his own troops was not conducive to making this body an independent municipal force. Towards the end of December 1918, however, Eichhorn reorganized it. He recruited some thousand returned soldiers who were trade unionists and members of the Independent Party. They were inducted and equipped on the day of the battle of the Marstall, 24 December. This fact (well known to everyone concerned) was soon twisted to 'prove' that Eichhorn had given out arms to workers in order to help the sailors in that battle.

On 3 January Eichhorn was summoned to appear before the Prussian government. He was handed a long list of offences, ranging from larceny to embezzlement, which he was supposed to have committed in office.[1]

A few days earlier, 29 December, Anton Fischer, the commandant of Berlin, had made a compact with a police commander, Gerken, one of Eichhorn's subalterns. Under this compact the Republican Security Wehr (Eichhorn's police force) was to be absorbed by the Republican Soldiers' Wehr (Fischer's force) which received higher wages than the police. To show that this was not an empty promise, Fischer paid a large amount of money to Gerken. Having completed this masterpiece of what Fischer regarded as high politics, he went a few days later to the Prussian government, with which he had nothing to do (being a servant of the Reich government), demanded the removal of Eichhorn, and to satisfy his vanity offered to induct the new police president to be appointed by the Prussian government. To give substance to this offer he declared that he had the Republican Soldiers' Wehr and the entire garrison of Berlin on his side as well as the greater part of Eichhorn's police force. This happened on 4 January, and the Prussian government promptly declared Eichhorn deposed.

The Prussian government's action became known at a meeting of the Berlin executive of the Independents and the Revolutionary Stewards on the evening of the same day, 4 January. The meeting had been convened to discuss general questions, but it naturally turned to the Eichhorn affair. A resolution was passed calling upon the workers and soldiers to come out for mass demonstrations the following day, a Sunday, to protest against Eichhorn's dismissal.

At the same time the Central Committee of the Communist Party discussed the same topic with the same result. Neither of these meetings contemplated any action that went beyond a

[1] Most of these charges were preferred by the Councillor of the Prussian Department of the Interior, Doyé, who a year later became another prime mover in the Kapp putsch. An investigation commission, set up by the Prussian Diet, later found that none of the accusations against Eichhorn was based on fact. They had perhaps been suggested by Eichhorn's past record rather than by his deeds at that time.

protest. The Communists acted in accordance with a programmatic leaflet they had distributed a few days earlier. It said in part in clear understanding of the situation prevailing in Germany then: 'Were the workers of Berlin to disperse the National Assembly [which, of course, was not yet in existence] today, were they to imprison Scheidemann and Ebert while the workers of the Ruhr and Upper Silesia and the agricultural workers of East Elbia remained quiet, the capitalists would be able to subdue Berlin tomorrow through starvation.'

3

The Sunday demonstrations were huge beyond expectation. They filled the inner city from the Tiergarten to the Alexanderplatz (where police headquarters was situated). Ledebour, Liebknecht, Däumig and Eichhorn made speeches from the balcony of police headquarters. Tens of thousands of Social Democratic workers were in the streets, too. They had followed the government's urgent summons: 'You must be prepared to support unreservedly the revolutionary order. To this end we call upon you to form a voluntary Republican Protection Wehr.' The men crowded the Wilhelmstrasse (where the Chancellery was situated). They were few compared with the workers who were demonstrating for Eichhorn. But though relatively small, the number of Social Democrats was large enough to prevent the demonstrators from getting into the Wilhelmstrasse and seizing the members of the government.

It is important to realize the implication of this. The revolutionary workers, including a numerical minority of Spartacists (no one called them Communists then although this was their official name) could, by sheer weight of numbers, have dislodged the Social Democratic workers. But in calling out the latter, the government relied on the fact that there was never for a moment any thought of workers fighting against workers, in spite of the bitterness and the ideas that separated the rank and file of the Social Democrats from that of the revolutionists. The thought of violence between workers was first mooted publicly by *Vorwärts* when it wrote on the occasion of the first occupation of its building (p. 198): in case Liebknecht and his followers should occupy any government buildings, 'it will be the duty of the organized workers to throw them out with their fists the very next day'. Incidentally, there was of course no clear distinction between 'Liebknecht's followers' and 'organized workers'. The hundreds of thousands of workers who demonstrated the day after the battle of the Marstall and again on 5 and 6 January 1919, must have included large numbers of organized workers who had nothing in common with the Deserters' Union and the *Lumpenproletariat*[1] who had been around Liebknecht in November and early December. Moreover, the greater part of them were not even technically followers of Liebknecht, that is, Spartacists, but followers of the Independents and the Revolutionary Stewards. However, the indiscriminate use of the epithet 'Spartacist' for everyone they disliked served the Social Democrats well.

Shortly after noon on 5 January, Commandant Anton Fischer appeared at police headquarters, accompanied by Eugen Ernst, the Social Democratic Minister of the Interior, who was to take over the office of police president in addition to his ministerial duties. Before setting out on this errand, Fischer had another consultation with the Prussian government. He had arranged things so that Noske was present, the new member of the Reich government of whom the powers that be expected great things in general, and Fischer for himself in particular. Fischer protested that if resistance should be shown he would know how to deal with it. But Noske did not think much of Fischer; naïvely, he declared later that he had no idea where Fischer's troops were posted, he only knew that they did not do anything.

When Fischer appeared at police headquarters, affairs took a

---

[1] When coined by Marx the word *Lumpenproletariat* meant 'proletariat in rags', that is, paupers as distinguished from the real proletariat in the Marxian sense, namely, the workers. But the word has a double meaning in German, and it is in its other meaning that I use it here: 'proletariat of rogues'.

turn he had not anticipated. Eichhorn refused to surrender his office. He demanded a written statement of the reasons for his dismissal; he would reply to it in writing. In any case, he would relinquish his office only if he were dismissed by the Central Council and the Executive Council; he did not acknowledge any jurisdiction of the Prussian Ministry of the Interior over him.

Fischer thereupon appealed to his followers at police head-quarters (the men he had bribed), but they declared they were an 'absolutely neutral, independent, and unpolitical police force' and would act only upon orders from the police president who, at the moment, was Eichhorn. Fischer and Ernst withdrew. Hundreds of thousands of workers were standing in the streets all the time, waiting for word, not speeches, from their leaders, Independents, Stewards and Communists. But these leaders were so busy deliberating, negotiating, and arguing that they forgot about their followers, and in the evening these followers went home.

Of the situation on 5 January 1919, Noske wrote later: 'If the masses had had determined, clear-thinking leaders instead of swashbucklers, they would have had Berlin in their hands by noon of that day.' (This was typical of Noske's way of thinking. The thought of how it would have helped the 'masses' never occurred to him. The winning of a fight was all that mattered.) And Count Bernstorff wrote: 'The Spartacists did not shoot, and it was because they did not shoot that Germany was not fated to become a soviet republic.' (He too, believed that the mere fact of shooting on that day would have changed history.) In reality, if Liebknecht might have succeeded without bloodshed on 9 November, he could not so succeed on 5 January, and if he had succeeded through blood-shed on 5 January, his success would have been nothing but a short-lived military victory. As things were, his rejection of violence made even such ephemeral victory impossible from the outset—while at the same time it made violence inescapable.

4

While the streets were growing empty in the late evening of 5 January, a combined meeting of the Revolutionary Stewards, the Greater Berlin Committee of the Independents, and two members of the Central Committee of the Communist Party, Karl Liebknecht and Wilhelm Pieck, took place.

One of the leaders of the Marine Division, Dorrenbach, the man of the Palace keys (p. 179), reported to the meeting that his Division and the whole garrison of Berlin (which Fischer had told the government was in his hands) were standing behind the Revolutionary Stewards, prepared to overthrow Ebert and Scheidemann by force of arms; moreover, a large force with 2000 machine-guns and twenty pieces of artillery was standing at Spandau (a short distance west of Berlin) ready to march against the government. Dorrenbach must have been hysterical, and his hysteria must have transmitted itself to the meeting, for after listening to him Liebknecht suddenly declared that in the circumstances it was not enough to ward off the blow against Eichhorn; the overthrow of the government was possible and absolutely necessary.

The Independent Däumig protested violently, and a soldiers' leader, Albrecht, maintained that the troops in Berlin would not support the action; he even doubted whether Dorrenbach had his own men, the sailors, behind him. Richard Müller, once more chairman of the Revolutionary Stewards (since Barth became a People's Commissar), declared that the revolutionary movement in the Reich was growing every day, and that it would be possible to wage a decisive struggle in a short time; but a premature, isolated action in Berlin might spoil everything.

However, the meeting resolved almost unanimously to overthrow the government and to this end to call a general strike and sanction the occupation of the newspaper buildings. A few hundred of the waiting workers had on their own initiative occupied nearly all of the newspaper buildings in Berlin, including that of

Vorwärts. The meeting then elected a Provisional Revolution Committee of fifty-three members, and adjourned. This Committee was to lead the action and provisionally take over the business of government after the overthrow of Ebert and Scheidemann. It had three chairmen with equal rights, the 'provisional government'; Ledebour and Scholze of the Independents, and Liebknecht. This monstrosity, then, was Liebknecht's idea of a government. This idea which, moreover, he could conceive only amid a host of madmen, explains why he remained so ineffective on 9 November.

The resolution to overthrow the government by force disavowed everything that all the men concerned had soberly held to be correct until the moment the meeting began. Its consequences were frightful.

5

On the next morning, 6 January 1919, the Revolution Committee made its headquarters in the Marstall. When many workers, too, drifted there to reinforce the sailors' garrison, the sailors protested against their being drawn into the affair. They resolved to arrest Dorrenbach for involving them without their knowledge and against their will, but he preferred to vanish. More important, they turned the Revolution Committee out of the Marstall, and thus the 'government' did not even have an office.

Before this happened, Fischer had come to the Marstall to draw the sailors over to the side of the government. The Revolution Committee arrested him, but the sailors set him free; they wanted to stay neutral.

Meanwhile, however, Ebert had got his own back. While Fischer was detained in the Marstall, the government handed over the military authority in Berlin to General von Lüttwitz, the commander of the former Lequis Division that was at Potsdam. Lüttwitz appointed a Captain Marcks commandant of Berlin. But this military reshuffle was merely a gesture for the time being, for the government called together the officers of the soldiers who were loyal to it, and the consensus of opinion was that the number of troops available was insufficient to do anything.

The revolutionary workers of Berlin demonstrated again in spite of their disappointment of the preceding day, and a general strike paralysed the life of the city. Noske and a few others were in Ebert's room. Among them was Colonel Reinhardt (not to be confused with Colonel Reinhard, p. 186), Scheüch's successor as War Minister. Noske demanded action. Reinhardt formulated an order appointing Lieutenant-General Hoffmann commander-in-chief. Hoffmann, once commander of the Lequis troop (p. 170), had succeeded Lüttwitz when the latter assumed the military authority in Berlin, a command that was as yet non-existent (p. 227). Objections were raised in Ebert's room; the workers, without party distinction, would get angry if a general were to be commander-in-chief. Even the soldiers would not like it. The soldiers' council of Berlin had just ousted the freshly appointed Captain Marcks. Marcks was retained as technical director of the *Kommandantur*, and the soldiers elected Klawunde commandant; he was the chairman of the soldiers' council of Potsdam and had informed Barth the day before the battle of the Marstall that the government had called Lequis's troop to Berlin (p. 181).

In Ebert's room somebody said to Noske: 'Why don't you do it?' Noske said: 'All right. Somebody has got to be the butcher (*Bluthund*).[1] I won't shirk the responsibility.' Noske was appointed commander-in-chief; it was not said (because nobody knew) of what.

Scheidemann made a speech to the Social Democratic workers outside the Chancellery. The soldiers would be called upon to protect the government; the government would proceed against the minority with all its energy, if necessary by force; the 'masses' would be suitably equipped, 'of course not with clubs but with arms'. When *Vörwarts* first mooted violence among workers it

[1] Literally *Bluthund* means bloodhound. But it has lost this literal meaning and is used to denote a bloodthirsty person.

spoke of fists (p. 202); Scheidemann was not even satisfied with clubs.

Noske disappeared from the scene; he stayed away for a few days.

6

When Noske left Ebert's room on 6 January 1919, Breitscheid, Oskar Cohn, Dittmann, Kautsky, and Luise Zietz, all of them Independents, went to the Chancellery to offer their services as mediators between the government and the striking workers. *Rote Fahne* (Red Flag), the Central Press organ of the Communists, wrote: '700,000 workers, thirsting for action, bursting with revolutionary energy, are roaming the streets without any instructions, and the revolutionary bodies negotiate and compromise with Ebert-Scheidemann.' *Rote Fahne* could afford to be sarcastic; the Communists were not taking part in the action as a body, they merely allowed two of their leaders, Liebknecht and Pieck, to take part as individuals. If the action failed, Liebknecht would be declared to have had no authority to commit the Communists. If the action succeeded, most of the credit would go to Liebknecht in view of the veneration he enjoyed from so many workers: Liebknecht, the Communist hero; Liebknecht, who indeed had most probably the greatest integrity of all German public figures of that time but who was quite incompetent as a leader.

The government accepted the offer of these Independents to mediate. So did the Revolution Committee. The negotiations began at midnight. The government suddenly demanded that the buildings occupied by the revolutionaries be evacuated or discussions could not proceed. The revolutionaries refused to evacuate the buildings; the occupation was the only bargaining point they had. The meeting broke off without any result.

On the same day, 6 January 1919, both the Executive Council and the Central Council dismissed Eichhorn as police president. That the Central Council would do so was to be expected; it consisted entirely of Social Democrats. Things were different with the

Executive Council, which usually had an Independent majority. It dismissed Eichhorn with twelve Social Democratic votes against two Independents. This showed clearly the lack of system with which the Revolution was conducted in its most essential aspects. These supreme political bodies had not even adopted sensible constitutions for themselves. The Executive Council had forty members. Considering the circumstances, fourteen should never have constituted a quorum. Nearly all of the important Independent members could not attend the session because they were busy with the mediation. Such a contingency ought to have been foreseen in a revolution. But matters had in any case passed beyond the stage where legal points had any meaning; they had passed into the hands of the Revolution Committee, and this ludicrous Committee tried first to overthrow the government and then to negotiate it out of existence. This would have been the first negotiated revolution in history.

7

On the following day, 7 January, the revolutionaries declared: 'We regard the occupation of the newspaper buildings...merely as a means of carrying out our struggle. From this it follows that an agreement that satisfies both parties would include the evacuation of the occupied buildings.' The government refused to pass over this bridge.

Another day later, 8 January, the Revolution Committee was prepared to evacuate the occupied newspaper buildings with the exception of that of *Vorwärts* in order to make negotiations possible. At no stage could the Revolution Committee pluck up the courage and the intelligence to do something, and yet indeed to do nothing was the most sensible thing they could do. After they had sobered from their hysteria of the night of 5 January, they must again have seen what they had seen all along, namely that they had no chance whatever of success.

The government did not yield. On 9 January many thousands

of workers from two large plants in Berlin held an open-air meeting and elected a deputation which took a message to the government; the message said that these workers had discussed the matter with the Executive Committee of the Independents and that this Committee desired to find a basis for negotiations in order to end the fratricidal strife. Ledebour, a member of the Independent Executive and of the three-man provisional government of the revolutionaries, was also the chief negotiator of the revolutionaries. First of all, the deputation suggested an armistice (street fighting was going on by then, as we shall hear). The revolutionaries were then to evacuate the *Vorwärts* building if the deputation received the government's assurance that the negotiations would be conducted in a *socialistic, conciliatory spirit* (italics in the deputation's message); if the points of disagreement were dealt with by a commission constituted of equal numbers of Social Democrats, Independents, and Spartacists; and if police headquarters were occupied by the government only after consultation with the Independents (whose representative, Eichhorn, was in possession).

The government refused because it 'undoubtedly had behind it the great majority of the socialistic workers of Germany'; and this fact would be denied by a commission that consisted of equal numbers of Social Democrats, Independents and Communists. Actually, the government refused because it saw the helplessness of the Revolution Committee. This Committee lost confidence in themselves and made one frantic concession after another, seeing that all the three calculations on which they had based their action turned out to be wrong: the support of the People's Marine Division, the support of the garrison of Berlin, and the reinforcements that were supposed to come from Spandau (p. 204). The government refused any concession; in addition to realizing the helplessness of its opponents it received good news from Noske; but it was still forced to play for time and therefore protracted the negotiations it did not intend to conclude at all.

8

On 7 January Anton Fischer made 'great politics' again. When he had been released from the Marstall the previous day (p. 205) he went to the government to be informed that he was no longer commandant of Berlin. His dismissal did not daunt him, however. He well knew the confusion in the revolutionary camp and the military weakness of the government. On 6 January he had gone to the Marstall to win the sailors over to the side of the government. On 7 January he went back to the Marstall, this time to win the sailors over against Ebert and Scheidemann, but not for the Revolution Committee—for Mr Anton Fischer. The sailors were not interested, though, and Germany was spared a revolutionary Anton Fischer government. Again Fischer was not daunted, and his next move was less ambitious but more sinister.

The facts that the government lacked an adequate military force and that the revolutionaries did not use their own (however unorganized and undisciplined it was militarily) had set a group of reactionary officers scheming. Either Fischer got in touch with them or they got in touch with him. They formulated three conditions that Fischer took to the government. No alternative was stated, but the inference was that these officers would act if the government did not conclude a deal with them. What they threatened by implication has not become known. In any case, the government accepted their conditions because it hoped that they had a certain number of troops behind them.

These were their three conditions: the buildings occupied by the revolutionaries were to be evacuated without negotiations; the revolutionaries were to surrender all the arms in their possession; the leaders of the revolutionaries were to be arrested and kept as hostages. The government objected to this third point; it was against their *Weltanschauung* as Social Democrats. They told Fischer, however, that they could not prevent the soldiers from taking hostages. Fischer was kept in the Chancellery as the deputy of Noske who was still absent.

Immediately, the new assistant commander-in-chief (Fischer) sent out men to arrest Liebknecht and Luxemburg. They were not to be found, however, and so as not to return empty-handed Fischer's huntsmen arrested Ledebour and Ernst Meyer; the latter was a member of the executive committee of the Communist Party and had nothing directly to do with the whole affair; he was not a member of the Revolution Committee. The prisoners were taken to the *Kommandantur* and handed over to the commandant, Klawunde. Klawunde declared he had no idea why they had been arrested, and put them in a motor car to send them home. Suddenly, a number of officers forced them to leave the car again. Their attitude was so threatening that Klawunde took the two prisoners to his office and stayed with them until their safety was reasonably assured.

The government was embarrassed by Ledebour's arrest. So was Fischer, but the arrest was a fact and there was nothing left but to have Ledebour tried for having engineered the upheaval of January 1919. He was not accused of high treason, though, because the only high treason law in existence was that of Imperial Germany and because the application of this law to protect the Ebert government would have provoked violent popular protests. Ledebour's trial which began in May 1919 and lasted five weeks became a political *cause célèbre*. The stenographic protocol of the proceedings is a mine of information for the student of that revolution.

The leader of the men who arrested Ledebour was a certain Hasso von Tyszka. He informed Ledebour's counsels (one of whom was a brother of Liebknecht) that he had orders from Fischer to shoot Ledebour. He never appeared in court because he allegedly feared for his life from the Spartacists. Conveniently he was certified a lunatic which did not, however, prevent his word from being accepted in a later political trial. He then testified that Ledebour's counsels had paid him considerable amounts of money for stating that he had the order to shoot Ledebour from Fischer. Why he did not execute this order, which he probably received, remained obscure. That he did not execute it was the cause of Fischer's and the government's embarrassment. A corpse would have been a short embarrassment; a protracted political trial was a long one. The trial was conducted with fairness; Ledebour was acquitted. If this appears surprising at first glance, considering that German judges were not likely to be friends of Ledebour, it must be remembered that Ledebour was a harmless enemy then, while the government was a powerful one (or so it must have seemed to outsiders). And the surprise will vanish on seeing that the judgement implied a definite censure of the government for the events of 'Spartacus Week', the week from 5 to 12 January 1919.

We must now return to these events.

9

On 8 January, fighting broke out between revolutionists and soldiers in various parts of Berlin. On the preceding day, the revolutionaries had occupied the building of the railway administration to prevent the transport of troops, if any, to Berlin. Likewise occupied by the revolutionists were the military food supply office, the main telegraph office, the Reich printing works, the Brandenburg Gate, and the Silesian railway station.

During the next few days, all these places and the newspaper buildings were stormed by government troops after bombardment by artillery and mortars. The swiftness of the action was possible because the revolutionaries had no plan, no co-ordination, and no direction whatever. On the storming of the police headquarters five revolutionaries were murdered in such a fashion that their brains were splashed all over the place. In the *Vorwärts* building, 300 prisoners were taken. Seven men, who came out first with white flags to announce the surrender of the garrison, were led to a nearby barracks and disposed of in the same brutal way. Before this action started, Major von Stephani who was in charge of it, asked Brutus Molkenbuhr, a right-wing Independent deputy and military adviser to the government, if he could not be spared this unpleasant mission, and if the *Vorwärts* building could not be regained by negotiation. Molkenbuhr replied that this was not possible and that force was the only way.

Although the fighting in Berlin was heavy, many of the places occupied by the revolutionaries were taken by the government troops with little effort. This was so because a number of these places had been occupied not only by revolutionaries but also by *agents provocateurs* of Anton Fischer, and the occupying forces were thus divided when the assault began.

On 9 January, the Revolution Committee held its last meeting. It published a last proclamation to encourage its followers. The proclamation had no effect. The workers were confused beyond hope by all these queer goings-on. Those who actually fought numbered no more than a thousand; another reason why the inadequate government forces could succeed easily. A day later, the Central Committee of the Communist Party forbade its members (Liebknecht and Pieck) to continue in the Revolution Committee which only its incompetence and callousness had allowed them to join in the first place. But apparently the Central Committee had hoped for a miracle, that is to say, hoped against their better knowledge that the action might succeed. And they did not possess the courage or the decency to disavow their ill-considered decision of 5 January until many people were killed to no purpose.[1]

On 13 January the Revolutionary Stewards and the Independents called upon the workers to go back to the factories in order that no more of the forces of the revolution be squandered in

---

[1] Pieck (born in 1876) fled to Russia when Hitler came to power. With General von Seydlitz and Field-Marshal von Paulus he formed the 'Free Germany Committee' after those generals were taken prisoners at Stalingrad. At the conclusion of the Second World War he returned to Germany to become first the leader of the Communist Party and then one of the two co-leaders of the Socialist Unity Party of Germany in the Russian Zone of Occupation. In the autumn of 1949, after the partition of Germany, he was made President of the 'German Democratic Republic', that is, the Russian-sponsored State consisting of the Russian-occupied part of Germany.

useless fights. They, too, considered the matter after the event instead of before. Had they done so before they would have known that any fighting would be useless.

The government had won the victory. But it was not its last victory; more were needed to reconsolidate the old militaristic State.

10

One of the causes that contributed to the confusion of the workers at large was quite accidental. Just as many workers believed that a government consisting of Social Democrats meant socialism, so they felt reassured when a (former) worker, Noske, was made commander-in-chief. Clearly, they reasoned, this showed that the old army, and above all the hated officers' corps, was finished for good. No one in the government foresaw the effect Noske's first proclamation had in this respect. 'Workers! The government has charged me with the leadership of the publican soldiers. Thus, a worker is at the head of the military might of the *Socialist* Republic....I will bring you freedom and peace with the young republican army' (my italics).

During 'Spartacus Week' great disturbances also took place in Bremen and the Ruhr valley. They were put down, too. Where did the sudden strength of the government come from? On the negative side there was of course the insane policy of the Revolution Committee. But there were also a number of positive causes.

When the unrest began in Berlin the government called upon 'the citizens' to join the Republican People's Wehr (p. 178). Another force was established by the manager of a Social Democratic publishing house, Baumeister, and the assistant editor of *Vorwärts*, Erich Kuttner. It obtained so many recruits that three regiments were formed from them. One of these assumed the name of 'Regiment Reichstag'. It was billeted in the Reichstag premises and during its short stay there so devastated the interior of the building that the damage cost many millions to repair.

Colonel Reinhard (p. 186) was empowered to form still another regiment of volunteers. He thought he knew where to get his men; he urged the officials of the Prussian bureaucracy to join his force. The Social Democratic Prime Minister of Prussia, Paul Hirsch, sent a circular letter to all departments under his jurisdiction instructing them to give leave of absence to any officials who were prepared to join Reinhard. But the colonel collected no more than a few hundred men (so great was the competition for volunteers) although the Citizens' Council of Greater Berlin, too, urged the citizens to sign up with him. Germans can hardly resist when they see a chance of organizing something. When workers, soldiers, and sailors had soviets, the *Bürger* could not contain themselves; they had to have a soviet too, and they formed that ridiculous thing, a citizens' soviet (council). But though ridiculous it was sinister, and it was the main source of Anton Fischer's finances.

Recruits were also solicited by three other government volunteer corps apart from Reinhard's; we shall hear more of one of them that became the model of the Reichswehr (p. 221). Finally, there was of course a 'Citizens' Wehr'. All these organizations were needed (ostensibly, that is) to crush a mere thousand fighting revolutionaries.

Reinhard was a good soldier but a stupid man. Nevertheless, he managed to usurp the nimbus of being the 'saviour of Berlin'. This claim was rudely, and correctly, disputed by Noske. The 'saviour of Berlin' was Noske.

What did he do during his few days' absence from the capital?

XXI. MILITARISM

I

The belief is widely held that the German, especially the Prussian, officer corps of the Empire constituted a class. This belief is erroneous. The Prussian officers never formed a class in themselves, but they used to belong to one class, namely, the landed aristocracy (Junkers); for the Junkers formerly had the privilege of holding all the officers' commissions in the Prussian army.

The decay of feudalism and the rise of a free enterprise economy (generally but unsatisfactorily called capitalism) impoverished many of the Junkers. This process reached its climax during the reign of Frederick II (the Great) of Prussia (1740–86). The impoverished Junkers remained aristocrats in nothing but name and sentiment. Hindenburg, for instance, was of this type.

It was expensive to be an officer in the army of feudal times, but as feudalism decayed the modern army with its masses of infantry grew, and aristocrats of limited means could afford to be officers in the infantry. In other arms of the service, however, the career was still expensive, above all in the cavalry, which the Germans continued to call feudal, the word having acquired the meaning of exclusive.

The modern army also produced important technical units such as, for instance, engineers and heavy artillery with its complicated ballistics. To be an officer in these required hard study and work. It was inescapable that commoners should worm their way into the fold, because the wealthy aristocrats preferred an easy life, and many of the impoverished ones went into the civil service. Thus the number of aristocrats of all types, though not decreasing absolutely, became too small in relation to the size of the army to make it possible for them to take up all the commissions. The non-

216

aristocratic officers were generally speaking of upper middle class origin, or they were the offspring of officers and civil servants. Formally, there existed no Reich army until the Revolution of 1918, there was merely a 'Supreme War Lord', the Kaiser. The larger federal States maintained more or less independent military establishments. Nevertheless, a German army existed in fact though not in the details of organization from 1871 on. And there existed, of course, the General Staff. With the foundation of the Reich in 1871, the German army assumed on the whole certain pseudo-democratic features. It never became as democratic, however, as the South German contingents had been until then, while the South German contingents assumed some Prussian features without becoming as reactionary as the Prussian army had been before 1871.

A strong impetus towards a greater democratization of the German army was provided by the First World War. In that war, 63,193 German officers were killed, 3077 aristocrats among them. The percentage of aristocratic officers killed was small in relation to the total number of officers killed, but it was large in relation to the number of aristocratic officers in the army. Still, these figures show the numerical insignificance to which the aristocracy had sunk in the officer corps. In that war, too, tens of thousands of lower middle class people, and even a few workers, were made officers.

It was a typical expression of this change in the social composition of the officer corps that General Groener could say that the oath of allegiance to the Supreme War Lord was a mere idea (p. 81). To be sure, there was to be found in the German officer corps a code of behaviour that was not to be found anywhere else. But a code of behaviour in a certain group of people does not make a class of them; on the contrary, it is designed to overcome the friction which might arise because various classes are represented in the group. The point is obvious; the German officers' code was to imbue all officers with the spirit of the Junker class. In this it succeeded to a great extent, but this success did not make Junkers of those officers who were not Junkers.

The officers' code of behaviour achieved something else that was infinitely more important. It succeeded in permeating the German nation, with the exception of the working class which however was confused on the subject, with the spirit of militarism. Militarism did not consist of the maintenance of a large standing army alone; the French, with a population only two thirds as large as Germany's, had a larger standard army in 1914. Nor did militarism consist of the spirit of the army as such; nothing ever happened in Imperial Germany that could compare with the French Dreyfus affair for turpitude. Militarism was the attitude of mind of certain German classes. It consisted of the forcing of military standards upon the whole non-military public, and to a large extent even private, life in the interests of the ruling classes (it goes without saying that any non-democratic State has one ruling class or a combination of ruling classes; in Germany this combination consisted of the Junkers and the great industrialists and financiers). It consisted of the seemingly voluntary but actually propaganda-induced acceptance of these standards by a majority of German subjects. It consisted of the primacy of the general over the statesman, the officer over the citizen, the uniform over the workman's dungarees. This attitude of mind was the result of the history of Germany and of the social structure of the Empire (and the Weimar Republic).

A fatal manifestation of this attitude was the terror that struck most of the men with inside knowledge when Groener threatened that the generals would have to go to the enemy with the white flag unless the government obtained an armistice within ten days (p. 75). True anti-militarists would have said, 'this is just what we need: the generals must raise the white flag'. Instead, the government raised it, thus saving the generals from humiliation, and militarism from the worst disaster that could have befallen it short of a transformation of the substance of the German State.

Militarism, then, was not the *effect* of the psychological make-up of so many Germans; it was the *cause* of this make-up. The social and historical development of Germany made militarism not necessary but possible. Crafty people seized upon this possibility, and they achieved a triumph of propaganda seldom paralleled.

The Revolution of 1918 shattered this psychological make-up for a short while. This was the reason why the Supreme Command could not easily and quickly produce a force appropriate to the government's intentions and needs at that time. Until 9 November 1918, the class differences within the officers' corps were bridged by the officers' code and the common oath of loyalty to the Supreme War Lord, the Kaiser. When this cement crumbled, spiritual chaos resulted and the class differences asserted themselves. The lower middle class men who had become officers in the war had no social interest in common with the ruling classes. They were good officers as long as the war went well, but towards the middle of the war their class grew disillusioned, and in the end it clamoured as loudly for abdication as the workers. The Kaiser fled, the oath of loyalty to him lost all meaning, and militarism broke down. The many lower middle class officers were suddenly nothing but lower middle class individuals.

Not being a class, the officer corps naturally reflects the attitude of the class it serves, that is, the ruling class (in a non-democratic State). Therefore the social and political attitude of the officer corps *as a body* is subject to change with any change in the ruling class. Any change of the latter kind necessitates a weeding-out process among the officers; for not all individual officers can be expected to change and to be loyal to the new ruling class (or to democracy).

No weeding-out process was undertaken in the German Revolution of 1918. It could not be undertaken for the simple reason that the ruling classes did not change fundamentally, though the great industrialists and financiers became more important than the

Junkers. By what standards should officers have been weeded out? By their rejection of the Republic? This would not have justified the wastage of good officers since the substance of the Republic did not differ from that of the Empire.

The professional officers who came from the ruling classes and who rejected the Republic and democracy in the beginning, realized in the early 1920's that the substance of the State had not changed, and the officer corps *as a body* became reconciled to the 'new' State. It again became united in loyalty to the State in spite of the class differences within it. Only a few officers remained unreconciled, and many of these retired (with pensions from the Republic of course) when the Treaty of Versailles limited the standing army to 100,000 men.

3

Hindenburg and Groener were among the chief exponents of militarism whom the Revolution failed to remove from posts of influence. Groener was middle class by origin and a half-hearted Liberal by ambition. Hindenburg was a Junker by birth and a reactionary by mental limitation. Both men offered their services to the Republic on condition that Bolshevism be crushed. In this negative attitude they were united, but they had nothing socially and politically in common that was positive. Moreover, their loyalty did not help Ebert and Scheidemann and Landsberg in their troubles of early 1919. To be sure, the immediate troubles of these men were solved. They were solved because the Social Democratic People's Commissars managed to rake up sufficient troops from among the Berlin garrison and volunteers to overcome the 1000 revolutionists (mostly Spartacists) who really fought. But their victory did not remove the powder-keg of socialist revolution; it merely removed the detonator that the Revolution Committee had insanely put in that powder-keg. The forces that removed the detonator were inadequate to render harmless the powder-keg itself; but it was rendered harmless in the ensuing few months.

There was only one type of officer who could do this job: a man who could put aside his political and social preferences and prejudices and place himself unreservedly at the disposal of the new government. His reasons did not matter. They may have been, to name but a few, love for his country as he understood it and he may have understood it rightly; or love of soldiering; or the vanity of playing a leading role. Hindenburg and Groener were not of this type; they were too narrow-minded. Groener, vaguely believing that the substance of the German State was changing, wanted to democratize the army politically, not only socially, in order to lay the foundation for militarism in the new democracy; this was not possible at all: a democracy cannot be militaristic. Groener's beginning, though, was carried to success by others later on, who naturally killed democracy in the process. Hindenburg wanted to carry on the army as it had been; this was not possible at the time. His beginning, too, was carried to success later on, in the Weimar Republic.

An officer of the right type turned up with a ready-made force just at the critical moment when the Revolution Committee's putsch had been crushed and the government did not know how to go on militarily (it never tried to go on politically, socially, and economically). He was General Maercker. While still in enemy country, though marching homewards, General Maercker evolved a plan for establishing a force in which the 'contrasts and short-comings that had arisen and were recognized during the war, were eliminated'.

His plan came to fruition at a meeting of commanding generals that took place in the Palace of the Bishop of Paderborn in West-phalia on 6 December 1918. He submitted this plan to his immediate superior and was authorized to go ahead with its execution. He made his headquarters in the Franciscan cloister at Salzkotten in Westphalia. A sufficient number of soldiers volunteered to join his corps. On 17 December, he was sent a new form of military oath by Supreme Command; the old oath had demanded allegiance to the Kaiser.

December 17 was the day on which the Reich Congress of Workers' and Soldiers' Councils adopted the Hamburg Points. Not to make their rejection of the Points (p. 172) appear outright insubordination, Hindenburg and Groener circulated that new form of oath to all units the same day. It began: 'I swear by my signature that I will be loyal to the provisional government of *Reich Chancellor* Ebert until the new Reich constitution is adopted by the National Assembly' (my italics). This showed the hand of Hindenburg; he did not recognize the Council of People's Commissars; to him, Ebert was Reich Chancellor. The Revolution abolished this imperial title; the National Assembly substituted for it the title of Minister President; and the Republic restored the 'Reich Chancellor' by way of the Weimar Constitution that was adopted on 11 August 1919.

Maercker, whose corps was under the jurisdiction of the Supreme Command but militarily independent of it, swore in his troops accordingly. A little later, however, he suggested a different form of oath, the government accepting his suggestion. It began: 'I pledge myself to serve the *socialistic democratic Republic* as a soldier with all my strength and the best of my will' (my italics).

XXII. 'LANDSKNECHTS'

Maercker believed at that time that Germany was going to be socialist. It has been said of him that he pledged his soldiers to serve the 'socialist Republic' only in order to force the government (which was widely believed to be socialist) to cover the reactionary measures he himself wanted to carry out. There is no evidence to support this view; rather, the available evidence indicates that he was honestly prepared to serve a socialist State.

He described his corps in the following way: '...especially the young soldiers realized that their political training was inadequate. ...They believed therefore that "it was best that they follow their officers". Their political interest was small altogether, "Spartacus must be biffed on the head", this was their political credo. The range of their inclinations was, generally speaking, occupied with questions of food and cigarettes, moving pictures and girls—and the desire not to have too much drill.'

And what about the officers these *Landsknechts* thought it was best to follow? Maercker himself was typical of them. When his corps was ready for action he addressed it: '...I am an old soldier. I have loyally served three Kaisers through thirty-four years. I have fought and bled for them in five wars and on three continents. Sentiments one has had for thirty-four years one does not throw away like an old dirty shirt....I love and venerate Wilhelm II today as I did thirty-four years ago when I swore loyalty to him. However, he is no longer my Kaiser and War Lord, but a private person. The government of Reich Chancellor Ebert has taken the place of the Imperial government....It is threatened by the group of Spartacists, by Liebknecht and Rosa Luxemburg.... Rosa Luxemburg is a she-devil, and Liebknecht is a fanatic who

knows exactly what he wants. Above all, this group wants to
prevent the sitting of the National Assembly because the National
Assembly is to bring about what these people do not want, namely,
peace and quiet and order in the country....In this situation we
want to help, be it to protect the frontiers of the Reich or to attend
to quiet and order at home....'

There was a man speaking. His speech was a psychological
masterpiece, considering his audience, and it had a genuinely sincere ring. It also reflected the professed ideas of the government
he was serving. He did not combat socialism; he believed that
Ebert, Scheidemann and Noske were Socialists. He combated
Liebknecht and Luxemburg because he read in the papers from the
reactionary Press to *Vorwärts* that they were trouble-makers.

A little over a year later, in April 1920, Maercker had to be
retired because he had taken an ambiguous position in the Kapp
putsch. This putsch was crushed by a general strike, the call to
which had been signed, among others, by the Social Democratic
members of the then Reich government and by Ebert who had
been elected the first President of the German Republic in February
1919. At the beginning of the putsch Ebert and the government,
including War Minister Noske, fled from Berlin to Dresden where
Maercker was military commander at that time. Seeing that
Maercker was no longer trustworthy, they fled on to the south of
Germany. Before so doing the Social Democratic leaders assured
Maercker that their names had been put under the call to the
general strike without their consent. Maercker, though an excep-
tional character for a German general, still was a German general.
And it is likely that his loyalty for politicians of the Ebert-Noske
type vanished when he realized the dishonesty that made them
play a double game with the loyalty of millions of their party
followers, the Social Democratic workers who, together with all
other workers, made the general strike a mighty success because
they believed that it was endorsed by their leaders.

2

When Noske left the city of Berlin on 6 January 1919 (p. 207) he
went to Dahlem, a western suburb. The work of organization and
co-ordination he had to carry out could not be undertaken in the
turbulent atmosphere of the capital. At Dahlem he made his
headquarters in the Louisa convent. Two days earlier, he and
Ebert had visited Maercker's force which had been moved to
Zossen near Berlin at the end of December 1918, and was now
called *Freiwilliges Landesjägerkorps* (approximately, volunteer
corps of sharp-shooters). On this visit Maercker paraded his men
before Ebert and Noske and the two were delighted at seeing
'real soldiers'. Noske, who was tall and lean, bent down to Ebert,
who was short and stout, slapped him on the shoulder, and said:
'Chin up, Fritz, all will be well.'

Noske was a particularly instructive example of the corroding
influence that power, and the striving for it, has on certain kinds of
character. He was all 'will to power' in the worst Nietzschean
sense. His energy was of superhuman concentration. He entered
the Reichstag in 1906 after having spent the preceding years
working his way up from a wood-chopper to a trade union functionary and editor-in-chief of one of the most influential provincial newspapers of the Social Democratic Party, the *Volksstimme*
(People's Voice) of Chemnitz in Saxony. In the Reichstag he
clung from the beginning to the extreme right wing (the opportunists) of his party. Quickly he became the party's specialist on
army and navy affairs and, soon after, assistant chairman of the
armed forces committee of the Reichstag. Naturally, the members
of this committee were coddled by the generals and admirals.
Noske showed himself very receptive. He gave his (unofficial)
blessing to the most extravagant demands of that most Pan-
German of the Pan-Germans, Admiral von Tirpitz, whose naval
policy was one of the immediate causes of the First World War.
Noske loved the navy with a blind passion. He listened sympa-
thetically to the generals, too. They let him into the innermost

secrets of the German war-machine. He repaid their confidence by working and hoping for, and believing in, German victory until even the blindest of lovers could no longer hope and believe. And then he became the most outspoken Republican among the Social Democrats. The explanation is simple. As we have read Scheidemann's character (p. 25) he needed the monarchy in order to shine as he wanted to shine. Noske needed the Republic. His love for things military and naval, though blind, was not platonic. He was not a military man, but his ambition was to become the political head of Germany's armed forces. This was impossible in the monarchy, not only because he was a Social Democrat, but also because he was of working class origin (which origin, in turn, was the cause of his being a Social Democrat, not a Conservative). Therefore he needed the Republic. His chance came when the monarchy proved incapable of maintaining the militarism that was dear to him. Only a substantially identical republic (not a democratic republic) could preserve it. Of course, he did not make the Republic. But the Republic was made, and in it he succeeded in realizing his ambition. The climax of his career began when he left Ebert's room in the Chancellery in January 1919.[1]

[1] He had to resign as War Minister after the Kapp putsch. Although he was not involved in this putsch, it became known that an officers' clique had planned to establish a military dictatorship with him as dictator, and that they had sounded him on the project. He was made President of the Prussian province of Hanover (the office of Provincial President was non-elective, and was roughly analogous to that of Lieutenant-Governor in the provinces of British dominions). He held this post until Hitler came to power, and embarrassed all democrats profoundly by telegraphing to Hitler on 30 January 1933, inquiring if the new (Nazi) government would pay for the transport of his furniture to some other city if he resigned his office. The Nazis did not molest him for a long time. But in their last frenzy, when a situation was clearly imminent in which he might attempt to repeat his success of 1918-19, they put him in a concentration camp where he was liberated by the British. He died in Hanover on 11 November 1946, aged 78.

3

When Noske became commander-in-chief he combined a number of corps in a group. Maercker's *Landesjägerkorps* was one of
them. Then there were two infantry divisions that had returned
from the front and had been combed out until only the required
Landsknechts characters were left; and the former Lequis Division,
now called *Garde-Kavallerie-Schützen-Division* (approximately,
cavalry sharp-shooters of the Guards). The chief financier of the
second division was the great iron merchant Otto Wolff of
Cologne.[1]

None of the other troops had the military qualities of Maercker's
corps, but the *Schützen Division* was a close second. The whole
organization, the size of which exceeded greatly that of a normal
'general command' of the German army, was entrusted to General
Baron von Lüttwitz and given the harmless name of 'Detachment
Lüttwitz' because a name that corresponded to its true size and

---

[1] After the First World War Wolff became entangled in the Rhenish separatist movement which wanted a Rhenish republic closely tied to France. After
the Second World War, left in full possession and control of his vast holdings,
Wolff and his surviving friends of the 1920's tried to establish military contingents after the model of 1919 and to sound the United States government on this
project.

The Rhenish separatist movement after the First World War was supported
by other outstanding German industrialists and financiers. These men elected
Dr Adenauer, then Lord Mayor of Cologne, their political spokesman without
his knowledge. He ignored them, but his unwitting involvement made him, in
the 1950's, the target of wild denunciations in the Communist German Press.
However, one of the leading authorities on the problem of federalism and
regionalism in Germany, Dr Arnold Brecht (see Bibliography, also pp. 151 and
157), writing before the end of the Second World War brought Dr Adenauer
to world prominence, described him as having taken part in certain activities in
the fall of 1923 (when there was another flare-up of Rhenish separatism) that
have a distinct aspect of treason. 'Some important persons in the Rhineland
were about to lose hope, for example the mayor of Cologne, Conrad Adenauer,
and the banker, Louis Hagen, who negotiated with the High Commissioner of
the Rhineland on the creation of a new currency. If the worst came to the
worst they were willing to consider the temporary separation of the western
parts of Germany.'

character would have aroused the suspicion of the workers of Berlin. But when Noske saw that the command turned out to be what he and Ebert, Scheidemann and Landsberg had been praying for, all reserve was dropped and the Detachment Lüttwitz became the General Command Lüttwitz.

On 10 January, Noske was called to the city to attend a meeting of the government. He was told that the worst was to be feared if he did not bring troops the very next day. He did bring troops the very next day, 3000 men, and marched through the city at their head. The general public acclaimed him. On 15 January, the whole of the General Command Lüttwitz descended upon the capital.

Brutus Molkenbuhr (p. 213) addressed the Workers' Councils of Berlin. 'Forces are at work which want to make the Revolution illusory. Like wildfire word has spread through the city: the White Guard is here. The generals personify a spirit that we must combat more vigorously than that of the Spartacists.' He was quite impartial in misunderstanding the character of both social revolution and counter-revolution and, for good measure, of militarism as well. He did not have to ask his audience how 'the generals' got to Berlin; he knew the answer, he had helped bring them there.

XXIII. NIGHTMARE

I

When the Revolution Committee gave up the ghost on 9 January, many of its members went into hiding, among them Liebknecht. Rosa Luxemburg, too, disappeared. On 15 January, both of them were tracked down by the Citizens' Wehr in the apartment of a friend somewhere in Berlin. They were taken to the fashionable Eden Hotel in the west end of the city. The *Garde-Kavallerie-Schützen-Division* had made its headquarters there. Captain Pabst was in command, the man who was revolted because he had to shoot at Germans (p. 181). After questioning the two revolutionary leaders, Pabst ordered them to be taken to the prison of investigation in Moabit, a northern district of Berlin. They were to be transported separately. It was evening, and dark outside.

On the next morning, Berlin was partly enraged, partly shocked, and partly amused when it read in the newspapers that Liebknecht and Luxemburg had been lynched by a crowd of furious citizens. The *Garde-Kavallerie-Schützen-Division* issued a detailed report. The gist of it was that large numbers of people had gathered in front of the Eden Hotel upon learning that Liebknecht and Luxemburg were there. Pabst gave orders for Liebknecht to be taken away first, through a side door. But there was a crowd by the side-door, too, and just as the car was beginning to move, somebody hit Liebknecht heavily on the head. To escape the crowd the car made a detour through the Tiergarten. The motor stalled in the centre of the great park. Liebknecht was told he must walk. Some fifty yards from the car he freed himself, stabbed a soldier in the hand, and ran away. The usual military warning to stop was shouted after him, but he did not stop. The soldiers shot him.

Rosa Luxemburg (still according to the first official report) was led from the hotel a little later. Again there was a crowd. It separated the soldiers from one another and beat the captive unconscious. The soldiers saved her from the crowd. Her car, too, made a detour through the Tiergarten. Part of the crowd had run ahead of it, and stopped it in the park. A man jumped on the running board and shot Rosa Luxemburg. The car drove away at great speed in the direction of the inner city. It was stopped again, near the Landwehr Kanal. People jumped on the running-boards, pulled the body from the car, and disappeared with it. The body had not yet been found, the report of the *Garde-Kavallerie Schützen Division* concluded.

2

It became known almost immediately that there were no crowds whatever at the Eden Hotel that night, and the truth was established as follows. Liebknecht left first. When he stepped out of the hotel a soldier, Runge, twice hit him across the head with the butt of his rifle. Bleeding profusely, Liebknecht was dragged into a motor-car. The car moved away. When it reached the Tiergarten the driver stopped and Liebknecht was told there was a puncture and he must walk. He had hardly alighted from the car when he was shot dead. Lieutenant Liepmann took the body to the first-aid station at the nearby Zoological Garden and deposited it there as the body of an unknown man. Navy Captain von Pflugk-Hartung was the leader of the transport.

When Rosa Luxemburg left, Runge was still in the street. He knocked her unconscious with the butt of his rifle. She was taken away in a car. The car drove to the centre of the Tiergarten, and she was shot dead. Her body was weighted with stones and thrown in the Landwehr Kanal. It was not found until several months later. First Lieutenant Vogel was the leader of the transport.

3

The murderers were tried in May 1919 by a court consisting of officers of their own unit, the *Garde-Kavallerie-Schützen-Division*. Pflugk-Hartung was acquitted. Five other officers involved in the murders were acquitted, too. Runge was sentenced to two years in prison; his moral inferiority and great excitability were regarded as extenuating circumstances.[1] Lieutenant Liepmann was sentenced to six weeks' confinement in his room. Vogel was sentenced to two years and four months in prison, not for murder but because he had abstracted a body and intentionally made a false official report. Three days later, a friend of his gained access to the prison on the strength of a false, but not forged, document. He liberated Vogel who fled to Holland. His travel papers had been prepared by the police in conjunction with the German Foreign Office.

4

The double murder had been preceded by an orgy of baiting. Anonymous handbills and posters were to be found everywhere calling upon their readers to kill Liebknecht and Luxemburg. The general Press echoed these sentiments in a more civilized style. *Vorwärts* was most civilized. Two days before the murders it published a 'poem' that mourned the deaths of many hundreds of proletarians who most certainly had been killed through Liebknecht's lack of self-control which led to an undertaking that was vehemently opposed by Luxemburg. The poem ended:

> A row of many hundred dead—proletarians!
> But Karl and Rosa are safe in bed,
> They are not dead, they are not dead—proletarians!

[1] See Preface, p. x.

XXIV. SIGNAL

The General Command Lüttwitz occupied Berlin on 15 January 1919. On that day, the counter-revolution won two victories: over the revolutionary workers and over Liebknecht and Luxemburg. But the Revolution was not yet at an end, and that was why the General Command Lüttwitz occupied Berlin.

Noske complained in his memoirs that he was reproached for putting his troops under the orders of Imperial officers. He explained that the soldiers had urged him to do so because they believed they would thus be spared unnecessary casualties. This demand of the soldiers was sensible, and it was sensible that Noske yielded to it, provided of course that fighting there had to be. The reproach levelled at him on this count was ill-considered. But the way in which he defended himself against it showed that he did not understand military problems in spite of his constant occupation with them. Naturally there must be officers in any army. But the question of who these officers are is not the only decisive question. Just as important, and in the circumstances of the Revolution of 1918 even more important, was the question of how these officers were organized and what they were told to do. They were given their orders by the civil authorities. And instead of arguing what he used the officers for, Noske argued that he used them: a point unarguable because of its inherent logic.

He stood on firmer ground when he discussed the question why the ranks of his troops were predominantly composed of *Bürger*, not workers. Here, he could point to numerous examples of the blindness of his party, the Social Democrats. For instance, a district assembly of this party that had jurisdiction over *Vorwärts* resolved in March 1919 to bar *Vorwärts* from accepting any advertisements soliciting recruits for Noske's volunteer corps. The same attitude was taken by many other Social Democratic district organizations and publications.

When the National Assembly passed the law establishing the future *Reichswehr* in February 1919, the Social Democratic Party voted for the law. But at the same time it forbade its members to join up. The idea was that an army was an instrument of murder, when the idea ought to have been to make the new army a stronghold of democracy. But this ran counter to the interests of the existing State. The Social Democrats at large did not want this State, and therefore they sabotaged the new *Reichswehr*, believing it would not find enough recruits if the workers kept away. They could not see that the *Reichswehr* would simply be filled with *Bürger* who, in the course of time, would be sifted so as to leave only reactionaries in the force.

It is doubtful, though, whether the ban on Social Democratic followers joining the *Reichswehr* was the only thing that influenced the masses of workers. They had another potent reason for staying away. In this respect, as in many others, General Maercker had a keener insight into social matters, or perhaps only more common sense. He wrote in his memoirs: 'One would have thought that the People's Wehr which was to be formed (p. 178) would have been much run after in view of the bad state of the labour market. Strangely enough, this was not so in general. The reason probably was that a great part of the proletariat believed the Revolution was not yet over, and they shunned a pronouncedly governmental force.'

2

After 'Spartacus Week', Noske used his military power for two purposes. The first was to continue the disarming of the workers. We have seen why this action (decreed by the government on 15 December) had not proceeded too well (p. 199). But it made great strides under the régime of General von Lüttwitz, especially in Berlin. However, even then a certain quantity of arms were not surrendered, as was proved by the fighting that broke out all over Germany a little later.

Then, there was the restoration of absolute quiet and order. Although the fighting of Spartacus Week was over, the inhabitants of many parts of Berlin were kept awake at night by constant shooting between 'Spartacists' and soldiers. It was strange that these soldiers were in every case from the volunteer units the government had established in the capital, and in no case of the Lüttwitz force. Moreover, no one was even hurt, nor were any Spartacists captured in the act of shooting.

General Maercker stated the case bluntly in a report to Lüttwitz. He declared his 'conviction that the shooting did not come from Spartacists but from men of the volunteer units; that it was partly done from fright and partly from the desire to be important. I even suspected that the guards shot merely to demonstrate the necessity of the existence of the volunteer units. (Revolution profiteers!) My forbidding shooting had the effect that hardly a shot has been fired since. . . . Thus, the population of Berlin was for almost ten days put in fear and trembling by unscrupulous elements among the volunteer units.' Maercker's order forbade all government soldiers to shoot in any circumstances. And as nobody shot at them, there was no shooting at all.

3

The second purpose for which Noske used his power at that time (the restoration of quiet and order) was of great political significance. The battle of the Marstall and the fighting of early January had interrupted any government action about the Hamburg Points. Of course, there was much in the Hamburg points impossible of realization; but what Noske did next brushed aside all that was possible and necessary, too, and it became one of the signals for the outbreak of battles that far outdid the January fighting in scope and ferocity.

On 19 January 1919, he issued 'Rules concerning the Provisional

Regulation of the Power of Command and the Position of Soldiers' Councils in the Peacetime Army'. It may be recalled that the Hamburg Points demanded that 'The Supreme Command be exercised by the People's Commissars under the control of the Executive Council'. Noske's Rules said: 'The Supreme Command is exercised by the Council of People's Commissars elected by the Central Council.' This was a polite bow at the Central Council but it eliminated all control of military affairs and made the exercise of this branch of State activity arbitrary. Furthermore, Noske's Rules rendered the soldiers' councils completely impotent though they did not dissolve them. Since the Central Council consisted entirely of Social Democrats there seemed to be no need for abolishing its right of control. But the Reich Congress (of which the Central Council was the executive organ) had voted unanimously for the Hamburg Points, it had repeatedly urged the government to put these Points into effect, and Noske would take no chances.

In fact, however, there was no risk at all. A few days later, the executive of the Berlin soldiers' councils, which also consisted entirely of Social Democrats, passed the following resolution: 'The powers of soldiers' councils have been newly regulated by the competent authorities. (Rules of 19 January.) In the opinion of the Executive Council the soldiers' councils of Greater Berlin have therefore no further field of action and no legitimation for action.' A full meeting of the soldiers' councils thereupon disavowed their executive and passed a vote of no confidence in it. But the machinations of the executive had created such confusion that nothing mattered.

Not to have any unnecessary trouble, Noske adopted peculiar methods to get rid of a number of soldiers' councils which did not fold up as meekly as the Berlin executive. In general, he deposed the commanders of units who had been elected by their local councils. But if they objected to being deposed he induced them to resign by paying them a bonus. These bonuses had to be high in certain cases in order to persuade the commanders concerned of the political and patriotic necessity of their resignation.

XXV. CARNAGE

I

But the wholly Social Democratic General Soldiers' Council of Münster in Westphalia would not be bought nor would it resign. Its field of activity was the Rhenish-Westphalian coal-mining district and the Ruhr valley.

Seeing that the government made no attempt at socializing the mining industry, the Workers' and Soldiers' Council of Rhineland-Westphalia had issued a manifesto on 3 January 1919, taking the matter in their own hands. They formed a 'Commission of Nine', consisting of three Social Democrats, three Independents, and three Spartacists. The Social Democrats were outwardly the most eager propagators of the action. A general strike which was in force at that time was broken off upon the formation of the Commission of Nine according to the view accepted by all the parties concerned that in a socialist economy workers could strike only against themselves.

To appease the miners the government issued a decree appointing proxies for each German mining district. Their task was to supervise 'all economic activities connected with the production, the sale, and the use of coal, and also with the calculation of prices'. The proxies for Rhineland-Westphalia were a high (old-time) Prussian civil servant, Röhrig; a coal magnate, Vögler;[1] and a trade union leader, Hue.

[1] Albert Vögler (born in 1877) was one of the leading German iron and coal industrialists. In 1919 he became a member of the National Assembly for the Conservatives, and served in the Reichstag from 1920 to 1924. In 1929 he was, together with Dr Schacht, on the German Committee for Reparations which negotiated with the Young Committee. Vögler resigned because he did not approve of the German reparations policy. In 1933, Hitler appointed him a member of the *Generalrat der Wirtschaft* (General Economic Commission).

Another decree stipulated the creation of 'Labour Chambers' which were to deal with the problem of socialization. They were to consist of equal numbers of employers' and workers' representatives. Among the recognized agencies of the workers were the National-Liberal Trade Unions which comprised approximately 4 per cent of organized labour, while the Free (Social Democratic) Trade Unions comprised 81 per cent and the Christian-National (mostly Catholic) Trade Unions about 13 per cent. The National-Liberal Trade Unions, which professed to be politically neutral, were usually called the Hirsch-Duncker working men's associations after the two men who initiated them in the 1860's. As the Hirsch-Duncker unions always voted with the employers, socialization was practically laid in the hands of the mine-owners.

2

In this situation Noske ordered the general commanding the district, Baron von Watter, to arrest the recalcitrant General Soldiers' Council. Watter held a position in the west analogous to that of Lüttwitz in Berlin. His corps was 30,000 strong. The arrest was made without a hitch, for everything had been prepared long in advance. Watter's soldiers were kept in the necessary spirit by gifts from the mining magnates. It would have been impossible, generally speaking, to keep the government troops together without the enormous amounts of money that came from private sources.

On 14 February 1919, the workers' and soldiers' councils of the entire industrial district met in Essen and resolved to strike unless the General Soldiers' Council were reinstated. Another meeting was called for 18 February to make the final decision. The government's reply was requested by 17 February.

On 16 February, a non-representative meeting of workers' and soldiers' councils at Mülheim-Ruhr resolved to strike immediately.

The government merely conceded that the Commission of Nine should continue to function until the Labour Chambers began their work. This concession was rejected by the new conference in Essen on 18 February. The Social Democrats then demanded that this conference disavow the resolution of Mülheim. The Independents and Communists protested against this step, as the Essen council had nothing to do with the Mülheim resolution which was passed by a body that was not competent to speak for the whole district. Thereupon the Social Democrats resigned from the Commission of Nine, which was backed by all the workers including their own followers; the whole affair being another of the many instances of terrifying childishness in both workers' camps. Naturally, the Social Democrats refused to participate in the general strike. Many of their rank and file, however, struck with their Independent and Communist fellows. As in the war, they deserted their party and trade union leaders. The strike assumed great proportions.

In his memoirs Noske wrote: 'Workers' and soldiers' councils who called themselves Social Democrats agreed to the resolution' (of the Essen meeting of 14 February, p. 237). This sentence might look as if he condemned them. But in the next sentence he said: 'This probably prevented the general strike', the meaning being that obstruction by participants is more effective than opposition by non-participants. As far as his memoirs are concerned, the strike did not take place.

On 21 February, the strikers seeing that they could not withstand Watter's forces, negotiated with him. Unorganized revolutionary fighters, however enthusiastic, cannot stand up to a rigidly disciplined and ideologically unbroken modern military force (but see p. 242). And there was another reason. As in the fighting in Berlin, so in the west, Russian agents were very much in evidence. No one, whatever his political opinions, who has seen these men in action could deny their valour. But the Germans were like the people of most other nations in this respect; in spite of their ideological affinity the German revolutionaries did not like the idea of being 'shown' by foreigners. And comparatively few of the revolutionists were Communists in the party sense, anyway.

Terms acceptable to both sides were arranged, and the strike was called off. The severe street fighting that was going on in many cities of Westphalia, the Rhineland and the Ruhr ceased. By 25 February, work in the pits was going on normally.

3

The National Assembly was sitting in Weimar at that time. It was removed from Berlin on the insistence of Ebert. Weimar was chosen for the cultural significance the town of Goethe and Schiller has for most Germans. Because it was chosen, the German Republic was often called the Weimar Republic. The National Assembly had been elected on 19 January 1919. The elections, as was to be foreseen, did not bring a majority to the Social Democrats. Even with the Independents they were in the minority. The Communists had boycotted the elections. Their vote would probably have been very small. The Social Democrats formed a coalition government with the Centre and the Democrats. On 11 February, Ebert was elected President of the *German Republic*; the *German Socialist Republic* was buried, and so was any democratic-capitalist change of the substance of the German State, not because the Democrats and the Centre did not want such a change, but because the Social Democratic policy, and especially their alliance with the generals, made it impossible. Scheidemann became Minister President (p. 222). He exclaimed in the National Assembly on 21 February: 'The ground on which we stand is heaving. It may break down any moment if we do not succeed in determinedly ending the insanity and the crime in the Ruhr.' By crime and insanity he meant the demand for the destruction of the militaristic State, which destruction the revolutionary workers in the Ruhr meant to accomplish in their own way (if they had any ideas at all, p. 243), but which he rejected in any shape.

This demand was not confined to the Ruhr. Two days after Scheidemann's outburst the same demand flared up in the huge soft-coal mining district of central Germany. And there it gripped not only the miners but also the industrial workers and a large part of the railroad personnel. Their representatives demanded the 'democratization of all factories as a first step towards socialization'. On 23 February they resolved: 'As all that could be tried to carry the demand of the miners has been tried, but rejected by the government, we use the last, terrible weapon and declare a *general strike* for Monday, 24 February.' The wish was then expressed that Berlin join the action. The conference consisted of 50 per cent Independents and 25 per cent each of Social Democrats and Communists, a composition that reflected the relations in the rank and file of the workers in that part of Germany.

The government realized the gravity of the danger. It issued a long proclamation on 1 March 1919: '...We shall reach the goal of economic democracy: the *constitutional factory* on a democratic basis. And we shall reach the *socialization* of those branches of economic activity that are ripe for transfer into public or mixed-economic management or that can be subordinated to public control, such as mining and the production of electric power....To work is a *socialistic duty* in the new Germany....Any human life is sacred to us....'

The Social Democratic *Fraktion* moved the same day in the National Assembly: 'The Reich government is requested to undertake with the greatest possible speed the conversion of mines and the production of power into public enterprises (socialization), and in this process to make use of workers and employees through suitable representations for the purpose of control and administration.' In reply, the government informed the House that a bill, corresponding to the wishes of this motion, was being drafted and would be put before the House very shortly.

Again the same day the Social Democratic Party issued a proclamation. It said in part: 'The soldiers' councils will not disappear....Nor will the workers' councils disappear....Socialization is coming....We cannot remove in four weeks the debris and rubble that four centuries of feudal mismanagement and four years of the most terrible war have left.'

4

The workers were not impressed. A general strike in Berlin was added to the action in central Germany. The threat of this strike had contributed a great deal to the hectic activity of the government and the Social Democrats in issuing those three pronounce-ments.

On 28 February 1919, the workers' councils of Greater Berlin had elected a new executive council. It consisted of 6 Independents, 6 Social Democrats, 2 Communists, and 2 Democrats. In the full council the Independents and Communists had a majority with 305 and 99 members, as against 271 Social Democrats and 95 Democrats. However, a general strike had no chance of success unless it were endorsed by the Social Democrats, and the latter showed no willingness to act in this direction. They and the Democrats were surprised by a *fait accompli*, though, at a meeting of the full council on 3 March when delegates appeared, representing a great number of large factories, declaring that the workers had resolved to act and were demanding a corresponding resolution by the councils. Upon this, the meeting passed a strike vote against the opposition of the Democrats.

The action started on 4 March. Furious battles between workers and Lüttwitz soldiers began immediately. On the fourth day of the struggle the greater part of the Independents supported by the Communists moved in the workers' councils of Greater Berlin that the strike be extended to include gasworks, waterworks, and power stations. Reasonable deputies of all parties pointed out that this measure would hurt the striking workers and the working population in general more than anyone else. But the motion was carried by a small majority. Thereupon the Social Democrats resigned from the strike committee.

The Lüttwitz soldiers took over the public utilities of the western residential districts and kept them operating. But they made no effort to capture those in the other districts, and consequently the poorer population had to live without water, gas and electricity. This did not raise their spirits.

If the movement were not to break down right then, it was necessary that the Independents and Communists should form a new strike committee. But the Communists refused, and the action did break down, on 8 March. The surrender of the strikers was unconditional; in western Germany the parties had agreed upon terms, but in Berlin the military would not negotiate. In central Germany, in turn, negotiations began on 4 March and led to mutual accommodation on 8 March, simultaneously with the end of the strike in Berlin.

5

Had the central German movement begun a week earlier, or else had the strike in the west not been called off prematurely (p. 243), the two actions combined might have broken the government, although the workers had not a sufficient number of trained soldiers and officers on their side, and not enough arms in general. These actions were quite different from the January putsch in Berlin which had been a purely military undertaking; they had a broad industrial basis and comprised the two most essential industrial districts of Germany. They further combined political and economic demands and might thus have become the beginning of a movement such as Liebknecht and Luxemburg had been working for (p. 195) until Liebknecht lost his head (p. 204). None of these conditions had been given in the Berlin putsch. That the great actions in western and central Germany could break out at all in spite of the crushing of the January putsch in Berlin, showed the powerful desire for a change among large sections of the workers.

The question whether or not these actions would have broken the old State if they had succeeded in overthrowing the government must remain open, of course. However, the failure of the actions was due to the lack of any plan and of a central leadership.

In the case of success, the lack of these two things might have produced chaos rather than a new State. There certainly was no conception on anybody's part of what to do with victory.

6

While Berlin, the centre, and the west of Germany were in flames, similar movements broke out in Baden, Brunswick, and Württemberg (Swabia). They, too, were put down quickly.

When the strikes in central Germany and Berlin were at their height, the Commission of Nine (consisting only of six after the withdrawal of the Social Democrats, p. 238) declared on 5 March 1919: 'A part of the Social Democratic leaders and the trade unions are trying to remove the Commission of Nine and sabotage the socialization of mining. We are, however, satisfied that the workers resolutely insist on socialization.'

It became evident that the action in the west had been called off prematurely; that the revolutionary energy of the workers was far from being spent. A new upheaval began when the military declared that the workers were not fulfilling the terms of the agreement of 21 February (p. 239). Watter's troops occupied the entire district although he had accepted the workers' condition that his corps should be withdrawn altogether. Soon, encounters occurred between workers and Watter's soldiers. The government proclaimed a state of siege. This was the signal for a new general strike that paralysed the whole district by the beginning of April. But the government was free then to concentrate all its military might upon this one battle-ground; it refused to negotiate, and the rest was simple and bloody.

Watter received his instructions from the Social Democrat, Karl Severing, who had been appointed Reich Commissar for the Industrial District. Severing was for many years Prussian Minister of the Interior later on. When von Papen became Reich Chancellor in 1932 he ousted Severing by sending a lieutenant and two men who informed him that he was deposed although the Prussian government of the time had a majority in the Diet. Severing asked Papen's minions if they would use force if he did not yield. Of course they said they would. He then resigned and told his followers, the Social Democratic workers who were standing outside clamouring for arms, that he had yielded to force. He was just another of those little men who used violence when he should have used power, and who cravenly threw away power if somebody else as much as mentioned violence against him.[1]

7

The upheaval of March 1919 was accompanied by grotesque capers by Communist politicians and the Communist Press. This upheaval was not the work of Communists, as we have seen, although many Communist agitators, including many Russians, were busy among the workers. These Russians were hirelings of the constitutionally hyper-sanguine Trotsky. And if the German Liebknecht misread the situation (or rather, acted against his reading of it) how could minor Russian agents do better? Anyway, when the movement spread to Berlin the Communists proclaimed once again that world revolution was on the march. But whatever the movement was, it was not world revolution, and it was not Communism. The workers of Berlin had just elected workers' councils and had sent to them a mere 99 Communists out of 770 members. The strike vote, as we have seen, was passed by 675 to 95. The demands of the strikers did not mention socialism, let alone world revolution, but they had a great deal to do with the destruction of the old army and the creation of a new one. To be sure, the fighting on the revolutionary side was largely carried out by Spartacists. If successful they might have set up a military dictatorship, which would certainly have been against the wishes of the vast majority of the strikers. Moreover, it could

[1] After the Second World War Severing, who had been left alone by the Nazis, became chairman of the Social Democratic Party for the district of Bielefeld, his home town. He died on 23 July 1952, aged seventy-eight.

hardly have maintained itself, isolated as it would have been in Berlin, and seeing that the piecemeal character of the upheaval had given the government absolute military superiority, and the military absolute superiority over the government.

However, the fantastic claims of the Communists about their role in the upheaval were just what Ebert, Scheidemann and Noske needed. Ignoring the fact that the council representatives who had voted for the strike included 305 Independents and 271 Social Democrats as well as 99 Communists, they denounced the whole action as a Communist affair, and as such it lived on in the memory of the Berliners (and a number of German and non-German historians, too).

XXVI. BESTIALITY

I

More than 1200 people perished during the March fighting in the capital alone according to official figures. The actual figure probably was nearer 3000. Several hundred of them were shot out of hand in consequence of an order by Noske: 'Any person found with arms fighting against government troops is to be shot instantly.' This order was barbarous. Its effect could be foreseen; in many cases, as we shall hear, the government soldiers forgot about its second part and shot people simply for possessing arms, and in some cases even for possessing alleged arms. When Haase accused Noske in the Reichstag of having overstepped his rights, Noske retorted: 'In such dangerous situations it is not paragraphs that count but results.' There have always been people who made these or similar words their principle; in public life they are called dictators, in private life, criminals.

In his memoirs Noske explained why he issued this order. A government soldier had been separated from his patrol in a Berlin district mainly inhabited by workers. He was hounded by a mob and put to death in a horrible fashion.[1] Such incidents could not be stopped merely by shooting armed men. In this particular case, arms figured only in that the soldier was given the *coup de grâce* by being shot with a rifle. And, of course, there was no

[1] The hapless soldier's pleadings still ring in my ears. There were only a few armed brutes who beat him with their rifles block after block, street after street. The onlookers were sick at heart, but anyone who dared to open his mouth was threatened with the fate of the soldier. Still, the onlookers stayed on, hoping they might save the man somehow. At one stage he managed to get into a military hospital, and the onlookers managed to confuse the brutes. But they got into the building and snatched him from the operating table where doctors were busy with him by then.

fighting. Two other similar cases occurred in the Revolution. Lieutenant-Colonel von Klüver, Maercker's public relations officer, was thrown in the river Saale in Halle by a mob. He tried to swim ashore, but the mob shot him. Klüver was in mufti at the time of his death, engaged in a spying mission; somebody recognized him. The third case occurred in Dresden several weeks after Noske issued his shooting order. The Social Democratic Saxon War Minister, Neuring, was thrown in the river Elbe by a mob of war cripples who were dissatisfied with their pay. He, too, tried to swim ashore but was shot by the mob. To quell the unrest in Saxony at that time, the Reich government sent a volunteer corps commanded by Colonel Faupel[1] who acted with great brutality.

That there were not more than three such cases was due not to Noske's shooting order but to the discipline of the revolutionaries in human respect, undisciplined though they were in other respects. These bestialities were committed by mobs, not by organized bodies of revolutionary workers. In any case, a shooting order was not likely to accomplish what was desired. But what it did accomplish was illustrated by the following case that was by no means the only one of its kind. A father and his son, both factory workers, were stood against the wall in Berlin because the handle of a hand grenade was found in their home; they had taken it there to 'make something useful out of it'.

2

The Republican Soldiers' Wehr, once the force of Wels and Fischer, appeared on the scene for the last time in the March fighting in Berlin. On the afternoon of 5 March, a detachment of this troop was ordered to clear the Alexanderplatz of plunderers who were said to be on the rampage there. The order came from Captain

---

[1] Faupel later became a general in the Reichswehr. During and after the Spanish Civil War he was Hitler's ambassador to General Franco. When Hitler's Germany collapsed in 1945 he committed suicide.

Marcks (p. 205) who was undisputed master of the *Kommandantur* after Klawunde ceased to be commandant in consequence of the self-dissolution of the soldiers' councils (p. 235). Police headquarters, a huge complex of buildings, was situated on the Alexanderplatz. It had a garrison of Lüttwitz troops whose General Command had occupied the capital once more. The Lüttwitz men opened fire on the approaching Soldiers' Wehr detachment who, infuriated, returned the fire. The ensuing battle lasted far into the night and cost both sides many casualties. There can be little doubt that Lüttwitz and his accomplice, Marcks, provoked this affair in order to get rid of the Soldiers' Wehr on the grounds that it had attacked their force. For one thing, the Lüttwitz men must have seen that the approaching troop was a disciplined military body; more probably, they were even informed of its approach. Still more telling was the fact that the Soldiers' Wehr was sent from another district of the city to the Alexanderplatz to restore order there when the Lüttwitz men were on the spot and consequently knew that there was no disorder.

Another force appeared on the scene for the last time in March 1919: the People's Marine Division. Although it took no part in events of that month it was declared dissolved. The sailors submitted without any resistance and were ordered to assemble at a certain place in the city to receive their last pay. Only a small number turned up, 150 of them. The district in which they assembled was under the command of the volunteer corps leader, Colonel Reinhard, the self-styled saviour of Berlin (p. 215). His troops were told that the sailors were planning a conspiracy and were to be arrested. First Lieutenant Marloh was put in charge of the action. He had only a small detachment at his disposal. Seeing that he could not handle the arrest of the sailors though they were peaceful and unsuspecting, he telephoned to Reinhard's headquarters for reinforcements. An adjutant of Reinhard's replied that the colonel was furious because Marloh was not making extensive use of the rifle. But Marloh could not shoot 150 sailors with his inadequate troop. He sent for help once more and was told that Reinhard was now beside himself with fury. 'You are to shoot as many as you can; it's all right if you shoot them all. There is no prison space available for them.' For a moment Marloh thought of selecting a number of the sailors (who were still unsuspecting) by lot, and having them shot. But then he felt this was cruel. Therefore he went up to them and pointed out to his men those sailors who looked most intelligent, thirty-one of them; they must be the ringleaders, he thought. They were led into the courtyard, following docilely, thinking they were to receive their pay. In the courtyard they were mowed down by machine-guns. Some did not die instantly and tried to get away. Their anguish and sufferings were ended quickly and effectively. Two, badly wounded, pretended to be dead and thus saved their lives. Dorrenbach, the man of the Palace keys who had later tried to involve the sailors in the January putsch, was arrested at the same time. He no longer had any connexion with the Marine Division, but his captors murdered him all the same. Lieutenant Marloh was tried in December 1919. He was acquitted because he had acted upon orders. Those who gave the orders were not called to account.

3

Bestialities, then, were committed against both sides in the fighting of March 1919, not only in Berlin but also in the Ruhr and central Germany. Recriminations never ceased. Statistically it was true that the number of atrocities committed against soldiers was negligible as compared with that committed against revolutionaries. But statistics cannot explain the causes of atrocities. The question is who and what turned the mob in the direction of bestiality; for with one exception (p. 265) the acts against soldiers were performed by mobs, not by organized workers.

In the fighting for the building of *Vorwärts*, seven revolutionaries were butchered in the most brutal fashion imaginable. The procedure was repeated a few days later after the capture of police headquarters by government troops. This was the beginning.

The mobs that replied in kind were not moved by the desire to get an eye for an eye. They had no clear desire at all. They were mobs composed of individuals, each of whom had his own vile motives for his evil deeds, and whom the circumstances of the revolution afforded a chance of banding together and perpetrating, under the cover of hysteria and mob anonymity, crimes of which their warped minds could only dream in other circumstances. Above all, they were shown something to which mobs succumb readily. Bestiality is contagious.

What was it, on the other hand, that made organized bodies of men, disciplined soldiers, act in that bestial fashion? Such bodies do not readily succumb to mob emotions.

It is worthy of note that no atrocities occurred wherever General Maercker's corps was in action, although this corps was otherwise quite as brutal, though never savage, as the rest of the government forces when military necessity demanded such behaviour. Likewise, when orders demanded it, for instance, they shot their share of people out of hand in accordance with Noske's barbarous order, but there is no case on record of Maercker's men stretching this order by killing innocent persons. There were two reasons for the satisfactory record of Maercker's corps. He selected his officers scrupulously, and his troops, as distinguished from all others, consisted largely of workers. The second-in-command of his recruiting staff, Captain Crasemann, a none too intelligent but honest man, gave many interesting glimpses of the working of Maercker's corps in a slim, clumsily written volume of reminiscences. At one place he complained (incidentally contradicting his chief (p. 233) who, however, saw the situation more clearly than he): 'The bourgeois element is lacking, the university students, the high-school students. The educated circles do not respond to...our commercial type of canvassing.' And: 'It was almost exclusively workers and unemployed who joined up; few country people; while the bourgeoisie stayed aloof, numbed by events.'

These recruits did not read any newspapers; consequently, they

did not read the general, and especially the reactionary, Press or
Vorwärts. But the officers and men of the other government
troops read these publications, and the regular reading of them
was apt to turn lambs into hyenas at that time.

4

In the fighting in Berlin, revolutionaries occupied the police
office of the borough of Lichtenberg. The Press reported, according to the temperament of the various editors, that 60 to
150 policemen had been butchered. The mayor of Lichtenberg,
a Democrat, stated publicly that 'all told, five officers were killed,
and it cannot be established whether these unfortunate men were
stood against the wall or fell in fighting'. Two other officers were
kidnapped by the revolutionaries but released later.

Four days after this event Noske said in the National Assembly
that a part of the Press had been guilty of distortion in its craving
for sensation. This nettled the only noon newspaper of the capital,
and it declared that it had been sent a report from the military to
the effect that all the police officers of Lichtenberg had been
butchered. The editors had not believed the story and omitted it
altogether. But a little later they received the same report from
the Social Democratic Prussian Ministry of the Interior. The
Ministry insisted that it be printed and urged that an extra edition
be brought out if the newspaper were already made up. The newspaper then printed a second edition with banner headlines of the
'Spartacist Mass Butchery', and drove the non-revolutionary
population of Berlin into a frenzy.

Just as there was some truth in the report that police officers had
been killed at Lichtenberg, so there was also some truth in another
report, spread by the 'Socialistic Press Correspondence'. It said
that the Spartacists in the Ruhr were paid by the 'enemy', and that
they collaborated with Poland in order to enforce the occupation
of Germany by the Entente. Conversations had indeed taken
place between certain French military men and certain Germans.

The spokesmen of the Germans were the 'Spartacists' August Thyssen (father of the notorious author of *I Paid Hitler*, Fritz Thyssen) and Hugo Stinnes, and the group for which they spoke was the German coal and steel industry. The workers' and soldiers' councils of the industrial district arrested Thyssen and Stinnes on various occasions for various reasons. They had to release them each time upon orders from Landsberg, although he was not responsible for the administration of justice. Landsberg argued that the only law that could be applied against the industrialists would be the high treason law of Imperial Germany, and that this law was not applicable because Germany was now a republic. There is irony in the fact that Landsberg refused to use that law against leftists (p. 211) as well as rightists. But when it suited the new old State it applied the Imperial high treason paragraph vigorously, as we shall see (p. 268).

The confusion of French politics did not permit any French government to expose those Germans as traitors to their country when, later on, they openly allied themselves with Hitler.

XXVII. CAESAR

After completing its task in Berlin in January 1919, the Maercker corps was given the honour of protecting the National Assembly in Weimar. Some fertile brains saw in the upheavals of late February and early March an attempt at Communist world revolution by capturing Weimar, and therefore the National Assembly had to be protected. But even those revolutionaries were not so unimaginative as not to see that their best chance of success was to take Berlin, the political nerve centre of the Reich, and to isolate the government in Weimar where it would be quite helpless. The capture of Weimar would be a meaningless gesture.

Not being needed at Weimar the Maercker corps was sent to other parts of central Germany to quell unrest there: Halle, Magdeburg, Leipzig, Eisenach, Erfurt and Brunswick.

Brunswick was an interesting case. The Revolution had established a government there under the Social Democrat, Jasper. In the subsequent elections to the Diet (Brunswick was a Free State, and its capital was also called Brunswick) the Social Democrats and Independents obtained a majority between them. Jasper resigned, and the two parties formed a coalition government that included the Independent, Sepp Oerter. The new government pledged itself to carry out socialization. The Reich government did not like the idea, impossible as it was anyway (p. 125), and looked for a pretext to act against the little Free State.

At that time, the commander-in-chief, Noske, sent the following telegram to the government of Brunswick: 'Have report soldiers on through-transport captured there yesterday to be shot tomorrow. If true warn urgently to abstain from acts of violence.

Release prisoners instantly and send on their way. Severe accounting will be demanded. Wire explanation to Reich government instantly. Reich government Noske.' The reply: 'Your believing imbecile falsehoods indicates complete nervous breakdown. Nobody taken prisoner here. Unlike Ebert Scheidemann government Brunswick government is not murderous. Spare us further nonsensical telegrams. Brunswick government. Oerter.'

This reply was more blunt than diplomatic. Noske's telegram, however, was not nonsensical; it served a purpose: to label the Brunswick government one that interfered with military transports. But before the Reich government took any action on this and similar trumped-up charges, a workers' meeting proclaimed the soviet republic of Brunswick on 28 February 1919, and elected a revolution committee. This committee, though, refused to carry out its mandate because in its opinion the participation in the vote in the factories by which the delegates to the meeting of 28 February were elected had been too small. The former Independent police president of Berlin, Eichhorn, now a Communist, was prominent in the Brunswick revolution committee. This committee proclaimed a general strike in order 'completely to consolidate the revolution', which of course was ludicrous in the circumstances.

Berlin, in turn, ordered Maercker to consolidate quiet and order in Brunswick. He did so, and deposed the government that had nothing to do with the affair. But he observed the rules of political democracy in that he installed a new government which again consisted of Social Democrats and Independents. Then he left Brunswick.

A few days after his departure the non-socialist parties of the Brunswick Diet declared they would stay away from the House unless a government were formed that included non-socialist ministers. These tactics deprived the Diet of the constitutionally required quorum, and it could not function. The Social Democrats thereupon dropped the Independents and formed a coalition government with non-socialists. Thus quiet and order was further consolidated.

2

The sailor Kuhnt, president of the Free State of Oldenburg, had some official business with Noske early in February 1919. A few weeks later he was arrested upon Noske's order because he was said to have been implicated in a Communist putsch that took place in Wilhelmshaven at the end of January. Kuhnt wrote: 'I have gained...the impression that the excitement of the last few weeks has left its mark on his [Noske's] mind.... When I left him I felt no anger or hatred of him, but profound pity for the changes I observed in his personality.... The old professional generals were brutal, but they had tradition, and this gave them a certain air and reserve. The new upstart general, however, has learned from them only how to clear his throat and spit; and he has inherited only their brutality, not their reserve. I am sorry to have to say the new Red Caesarian madness seems to be worse than the old one of the Junkers.'

Kuhnt, of course, was prejudiced. There were people who thought differently of Noske; for instance, Baron von Oldenburg-Januschau, an intimate friend of Hindenburg and the most typical of Prussian Junkers. The people called him the 'Januschauer', a word that had no particular meaning yet expressed hatred and contempt to German ears. All classes hated him, and even many of his fellow Junkers frowned at the uncouth manner in which he liked to express his reactionism.[1] The Januschauer said: 'It would have been better had a Noske, not Prince Max of Baden, stood behind the Kaiser at the decisive moment....'

[1] In answer to the democratic slogan, 'vox populi, vox dei', he coined the counter-slogan, 'vox populi, vox Rindvieh' (cattle).

XXVIII. CARNIVAL

I

Munich took pride in the gaiety and colourfulness of its carnival. In 1919 this carnival was followed by an Ash Wednesday that never ended.

The first of the German Republics, the Republic of Bavaria, was proclaimed in Munich on 7 November 1918. Kurt Eisner became its Prime Minister. He was an intellectual, born in Berlin in 1867, a man of inexhaustible energy, an inexhaustible well of ideas, and a spirit of inspiring idealism. It took him many years to acquire a slight notion of the intricacies of social and political reality. But he kept on forgetting it and could never free himself from relapses into dreaming.

One of his first attempts at politics taught him a lesson, eight years before the turn of the century. He wrote a pamphlet then in support of a Radical-Liberal candidate in an election in the Grand-Duchy of Hesse. '... How is it, you farmers of Hesse, that you do not know that your candidate, Böckel, has sixteen illegitimate children? Is it to such a person that you want to give your votes?' The farmers had not known it, and Böckel, who had unsuccessfully run on several previous occasions, received more votes than ever before. Eisner learned that the unexpected is liable to happen in politics, and that certain manifestations of sturdiness endear a candidate to many people.

By 1899 he was a reformist Social Democrat, that is, a follower of Bernstein (p. 20), and by 1917 a left-wing Independent. Anyone who knows the Bavarians must marvel at the popularity Eisner gained among their workers, he, the Berliner and Jew, the very 'type of humanity' his friend, Professor Foerster, called domineering (p. 165). But his popularity was real, and it swept

Carnival

him into power in November 1918 to establish his 'realm of light, of beauty, and of reason'.

He did not oppose the idea of a National Assembly, but he wanted first to create a 'living, active democracy', that was then to be carried on by the 'formal' democracy of the Assembly. Of socialization he said: 'One cannot socialize when there is hardly anything to be socialized.' The industrial and financial backers of militarism perked up their ears. They had ridiculed him because they feared and hated him, but now they thought he was a man they could use. They were mistaken.

On 15 November 1918, Eisner's government, consisting of Independents and Social Democrats, published a comprehensive programme that clearly showed his imprint. At the end of December, he put his name to an appeal for the formation of a citizens' Wehr. The chief man behind this project was his ministerial colleague, the Social Democrat, Auer. But the idea of the citizens' Wehr had to be abandoned (for the time being) because it made the workers angry. Moreover, Colonel Ritter von Epp, the commander designate, and several other members of the embryo force were arrested for conspiring to make it the nucleus of reaction. Meanwhile, Auer wove invisible nets.

The elections to the Bavarian Diet, in January 1919, gave the Independents a mere three seats in a house of 180. The disappointed workers' and soldiers' councils refused to permit the convening of the Diet. But Eisner was not a dictator; he hesitated for some time and then convened the Diet intending to declare his resignation. On his way to the session, however, he was shot dead by the youthful Count Arco-Valley[1] on 21 February 1919.

The Diet began its session. Auer was shedding tears over the crime just committed when the door of the chamber opened.

---

[1] The Count was tried in 1920 and sentenced to death. The sentence was commuted to imprisonment for life 'because the deed of the politically immature young man sprang not from base motives but from the most glowing love of his people and country'. He was set free in 1924 because of 'ill health'.

A man walked slowly across the floor, the worker, Lindner.[1] He
shot two bullets at Auer who he thought was responsible for
Eisner's death. Then he killed a police officer who tried to stop
him. Auer was severely wounded but soon recovered.

2

The workers raged as only Bavarian workers could rage. The
workers' and soldiers' councils arrested hundreds of officers,
aristocrats, and wealthy citizens as hostages, but they released
them soon, unharmed. They would not, however, allow the non-
socialist majority of the Diet to form a new government. Instead,
they appointed a government of Social Democrats and Independents which was given unlimited power by the frightened majority
at a short session in the second half of March. The new prime
minister was the Social Democrat, Hoffmann.

Colonel von Epp,[2] released soon after his arrest and forced to
resign his commission in the army, was in Berlin, negotiating with
the commander-in-chief, Noske, telling him that the Bavarian
workers would not tolerate the formation of a new army, and the
Bavarian government would not provide any money for it.
Noske gave Epp the money needed for the purpose, out of the
coffers of the Reich. Hoffmann knew of this transaction and forbade the recruiting of soldiers in Bavaria on the grounds that the
workers would revolt. He was sincere in this fear, but he did not
proclaim the ban on recruiting without obtaining Noske's consent
first. Noske sympathized with his party friend and agreed to the

[1] Lindner was sentenced to fourteen years hard labour. His health stood up
well. He would have been sentenced to death, but he had fled to Austria, and
the Austrians extradited him only on condition that he would not be punished
more severely than under their law.

[2] Franz von Epp joined the Nazis early, and became a member of the Reichstag for them in 1928. In 1933 Hitler made him Governor of Bavaria (*Reichs-
statthalter*). In 1939, like many other rats, he left the sinking ship and joined a
resistance movement. He died in February 1947, aged 78. In a dispute involving his estate, the Bavarian courts decided that 60 per cent of his estate be confiscated because of his Nazi activities.

ban, but in his memoirs he sneered at the Bavarian Social Democrats who would not show the courage of their convictions.

The ban on recruiting prevented Epp from raising more than a few hundred men, mostly Bavarian students. He ran his troop as a free corps and drilled it at the old army camp at Ohrdruf in Thuringia, near the Bavarian frontier.

Toward the end of March 1919 the Bavarian Social Democrats began to clamour for a soviet republic. It was said later that they did so in order to give Noske a pretext for occupying Bavaria, which may or may not have been true. A soviet republic was indeed proclaimed on 7 April. The Hoffman government fled to Bamberg, in the north of Bavaria, where they were protected by Epp's troops. The carnival began.

3

All over Germany the working class was licking the wounds it had received in the March fighting. Its spirit was crushed, its revolutionary fire dowsed. And at that moment the attempt was made to establish a soviet republic in a part of Germany that could not, economically, stand on its feet at the best of times. The courage of the workers who embarked on this venture was superb, the excesses some of them committed were commensurate. But they committed them only after being basely slandered, brutally attacked, and while being cruelly subjugated. Violence breeds violence. The question is always who started it. Whatever the spirit of the undertaking, its logic was weak, and its leaders were preposterous, that is, as political leaders.

There is not much to be said about Lipp, the Commissar for Foreign Affairs. He wired to the Bavarian ambassador in Berlin: 'As I must not abandon the privileges of Bavaria[1] won by Bavarian blood at Wörth and Sedan[2] I order you instantly to

---

[1] These privileges were those referred to on p. 131.
[2] Wörth and Sedan were places of decisive battles in the Franco-Prussian war of 1870–71 in which Bavaria fought on the side of Prussia.

announce your withdrawal to Count Brockdorff-Rantzau.'[1] Forty-eight hours later Lipp was taken to an asylum; the poor man had gone insane.

The finance minister of the Bavarian soviet republic (he walked out at the end of the first day and was succeeded by the professor of economics at Munich University, Edgar Jaffé) meant to cancel the effect of Lipp's breaking off diplomatic relations with the Reich and sent the following telegram to Berlin: 'Extension of diplomatic break to currency affairs would deplorably obstruct unity. I will put our currency on sound footing by radical means, will abandon ways of systemless money economy, go over to absolute currency, and request inform me your attitude.' This finance minister was Silvio Gesell.[2]

Another prominent member of the soviet-Bavarian government was the 'anarcho-socialist' Gustav Landauer who preached the gospel of an 'ideal community life without magisterial compulsion and capitalist rule'. There was, further, the intellectual, Erich Mühsam, to whom 'the world must become a meadow full of flowers where each can gather his share'. And then, there was a doctor, Wadler; the poet Ernst Toller; and half a dozen or so others. The sailor Eglhofer (p. 67), twenty-one years old but mature beyond his age, was commander-in-chief of the soviet-Bavarian army.

---

[1] Ulrich Graf von Brockdorff-Rantzau was foreign minister of the Weimar Republic then. He opposed Germany's early entry into the League of Nations because it was the best bargaining counter Germany had, in his opinion. He was one of a number of leading Germans who without being Communists, naturally, looked toward Moscow, where he died as German Ambassador in 1928.

[2] Gesell (1862–1930) was not really as silly as this telegram suggests. Son of a German father and a French mother, he emigrated to Argentina where he made a considerable fortune as a merchant. He retired from business in 1906 to live in Switzerland. The economic crisis of the 1880's led him to the study of monetary problems and a substantial output of writings on economic subjects between 1891 and his death. Lord Keynes called his strivings 'profoundly original' and said he believed that 'the future will learn more from the spirit of Gesell than from that of Marx'.

The soviet-Bavarian government derived its mandate from the Bavarian Central Council of Workers' and Soldiers' Councils, and consisted of Social Democrats, Independents, and one peasant. On 12 November 1918, the Reich government of Ebert had issued a proclamation calling upon the peasants at large to form peasants' councils. Ebert knew that another conservative, and in many ways reactionary, force was available in the peasants if they could only be organized. The peasants were conservative and reactionary not by nature but because the controlled economy of the war had treated them with particular shabbiness (see next chapter). Socialism meant controls, and controls were anathema to the peasants at that time. But the call to form peasants' councils fell, generally speaking, on deaf ears. In Bavaria, however, such councils had been in existence for some time. The majority of them were non-revolutionary. Nevertheless, they supported the Revolution because they feared Bavaria would become a battle-ground after the defection of Austria, and because they regarded the war as a private business between monarchs. Moreover, they saw in the aristocracy that surrounded them the 'main advocate of the demands for annexations and indemnities which prolonged the war'. After the war was over, the Bavarian peasants' councils remained important; they wanted to have a say in the administration of their country; they wanted their complaints and wishes to be heard; and they wanted in general that everything should not be left to the bureaucracy. However, although one of their leaders was in the soviet government they blockaded the capital; no victuals were delivered to Munich.

4

The soldiers' councils of Munich were Social Democrats. They kept the soldiers quiet in their barracks but did not support the soviet government in which Schneppenhorst, one of the Social Democratic leaders, was war minister. He had demanded the soviet republic long before it was proclaimed. A day after its proclamation he said he would go to the north of the country to make propaganda for the soviets. He went north, and resumed duty as war minister with Hoffmann's 'government-in-exile' at Bamberg.

Hoffmann was in Berlin, negotiating with Noske. He wanted to get back to power in Munich, but he would not consent to Prussian troops marching into Bavaria; and Epp's force was not strong enough. In the circumstances, Noske could not help him, but he knew that Hoffmann would soften.

The Communists declared: 'This soviet republic is not the work of a proletariat that has awakened to class consciousness but the product of the dilemma of leaders whom the masses have refused to follow.' They did not join the soviet government, but they formed a 'council of revolutionary factory councils and revolutionary soldiers' councils' which demanded that the Central Council (p. 261) resign and hand over the power to them, the revolutionary council. Thus, the Communists who condemned the existing 'pseudo-soviet republic' appeared prepared to form a soviet government of their own. Such a soviet government would have received even less support from the masses of the workers and peasants than the existing one. But the Communists did not intend to act to follow up their demands.

The Social Democrats acted, however, on the night of 13 April. They had persuaded a large number of soldiers of the garrison (which, of course, consisted of remnants of the old army, as no new army could be formed) to side with them, and they thought they were strong enough to overthrow the soviet government. The Bamberg government of Hoffmann consented to their action. There was also a connexion with the Thule Society, an organization of monarchists. The soldiers occupied the Wittelsbach Palace, arrested several members of the soviet government, instantly sent them north, and declared the Central Council deposed.

This called the Communists to the scene. They had gathered a military force of a few hundred men, and a furious battle ensued between them and the soldiers. The number of dead in this battle was never established; it probably was considerable. The Communists won, and the revolutionary council appointed a new soviet government that was led by the Communists Levien, Leviné-Nissen and Axelrod. Presumably the proletariat had all of a sudden awakened 'to class consciousness' (p. 262), but nobody bothered to explain this point. What happened, of course, was that mass hysteria swayed the leaders against their better judgement, just as mass hysteria had swayed Liebknecht and Pieck on 5 January (p. 204) a few days after they declared that Berlin would be subdued by starvation if Ebert and Scheidemann were imprisoned (p. 201).

However, unlike the first Bavarian soviet government the new one acted determinedly. It proclaimed a general strike. A general strike undoubtedly is sound revolutionary tactics in certain revolutionary situations, but it had become a routine with those revolutionaries. This whole affair was not a revolution at that, it was a putsch. By declaring a general strike the Bavarian Communists sawed off the very branch on which they were sitting, a branch that was already sagging and cracking.

Axelrod was a Russian agent, another emissary of the sanguine Trotsky with whom world revolution was an obsession divorced from all reality; and there were many more Russian agents in Bavaria then. These people were of course right in believing that world revolution could succeed only if Germany went Communist. But it took them a long time to realize that there were few Communists in Germany then, even among the revolutionary workers. And it took the lives of great numbers of Communist and non-Communist Germans, and many of their own Russian agents, to convince them that their appraisal of the German situation was wrong.

4

Hoffmann softened towards the end of April. Noske's army began to move on Bavaria, 100,000 soldiers under the command of Lieutenant-General von Oven against five hundred, perhaps six hundred brave men who were political infants. Noske knew that there were no more than five hundred or so Red soldiers. His army was not to crush a handful of men; it was to crush any idea that the substance of the German State could be changed in any way whatever. Certainly, those five hundred could not change this substance, not only because they were few in number, but also because those who shared their ideas were few in number. But what was done to them was to serve as a warning to the millions of Germans who wanted to eliminate militarism by different means.

The revolutionary councils realized the hopelessness of fighting against Noske's army and declared their solidarity with the survivors of the first soviet government who were negotiating with Hoffmann in order to avert a catastrophe and forestall the Prussian invasion. Simultaneously the second soviet government was deposed by another group of putschists and a new one formed with Toller as its head. Part of the Red soldiers, ludicrously over-estimating their own strength but resolved to do or die, decided to fight against Noske. Led by still another group of putschists they prepared to overthrow Toller and establish a military dictatorship under Eglhofer.

Amid this grotesque confusion Oven's troops occupied Munich in the first week of May 1919.

One of the last Red posts to surrender was that on the *Stachusplatz*, a square in the inner city. Morning and night the general Press of all Germany was filled with formidable war reports about the battle of *Stachus*. The square was besieged by two regiments. It was defended by five men with two machine-guns. For two days they held the division at bay; their machine-guns controlled the streets that ran into the square. On the third day the soldiers sent a negotiator. The commander of the defenders, Alois (his family name is not recorded), met the negotiator in front of a small hotel on the Sendlingerstrasse. The negotiations did not go well. A woman who was listening at a window of the hotel called: 'What, you don't want to make peace, you damned rascal? We haven't been able to get out of the house for three days, and our guests can't get away. When you were a bootblack here you made me angry, you said the shoes were polished well but I said they wasn't and you was botching the job. You haven't improved any since then, you've gone to the Reds. Now you make peace instantly, or I'll come down after you.' Alois said: 'If you say so, Frau Sonnenhuber.' And to the officer: 'Well, now you have your peace, you rotten bums.' He went back to his comrades and they vanished across the roofs.

Fighting ceased. The carnival was over. Ash Wednesday was come.

5

When Noske's troops began to move on Munich, a detachment of Red soldiers shot ten prisoners, among them a woman, without the knowledge of the soviet government or any individual leader. An outcry went through Germany. The reactionary Press accused 'the Jews'. To them, everything that was happening anywhere was part of a great Jewish conspiracy. They did not mention the fact that there was a Jewish artist, the painter Professor Berger, among the murdered persons; it would have disturbed their myth. The Liberal press, many of its business undertakings being Jewish-owned, did not mention it either; the 'Jewish problem' was delicate, but if the word Jew was not mentioned the problem did not exist. The general Press reported, however, that the ten victims had been hostages; Eglhofer had indeed ordered the arrest of hundreds of prominent citizens as hostages. The idea seems to have been that the murder of hostages was worse than the murder of prisoners. The victims were not hostages, though, but had for the most part been arrested for being members of the Thule Society

(p. 262) which, of course, was no excuse for the abominable crime. The hostages were neither killed nor maltreated.

Instead of calming the excitement in Germany the general Press excelled itself by reporting that the genitals of the victims had been found in nearby refuse bins. The anti-revolutionary propaganda of the whole Revolution period showed altogether an astounding degree of orgiastic versatility. When it was stated two days later that the pieces of flesh found in the refuse bins were parts of slaughtered pigs, the infuriated soldiery had already killed scores of workers in reprisal for the alleged mutilations.

In the Augustinerstrasse in Munich the soldiers of General von Oven found twenty-one members of the Catholic Artisans' Society of St Joseph. They had gathered to discuss the amateur theatrical performance they were getting up. The martial law that was in force banned meetings of any kind on pain of death. This was sufficient reason for the soldiers to stand seven of the artisans against the wall and kill the other fourteen by less direct methods.

Eglhofer was shot as he tried to get away in a motor-car put at his disposal by the wife of a doctor. He was lucky; he was not tortured. Landauer was clubbed shapeless by Major Baron von Gagern. When he sank to the ground a sergeant shot him in the back. As he still moved, the sergeant jumped on him and trampled him to death.

Every nook and cranny of Munich was searched for arms. Thousands of people were mercilessly beaten up in the process, among them bankers, aristocrats, merchants, officers, doctors, lawyers. No one was treated with any decency or respect. It was a passing, though significant, manifestation of the later Nazi spirit in Noske's *Landsknechts*.

An official report stated that 557 persons perished in Munich in the first week of May 1919, that is, during the process of occupation. Partisans of the soviet government estimated that their own dead amounted to a thousand. It is possible that the official figures were not quite correct. For instance, the official report said that the figure of 557 dead included 38 soldiers. The brunt of the fighting was borne by the brigade of Naval Captain Ehrhardt.[1] Ehrhardt wrote in his memoirs that his troop had four dead. It is difficult to see where the other thirty-four should have come from. Some four hundred persons were shot out of hand on the strength of Noske's shooting order. The twenty-one Catholic artisans were listed as 'victims of fatal accidents'.

The law student Schleusinger, a Social Democrat, was sentenced to death by a drum-head court-martial. He was led out, with some twenty other prisoners, to be executed. The officer commanding the firing squad singled out Schleusinger for his intelligent appearance and made him look on as the others were butchered. Suddenly, the mayor of Starnberg, where this happened, came running, waving an order: the military no longer had the right to shoot anyone; all offenders must be handed over to the regular courts. Schleusinger's life was saved. This order could and should have been given long before. In fact, no other order should ever have been given.

6

The regular courts set to work, then. Mühsam was sentenced to fifteen years of detention in a fortress.[2] Toller was given five years in a fortress; he served his full term.[3] Axelrod was sentenced to fifteen years' hard labour. All told, 184 persons were sentenced to 616 years of prison, hard labour, and fortress.

Toller was defended by the Independent ex-People's Commissar, Hugo Haase.[4] Haase argued that it was absurd that a government which had come to power by a revolution should try people who had done the same thing. Moreover, he argued, there was as yet no constitution and no law that defined high treason; the high-

[1] Next to Lüttwitz and Pabst, Ehrhardt became the most important military figure of the Kapp putsch.
[2] Mühsam was released in 1924, to be clubbed to death in a concentration camp after the advent of Hitler.
[3] Mental depression made Toller end his life in New York in May 1939.
[4] Haase was murdered by a madman a few months later.

treason paragraph the public prosecutor was invoking did not apply because it was designed to protect the monarchy. In fact, Haase contended, for the very reason for which he was demanding that the application of the high-treason paragraph be rejected in the case of Toller, the government itself had rejected its application in the cases of Ledebour (p. 211) and Thyssen (p. 252). Haase overlooked the fact that the Social Democrats had not *overthrown* the old State, they had *taken* it *over*. And therefore the government of the Social Democrats was entitled to invoke or not to invoke the law of the old State as it pleased. Ironically, that law was indirectly invoked against Ebert later on (p. 64).

Leviné-Nissen was sentenced to death and executed without delay. He died bravely. His case had challenged the ingenuity of the judges. That he was to be sentenced to death was a foregone conclusion. But it was not easy. The death penalty applied only to murder and high treason. He could not be accused of murder, he had not murdered anyone. But he could not be accused of high treason either. What had he done? He had overthrown the first soviet government which clearly could not be protected by the high-treason paragraph. He had not overthrown the legitimate government of Hoffmann, which was legitimate in that it had the power to enforce (with Noske's help) whatever it declared to be law, but which was not even constitutional in that it had no majority in the Diet; the majority of the Diet was non-Social-Democrat. Leviné had of course committed an offence; he had withheld the function of government from the 'legitimate' government from which it had been taken by third parties. In other words, he was guilty of being an accessory to high treason after the fact. This could not satisfy the judges because *post facto* accessoriness was not punishable by death. However, the judges rose to the challenge. They decided that the first soviet government had not committed high treason; that it was merely guilty of insurrection; and that high treason came into play only when the second soviet government started. This interpretation made everything legal, and satisfactorily disposed of Leviné-Nissen.

But did it not exonerate the members of the first soviet government of the charge of high treason? They were prosecuted for high treason, too. Why should judges not have different legal opinions? Wadler, for instance, was sentenced to eight years with hard labour.

The accused men were naturally photographed by the authorities. They were not allowed to shave for several days or to have their hair cut; they were not allowed to change their shirts and collars; they were forced to put on tattered caps and greatcoats. And then they were photographed. Their pictures went through the entire Press. Wrongdoers they certainly were. Politically immature and reckless they were, too. But their motives, intentions, and many of their actions were cleaner than the calculated immorality of the judiciary that dealt with them. However, this judiciary achieved what it desired; all Germany thanked heaven and Noske that it was rid of these monsters. When all was over, the judges asked the government for an increase in salaries; they felt they had performed a deserving piece of work.

German judges? Yes, but German judges of *that* Monarchy, of *that* Republic. Their real day came later, when they did not have to confine themselves to Spartacists and Russians but could practise their legal talents in addition on Catholics, Jews, Social Democrats, Liberals, could set husbands against wives, children against parents, could defend Nazi leaders in international courts of justice, and acquit, or deal leniently with, the murderers of Catholics, Jews, Social Democrats, Communists, and Liberals. German judges of yesterday?[1]

The commander-in-chief and Reichswehr minister Noske sent a telegram to Lieutenant-General von Oven, the commander of the 100,000 victors over a handful of criminal and dangerous fools: 'I express to you my full appreciation for the circumspect and successful operation in Munich, and to the troops my cordial thanks for their accomplishment.'

Less than a year later, in the reactionary Kapp putsch, Lieutenant-General von Oven refused to obey Noske's orders.

[1] See Preface.

XXIX. NORMALCY

I

Private economic power which aspires to political dominion in general, and to the changing of political frontiers in its own interest in particular, cannot tolerate political democracy. The first prerequisite for private power to maintain its dominion is to prevent political democracy where it does not exist; while its first prerequisite to obtain dominion is to destroy democracy where it does exist.

Private economic power cannot obtain or maintain dominion in the presence of trade unions. However, the mere existence of trade unions does not safeguard democracy. It is possible that the leaders of trade unions may conspire with the owners of private economic power to prevent or destroy democracy. This was what happened in Germany in 1918 and 1919. Whether or not the trade union leaders concerned did so wittingly or unwittingly is impossible to determine. It would, of course, have required great powers of prescience on their part to realize that their actions then would lead to the destruction of their organizations, and of political democracy, in 1933. But it required nothing but common sense to foresee in 1918 that democracy was doomed in Germany through, though not exclusively through, the actions of those trade union leaders.

2

Five days after the collapse of the monarchy a number of men met at the *Stahlhof* (Steel Yard), the headquarters of the German steel cartel, in Düsseldorf. They were representatives of the free (Social Democratic) trade unions; the Christian trade unions; the Hirsch-Duncker trade unions; the entrepreneurs of the coal, iron, and steel industries; the machine industries; and the electrical equipment industry.

The employers' side was dominated by Hugo Stinnes who, a few years later, became the greatest profiteer of the German inflation. The men at the *Stahlhof* concluded an agreement that became known as the 'Working Community between Employers and Employees'. It stipulated, among other things, the right of free association of the workers; the joint administration of employment exchanges; the regulation of working conditions through collective bargaining; workers' committees for all plants of fifty and more workers; the eight-hour day; and a central commission on the basis of parity to carry out the agreement.

Many Social Democrats and Communists condemned the trade union leaders later on the grounds that they had the power to demand much more than they did when they concluded the Working Community; moreover, these critics held, the trade union leaders ought not to have negotiated with the employers at all.

There was no adverse criticism on the employers' side. J. Reichert, secretary of the Association of German Iron and Steel Industrialists, made a speech in which he explained the motive of the employers in making the agreement: '...The question was, how can we save industry? How can we spare capitalism from the threatening socialization...? Unfortunately, the bourgeoisie as it is in Germany could not be relied upon in things economic-political.' Reichert was one of very few Germans who realized that the 'bourgeoisie' (i.e. the numerically preponderant lower middle class) wanted neither socialism nor militarism and expansionism, and because it did not want the last it was unreliable from the point of view of the heavy industries (the upper middle class). 'We concluded that in the midst of the general great insecurity and in view of the tottering of the power of the State and the government there were strong allies of industry only among the working class, and these allies were the trade unions....Moreover, there was a revolutionary government that consisted entirely of workers' representatives; and it was to be feared that the eight-

hour day would become law if the employers did not compromise....' Therefore, the employers conceded the eight-hour
day in private negotiations in order to prevent if from becoming
law. The inference is obvious.

The trade union leaders did not rebel at the cynicism of
Reichert's speech (which anticipated the Nazi ideology), they did
not even protest. Whatever they thought of it, they were not in a
position to object, for Reichert was careful to make his speech a
few days after the battle of the Marstall when the trade union
leaders realized as well as he in which direction the social and
economic wind was blowing in the young Republic.

3

It seemed a long time, yet it was less than two months earlier that
Paul Baecker had despaired of Germany's future. Paul Baecker
was the editor-in-chief of the *Deutsche Tageszeitung*. This central
organ of the Junkers made common cause with heavy industry up
to, but excluding, the point where heavy industry demanded
lower tariffs on imported grain; heavy industry sometimes demanded such tariffs (as it well knew without any chance of success) for the purpose of proving that it could not better the standard
of living of its workers. On 14 November 1918, Paul Baecker
wrote: 'We now have a revolutionary government whose revolutionary character is emphasized by the power of the workers' and
soldiers' councils, but we have no representation of the people,
neither of its majority nor its entirety.' Baecker's despair was not
without relief, however; Herr Stampfer published this article
implicitly denying the right of revolution (p. 99). Baecker
quickly responded: 'We are glad to see that this [Herr Stampfer's]
attitude completely agrees with what has been said here.... But the
actions of the government do not always seem to fit into that
framework.' How could a new German State be built when the
Januschauer praised Noske (p. 255) and Paul Baecker agreed with
Herr Stampfer on fundamental questions?

Two days before the Stahlhof meeting took place, a deputation had appeared in the Reich Chancellery consisting of a number of men all of whom were to take part on the employers' side in concluding the Working Community. They suggested to the government that something be done in order to assist industry in its conversion to peace-time activity. The government agreed that such assistance was necessary, and established the Reich Office for Economic Demobilization on 12 November 1918. The industrialists declared they had a man who was suitable to head this office, in fact they had brought him with them, Lieutenant-Colonel Joseph Koeth, honorary doctor of engineering, who upon the advice of Walther Rathenau had been made head of the War Raw Materials Department of the Prussian War Ministry in 1915. The Council of People's Commissars promptly appointed Koeth Reich Demobilization Commissar. He resigned on 1 April 1919, declaring that the economic demobilization was completed. In other words, it took him less than five months to eliminate that admixture of public enterprise which the war had injected into the German economy. His rapid success was due not to his being an organizing genius (which he was not) but to the fact that there was not much public enterprise to be eliminated. German heavy industry, and especially its armaments-manufacturing sector, had managed throughout the war to escape any far-reaching State intervention; or rather it had spared itself such intervention, for it ruled the State and the military dictators were its handymen.[1]

4

The mark, the German unit of currency, was divided into 100 pfennig. At the end of the war the internal value of the mark was 80 pfennig for rents, 40 pfennig for agricultural products, and 10–30 pfennig for industrial products. In other words, the prices of certain industrial products, especially munitions and farm

[1] During his short occupancy of the Reich chancellor's office in 1923, Stresemann made Koeth his minister for economic affairs.

implements, had risen up to four times as much as the prices of agricultural products. This showed the victory of financial and industrial interests over agricultural interests. Outwardly, this victory was expressed in all-comprising and rigorous controls of agricultural products and prices. The Junkers, however, who represented agricultural interests, were compensated in that these controls were laid in their hands.

While the peasants thus had to pay high prices for everything they bought and obtained low prices for everything they sold, their dissatisfaction did not turn them against industry. On the contrary, as industry was vociferously opposed to controls for itself, the peasants who were suffering from controls drew the conclusion that industry was their ally. And they pulled together with the very interests who, through their political power, had inflicted that suffering upon them. Naturally, the war-time controls of agricultural products and prices could not be abolished overnight at the end of the war. In fact, they were kept on for more than two years after Koeth declared the industrial demobilization completed. By then, of course, peasants no longer blamed the controls on the war or on the old régime, but on the new régime. This was one of the reasons why the peasants at large never became reconciled to the Republic.

The man who organized the agricultural controls during the war (very efficiently as far as they went) was a high-ranking Prussian civil servant, His Excellency Adolf von Batocki-Friebe Tortilowicz, a Junker. The leader of the Bavarian Centre Party, Schlittenbauer, said to Batocki in 1917: 'Your Excellency, if things continue as they are, if the prices of agricultural products are fixed while those of agricultural implements rise unchecked, we shall get an economic breakdown.' Batocki replied: 'We cannot prescribe prices to industry, or it will stop working.'

5

Two days after the conclusion of the Working Community, the government declared the eight-hour day law. The government persistently refused to initiate socialism; it maintained that the question of whether or not Germany was to be capitalist or socialist was to be decided by the people through the elections to the National Assembly. But while it refused to confront the National Assembly with the *fait accompli* of initial socialism it did not hesitate to confront the Assembly with the *fait accompli* of the revival of the old rule by sanctioning the Working Community, whose purpose was to establish a permanent economic and social order. This sanction naturally had to include the legalization of the eight-hour day. Thus, the eight-hour day was declared law not because the revolution demanded it but because the employers favoured it for reasons of their own—though they did not want it to become law. But this wish was impossible of fulfilment.

The workers responded to the Working Community by ousting numerous trade union functionaries everywhere in Germany, and wellnigh all of them in Berlin. Many large industrial concerns had made individual agreements with the workers' councils in their plants. When the Working Community recognized the trade unions as proper bargaining agents, the employers declared that those agreements had not been properly concluded and were therefore invalid. The trade union leaders sided with the employers in this matter, and this was the reason why the workers ousted many of them.

The executives of the trade unions then declared that the workers' and soldiers' councils were a political institution and had no right to interfere with industrial affairs. Actually, the workers' (and soldiers') councils were the source of political power, and there was nothing that anyone or anything could debar them from doing. However, the workers were handicapped by the fact that their non-union representatives were inexperienced in negotiating and that the new union functionaries were less trustworthy than the old ones who had been ousted. This was so because the new men were partly bought by the entrepreneurs and partly bribed by the promise of good positions in the trade union hierarchy and in the Social Democratic Party. Even a man like Emil Barth became a party secretary and held this post from 1921 until his death in 1930. All these happenings go a long way towards explaining the desperate mood that made the workers plunge into the adventures of January to March 1919.

Of course, it is impossible for any economy to exist if inexperienced workers' councils interfere in the plants. But it is also impossible for any social revolution to succeed if it lays the regulation of management-labour relations exclusively in the hands of groups and persons interested in maintaining the *status quo*. At this point it becomes quite clear why the Ebert government singled out the Executive Council of the Workers' and Soldiers' Councils for especially relentless persecution. The Executive Council (not the employers and the trade union leaders) would have been the proper body to regulate working conditions and economic affairs in general. And if the Executive Council was incompetent, it would have been the duty of the government to assist it by its counsel. The Executive Council was indeed highly incompetent, but part of its incompetency was relative. Even the best of bodies of this kind would not have been able to stand up against the leadership of a huge party and a huge trade union organization which pretended to act in the interests of the workers and the revolution; especially as the joint opposition of this team was crowned by a campaign of slander that had an effect commensurate to the millions in money which were poured into it by non-socialist parties, the non-socialist Press, and innumerable organizations and individuals. As a result, the Executive Council appeared to be a gang of hoodlums even to many workers.

6

On 21 November 1918, the government found it seasonable to appoint a commission of experts on questions of socialization. It meant to show the workers that everything was being prepared in case the elections to the National Assembly brought a majority for socialism. The Commission consisted of a number of university professors of economics, all of them Social Democrats and Independents, and of Walther Rathenau.[1]

Deutsche Tageszeitung, the organ of the Junkers, wrote: 'We warn the government...not to proceed on this path, which must lead to disaster....The entire German bourgeoisie must close its ranks with all its might against a policy that eventually must destroy the basis of co-operation between the bourgeoisie and the present régime.' This threat sounded so terrible to *Vorwärts* that it wrote: 'It is the task of the socialization commission to allay fears of unreasonable experiments....Any nationalization and socialization presupposes a *constituted State*, a constituted society, a constituted nation, such as does not exist here at this moment.' Instead of despairing at reading this nonsense (which incidentally implied that the Ebert government was based on nothing but the right of revolution) the old ruling classes took heart from it. The *Nationalzeitung* wrote: 'The gravest troubles of the stock exchange, namely the danger of bolshevism as well as the general socialization of industry, may today be regarded as *completely overcome....* The Berlin stock exchange, which has been truly haunted by spectres has every reason to heave a sigh of relief.' Written on 5 December 1918, this almost reads as if the *Nationalzeitung* knew what would happen the next day, namely the putsch of 6 December, the dawn of reaction.

[1] Rathenau, a multi-millionaire in his own right as well as by inheritance, was a strange mixture of hard-headed businessman and social dreamer. Politically he was a radical Liberal. As Reich Foreign Minister he concluded the German-Soviet treaty at Rapallo in April 1921 against the protests of France and Great Britain. Three months later he was murdered by two young men who committed suicide when trapped. They were pronounced national heroes by the Nazis.

The great strike movement in the Rhineland in March 1919 caused the government to put a socialization bill before the National Assembly (p. 240). The Social Democratic minister of economics, Wissell, presented this bill with a stirring speech: '...There are no dams and dikes that could resist the idea of socialism....The working people want to see deeds now, and everywhere they are proceeding to act for themselves....' The non-socialist majority of the Assembly tried to bury the bill in a committee of the House because it was presented under 'pressure from the street'. They well knew that nothing would ever come of it, but they were not even prepared to make the gesture of discussing it. However, their courage deserted them in view of the violent fighting that was going on in the Rhineland, Central Germany, and Berlin. The bill became law against the votes of the German Nationals (p. 145).

Shortly after, the Socialization Commission resigned. It declared that collaboration with Reich Economics Minister Wissell was impossible; the Commission had tendered him a report on the socialization of coal-mining but the report had been withheld from the National Assembly and the public after the vague government bill was hurried through.

A few days later, the German Manufacturers' Association was founded, a body of such asocial tendencies that the Empire would not have tolerated it. Reichert became its director.

7

This happened in March and April 1919. Some weeks earlier, in the middle of February, heavy industry had felt strong enough to press for the appointment of Hugo Stinnes as an expert of the German armistice commission; they scented enormous profits through reparations. Without asking Erzberger, the head of that commission, the government sent Stinnes to Spa, the place of the armistice negotiations. Erzberger demanded his immediate recall 'because I cannot offer our enemies as an expert a gentleman who participated prominently in the exploitation of Belgium and was the main moving force behind the deportation of the Belgian unemployed'. Erzberger succeeded, for the moment. But Stresemann's German People's Party moved in the National Assembly that the armistice commission be made a branch of the Foreign Office (until then, it had been directly responsible to the government without the Foreign Minister as intermediary). This disposed of Erzberger who was not a member of the Foreign Office. At the same time, the Association of German Steel Manufacturers declared that they would not provide any expert at all if Stinnes were rejected. The gentlemen had their way.

Versailles drew near. The government of Scheidemann resigned because he would not sign the treaty. He exclaimed in the National Assembly: 'What hand were not bound to wither which put itself and us in such chains?' 'Corpse-Müller' (p. 157) found a counterpart in 'The Man with the Withered Hand'. But the treaty was signed. Naturally, the question whether to sign or not gave rise to vehement controversies. Wagnerian and Hitlerian trends of thought manifested themselves in the minds of the most respectable of Germans. Count Bernstorff said: 'Looking back it must be admitted that a rejection of the Treaty would only have been possible if the German nation from the Adige to the Belt had been at one in the resolve to dedicate itself, if need were, to destruction....But so heroic a mood did not prevail.' And Bernstorff's friend, the then German Foreign Minister, Count von Brockdorff-Rantzau, drafted a speech he intended to deliver in the National Assembly when he still hoped that the Assembly would reject the Treaty. This draft speech concluded as follows: 'The decision I expect from you is the relentless declaration of struggle against the capitalism and imperialism that is expressed in the draft treaty of Versailles.'

An unpleasant incident had occurred a week earlier; the German fleet was scuttled at Scapa Flow. It had steamed across the North Sea, to its place of internment, under the command of Admiral von Reuter, its officers controlled by sailors' councils. When the first detachment arrived at Scapa Flow on 16 November 1918, a German admiral, Meurer, went on board the British flagship, *Queen Elizabeth*, to report surrender to Admiral Beatty. Meurer was accompanied by representatives of the sailors' councils. Beatty refused to talk to the councils, and assisted the German officers in sending them home. By and by nearly all the German sailors were sent home. Only officers and skeleton and crews of picked men were left in the end. The last transport of men who might have sabotaged the intended scuttling departed on 17 June 1919, after the Treaty conditions had become known to Admiral Reuter.

A few weeks after Admiral Beatty had refused to recognize the German sailors' councils, Erzberger inquired whether the Entente armistice commission would recognize soldiers' councils in the German commission; the soldiers' councils were demanding a voice in the negotiations. Marshal Foch and Admiral Wemyss replied that they would not recognize them. Their reason was that the armistice negotiations were a military matter, and they regarded the soldiers' councils as a political institution; in any case, they would deal only with persons who had been properly accredited at the beginning of the negotiations. The latter part, in itself absurd, looked as if it had been added on second thought when it occurred to them that Erzberger, too, was a political institution.

Vorwärts promptly wrote in bold type: '*Temps* reports that the Allies have prepared a note to Germany demanding an immediate dissolution of all workers' and soldiers' councils. The note...sets a time limit of four weeks in which to reinstate the legitimate authorities, failing which the Allies themselves will take in hand the fight against Bolshevism in Germany.' In other words, the workers' and soldiers' councils were Bolshevist, but the National Assembly and the Council of People's Commissars, both of whom had accepted their mandate from these councils, were not Bolshevist. And who were the 'legitimate authorities' if the Assembly and the Council were not legitimate? The Zürich correspondent of the Liberal *Frankfurter Zeitung* wrote: 'I have... re-read *Temps* for the whole of last week and not been able to discover that information.'

Erzberger's question was not repeated. Germany got rid of her workers' and soldiers' councils quickly and without the foreign intervention for which *Vorwärts* was longing. French and British generals and admirals, statesmen and politicians were no longer expected to negotiate with would-be and actual upstart Germans. Those of these upstarts who rose to power in the Revolution crushed those who attempted to rise to power. Then they effaced themselves and relinquished their places to respectable Germans such as Hindenburg and Papen, Goebbels, Ribbentrop, and Hitler. The *Götterdämmerung* of which Count Bernstorff and Count Brockdorff had been dreaming began to stalk about in heavy boots. And soon the German return to normalcy was complete, the return to *this* German normalcy of an almost unbridled economic liberalism in which iron and dyestuff merchants owned the State and their *Landsknechts* sang, 'Today Germany— Tomorrow the World.'

BIBLIOGRAPHY

'A'. *Eberts Prozess*. Berlin, 1925.

ALTROCK, W. F. K. VON. *Deutschlands Niederbruch*. Berlin, 1919.

ARTELT, KARL. See Popp.

BARTH, EMIL. *Aus der Werkstatt der deutschen Revolution*. Berlin, 1919.

BATOCKI, A. VON. *Schluss mit der Kriegszwangswirtschaft*. Berlin, 1921.

BAUER, MAX. *Der Grosse Krieg in Feld und Heimat*. Tübingen, 1921.

BECKMANN, EWALD. *Der Dolchstossprozess in München*. München, 1925.

BELOW, GEORG VON. *Die Deutschnationale Volkspartei (in Handbuch der Politik)*. Berlin, 1921.

BERGSTRÄSSER, L. *Geschichte der politischen Parteien in Deutschland*. München, 1952.

BERNSTEIN, EDUARD. *Die deutsche Revolution*. Berlin, 1921.

BERNSTORFF, GRAF JOHANN HEINRICH. *Deutschland und Amerika*. Berlin, 1920.

—— *Erinnerungen und Briefe*. Zürich, 1936.

BETHMANN HOLLWEG, TH. VON. *Betrachtungen zum Weltkriege*. (2 vols.) Berlin, 1919.

BRAUN, OTTO. *Deutscher Einheitsstaat oder Föderativsystem?* Berlin, 1927.

—— *Von Weimar zu Hitler*. New York, 1940.

BRECHT, ARNOLD. *Federalism and Regionalism in Germany*. New York, 1945.

BREITHAUPT, WOLFGANG. *Volksvergiftung 1914–1918*. Berlin, 1925.

CRASEMANN, FERDINAND. *Freikorps Maercker*. Hamburg, 1920.

DAVID, EDUARD. *Die Sozialdemokratie im Weltkrieg*. Berlin, 1915.

Deutsche Wirtschaftskunde. Bearbeitet im Statistischen Reichsamt. Berlin, 1930.

DIETZ, OTTO. *Der Todesgang der deutschen Armee*. Berlin, 1919.

DITTMANN, WILHELM. *Die Unabhängige Sozialdemokratische Partei Deutschlands (in Handbuch der Politik)*. Berlin, 1921.

DOMBROWSKI, E. F. O. *Das alte und das neue System*. Berlin, 1919.

DRAHN, ERNST and LEONHARD, SUSANNE. *Unterirdische Literatur im revolutionären Deutschland während des Weltkrieges*. Berlin, 1920.

EBERT, FRIEDRICH. *Schriften, Aufzeichnungen, Reden*. (2 vols.) Dresden, 1926.

—— *Kämpfe und Ziele*. Dresden, 1929.

EHRHARDT, HERMANN. *Kapitän Ehrhardts Abenteuer und Schicksale* (ed. F. Freksa). Berlin, 1924.

EISNER, KURT. *Treibende Kräfte*. Berlin, 1915.

—— *Schuld und Sühne*. Berlin, 1919.

ENDRES, FRANZ KARL. *Die Tragödie Deutschlands*. Stuttgart, 1929.

—— *Soziologische Struktur...des deutschen Offizierskorps vor dem Weltkriege* (in *Archiv für Sozialwissenschaft und Sozialpolitik*, 1927).

Bibliography

ERZBERGER, MATTHIAS. *Erlebnisse im Weltkrieg.* Stuttgart, 1920.

FALKENHAYN, ERICH VON. *Die Oberste Heeresleitung 1914–1916.* Berlin, 1920.

FELDEN, EMIL. *Eines Menschen Weg.* Bremen, 1927.

FISCHER, ANTON. *Die Revolutions-Kommandantur Berlin.* (Printed as manuscript, n.d.)

FOERSTER, F. W. *Mein Kampf gegen das militaristische und nationalistische Deutschland.* Stuttgart, 1920.

FORSTHOFF, ERNST. *Deutsche Geschichte von 1918 bis 1938 in Dokumenten.* Stuttgart, 1943.

Gebhardts Handbuch der Deutschen Geschichte. Edition of 1930. *Nachgedruckt auf Veranlassung der Kriegsgefangenenhilfe des Weltkomitees der Christlichen Vereine Junger Männer, Genf, Schweiz.* Photolithographed and printed in the United States of America.

GENGLER, L. F. *Die deutschen Monarchisten 1919–1925.* (Thesis.) Kulmbach, 1932.

GIESE, F. *Die Verfassung des Deutschen Reiches.* Berlin, 1931.

GOETZ, WALTER. *Die Deutsche Demokratische Partei* (in *Handbuch der Politik*). Berlin, 1921.

GOLTZ, GRAF RÜDIGER VON DER. *Meine Sendung in Finnland und im Baltikum.* Leipzig, 1920.

GROENER, WILHELM. *Der Weltkrieg und seine Probleme.* Berlin, 1920.

GRZESINSKI, ALBERT C. *Inside Germany.* New York, 1939.

HAASE, ERNST. *Hugo Haase. Sein Leben und Wirken.* Berlin, 1929.

HAASE, HUGO. *Reichstagsreden gegen die deutsche Kriegspolitik.* Berlin, 1919.

HAMMANN, OTTO. *Bilder aus der letzten Kaiserzeit.* Berlin, 1922.

HARDEN, MAXIMILIAN. *Köpfe.* (4 vols.) Berlin, 1910–24.

HAUSSMANN, CONRAD. *Schlaglichter.* Frankfurt a.M., 1924.

HELFFERICH, KARL. *Der Weltkrieg.* (3 vols.) Berlin, 1919.

HERTLING, KARL GRAF VON. *Ein Jahr in der Reichskanzlei.* Freiburg i.B., 1919.

HERZ, LUDWIG. *Die Abdankung.* Leipzig, 1924.

HILFERDING, RUDOLF. *Revolutionäre Politik oder Machtillusionen?* Berlin, 1920.

HINDENBURG, PAUL VON. *Aus meinem Leben.* Leipzig, 1920.

HINTZE, PAUL VON. *Aufzeichnungen* (in Niemann, *Revolution von Oben*, q.v.).

HIRSCH, PAUL. *Gemeindeverfassung* (in Thimme and Legien, *Die Arbeiterschaft* etc., q.v.).

—— *Die Mehrheitssozialisten* (in *Handbuch der Politik*). Berlin, 1921.

HOFFMANN, ADOLPH. *Die zehn Gebote und die besitzende Klasse.* Berlin (n.d.).

HOFFMANN, MAX. *Der Krieg der versäumten Gelegenheiten.* München, 1923.

HOHLFELD, JOHANNES. *Deutsche Reichsgeschichte in Dokumenten 1849–1926.* (2 vols.) Berlin, 1927.

HORKENBACH, CUNO. *Das Deutsche Reich von 1918 bis heute.* (4 vols.) Berlin, 1930–33.

Bibliography

HUGENBERG, A. *Streiflichter aus Vergangenheit und Gegenwart.* Berlin, 1927.

HUGO, OTTO. *Die Deutsche Volkspartei* (in *Handbuch der Politik*). Berlin, 1921.

JAFFÉ, EDGAR. *Die Vertretung der Arbeiterinteressen im neuen Deutschland* (in Thimme and Legien: *Die Arbeiterschaft* etc., q.v.).

KUHL, H. VON. *Der deutsche Generalstab in Vorbereitung und Durchführung des Weltkrieges.* Berlin, 1920.

KUTTNER, ERICH. *Die deutsche Revolution.* Berlin, 1918.

—— *Der Sieg war zum Greifen nahe!* Berlin, 1924.

LEDEBOUR, GEORG. *Der Ledebour Prozess.* Berlin, 1919.

LEGIEN, KARL. *Die deutsche Gewerkschaftsbewegung.* Berlin, 1911.

—— *Die Gewerkschaften* (in Thimme and Legien: *Die Arbeiterschaft* etc., q.v.).

LEWINSOHN, LUDWIG. *Die Revolution an der Westfront.* Berlin (n.d.).

LIEBKNECHT, KARL. *Militarismus und Antimilitarismus.* Zürich, 1911.

LUDENDORFF, ERICH. *Entgegnung auf das amtliche Weissbuch: 'Vorgeschichte des Waffenstillstandes.'* Berlin, 1919.

—— *Meine Kriegserinnerungen.* Berlin, 1920.

—— *Urkunden der Obersten Heeresleitung.* Berlin, 1920.

—— *Kriegführung und Politik.* Berlin, 1922.

LUTZ, RALPH HASWELL (ed.). *Documents of the German Revolution.* Stanford, Cal., 1932.

LUXEMBURG, ROSA. *Gegen den Reformismus.* Berlin, 1925.

—— *Gewerkschaftskampf und Massenstreik.* Berlin, 1928.

MAERCKER, L. R. G. *Vom Kaiserheer zur Reichswehr.* Leipzig, 1921.

MARSCHALL, FREIHERR. See Schulenburg.

MATTES, WILHELM. *Die bayerischen Bauernräte.* Sutttgart, 1921.

MAX, PRINZ VON BADEN. *Erinnerungen und Dokumente.* Berlin, 1927.

MEHRING, FRANZ. *Geschichte der deutschen Sozialdemokratie.* (5 vols.) Stuttgart, 1913.

MEINSHAUSEN, HANS. *Die Befugnisse des Kaisers in der Deutschen Reichsverfassung von 1871.* (Thesis.) Greifswald, 1911.

MICHAELIS, GEORG. *Für Staat und Volk.* Berlin, 1922.

MÜLLER, RICHARD. *Vom Kaiserreich zur Republik.* Wien, 1924.

—— *Die November-Revolution.* Wien, 1925.

—— *Der Bürgerkrieg in Deutschland.* Berlin, 1925.

MÜLLER-FRANKEN, HERMANN. *Die November-Revolution.* Berlin, 1928.

NAUMANN, VICTOR. *Profile.* München, 1925.

—— *Dokumente und Argumente.* Berlin, 1928.

NEU, HEINRICH. *Die Revolutionäre Bewegung auf der deutschen Flotte 1917-1918.* (Thesis.) Stuttgart, 1930.

NICOLAI, W. *Nachrichtendienst, Presse und Volksstimmung im Weltkrieg.* Berlin, 1920.

Bibliography

NIEMANN, ALFRED. *Kaiser und Revolution*. Berlin, 1922.
—— *Die Entthronung Kaiser Wilhelms II*. Leipzig, 1924.
—— *Wanderungen mit Kaiser Wilhelm II*. Leipzig, 1924.
—— *Revolution von Oben—Umsturz von Unten*. Berlin, 1927.
—— *Kaiser und Heer*. Berlin, 1929.
—— *Der Weg Kaiser Wilhelms II*. Stuttgart, 1932.
NOSKE, GUSTAV. *Der Krieg und die Sozialdemokratie* (in Thimme and Legien: *Die Arbeiterschaft* etc., q.v.).
—— *Von Kiel bis Kapp*. Berlin, 1920.
OLDEN, RUDOLF. *Stresemann*. Berlin, 1929.
OTTO, RUDOLF. *Die Organisation des Heeres in der Uebergangszeit*. (Thesis.) Greifswald, 1921.
PANNIER, KARL. *Die Verfassung des Deutschen Reichs (1871)*. Leipzig (n.d.).
PAYER, FRIEDRICH. *Von Bethmann-Hollweg bis Ebert*. Frankfurt a.M., 1923.
PFEIFFER, MAXIMILIAN. *Die Zentrumspartei* (in *Handbuch der Politik*). Berlin, 1921.
PLESSEN, H. G. H. VON. *Die Abdankung des Kaisers* (in Niemann: *Revolution von Oben*, q.v.).
POPP, LOTHAR and ARTELT, KARL. *Ursprung und Entwicklung der November Revolution 1918*. Kiel (n.d.).
RADEK, KARL. *Der deutsche Imperialismus und die Arbeiterklasse*. Bremen, 1912.
—— *Die deutsche Revolution*. Moskau, 1918.
—— *Rosa Luxemburg, Karl Liebknecht, Leo Jogiches*. Hamburg, 1921.
RATHENAU, WALTHER. *Autonome Wirtschaft*. Jena, 1919.
—— *Die neue Wirtschaft*. Berlin, 1921.
RHEINBABEN, ROCHUS VON. *Stresemann*. Dresden, 1928.
ROSENBERG, ARTHUR. *Die Entstehung der deutschen Republik*. Berlin, 1928.
RUDIN, HARRY R. *Armistice 1918*. New Haven, 1944.
RUNKEL, FERDINAND. *Die deutsche Revolution*. Leipzig, 1919.
RUPPRECHT, KRONPRINZ VON BAYERN. *Mein Kriegstagebuch*. (3 vols.) München (n.d.).
SCHÄFER, HEINRICH. *Tagebuchblätter eines rheinischen Sozialisten*. Bonn, 1919.
SCHEER, REINHARD. *Deutschlands Hochseeflotte im Weltkrieg*. Berlin, 1920.
—— *Vom Segelschiff zum U-Boot*. Leipzig, 1925.
SCHEIDEMANN, PHILIPP. *Zur Neuorientierung der inneren Politik* (in Thimme and Legien: *Die Arbeiterschaft* etc. q.v.).
—— *Der Zusammenbruch*. Berlin, 1921.
—— *Memoiren eines Sozialdemokraten*. Dresden, 1928.
SCHULENBURG, GRAF FRIEDRICH VON DER. *Denkschrift vom 7. Dezember 1918*.
——*Denkschrift vom 26. August 1919*.

Bibliography

SCHULENBURG, GRAF FRIEDRICH VON DER. *Die Abdankung Seiner Majestät des Kaisers und Königs. Gemeinsame Denkschrift der Generale von Plessen, Freiherr Marschall und Graf von der Schulenburg vom 6. April 1919.* (All three items listed here under Schulenburg, in Niemann, *Revolution von Oben,* q.v.)

SEVERING, CARL. *1919–20 im Wetter- und Watterwinkel.* Bielefeld, 1927.

STAMPFER, FRIEDRICH. *Sozialdemokratie und Kriegskredite.* Berlin, 1915.

—— *Die vierzehn Jahre der ersten deutschen Republik.* Karlsbad, 1936.

STRÖBEL, HEINRICH. *Die Kriegsschuld der Rechtssozialisten.* Berlin, 1919.

—— *Die deutsche Revolution.* Berlin, 1922.

THIMME, FRIEDRICH and LEGIEN, KARL (edd.). *Die Arbeiterschaft im neuen Deutschland.* Leipzig, 1915.

THIMME, HANS. *Weltkrieg ohne Waffen.* Stuttgart, 1932.

Time. Weekly Newsmagazine. 'West Germany: Higher Education.' 12 April 1954.

TIRPITZ, ALFRED VON. *Erinnerungen.* Leipzig, 1919.

TOLLER, ERNST. *Eine Jugend in Deutschland.* Amsterdam, 1933.

TROELTSCH, ERNST. *Spektator-Briefe.* Tübingen, 1924.

Ursachen, . . .des deutschen Zusammenbruchs im Jahre 1918. Das Werk des Unter-suchungsausschusses der Verfassunggebenden Deutschen Nationalversammlung und des Deutschen Reichstages 1918–1928. (12 vols.) Berlin, 1928.

VALENTINI, RUDOLF VON. *Kaiser und Kabinettschef.* Oldenburg i.O., 1931.

VALLENTIN-LUCHAIRE, ANTONINA. *Stresemann.* Leipzig, 1930.

VOLKMANN, ERICH OTTO. *Der Marxismus und das deutsche Heer im Weltkriege.* Berlin, 1925.

—— *Revolution über Deutschland.* Oldenburg i.O., 1930.

VOLLRATH, WILHELM OTTO. *Der parlamentarische Kampf um das preussische Dreiklassenwahlrecht.* (Thesis.) Leipzig, 1931.

WAHNSCHAFFE, ARNOLD. *Der letzte Akt der Kaisetragödie* (in Niemann, *Revolution von Oben,* q.v.).

WERMUTH, ARNOLD. *Ein Beamtenleben.* Berlin, 1922.

WESTARP, GRAF K. F. V. VON. *Konservative Politik.* (2 vols.) Berlin, 1933.

WETTERLÉ, ABBÉ E. *Behind the Scenes in the Reichstag.* New York, 1918.

WILHELM (KAISER). *Ereignisse und Gestalten.* Berlin, 1922.

WILHELM (CROWN PRINCE). *Meine Erinnerungen aus Deutschlands Heldenkampf.* Berlin, 1923.

WINNIG, AUGUST. *Der Krieg und die Arbeiter-Internationale* (in Thimme and Legien, *Die Arbeiterschaft* etc., q.v.).

—— *Die deutschen Gewerkschaften im Kriege.* Stuttgart, 1917.

—— *Am Ausgang der deutschen Ostpolitik.* Berlin, 1921.

—— *Das Reich als Republik.* Stuttgart, 1930.

WRISBERG, ERNST VON. *Heer und Heimat 1914–1918.* Leipzig, 1921.

INDEX

Adalbert, Prince, son of Kaiser, 14
Alexander of Hohenlohe, Prince (pacifist), 6
Arco-Valley, Count, assassin of Eisner, 257
Armistice: demanded by Ludendorff, 2; negotiations, 86; and new German government, 99; and food supplies for Germany, 128; Article XII, 137
Arms, private, surrender of, 171, 199, 233
Artelt, Karl (sailor), 68
Auer (politician), 257
Axelrod (Communist): and putsch in Bavaria, 263; goes to prison, 267

Baecker, Paul (journalist), 272
Ballin, Albert (shipping magnate), 79
Barth, Emil (trade unionist and politician): becomes chairman of Revolutionary Stewards, 64; organizes shock troops, 66; demands action on November 4, 71; advances date of action, 73; on 9 November, 73; becomes People's Commissar, 92; at Busch meeting, 97; character, 126; says Groener must go, 137; prevents arrest of Executive Council, 151; learns of Lequis, 170; explodes at Groener, 174; accuses Ebert of treachery, 181; resigns as People's Commissar, 188; becomes party secretary, 276
Batocki, Adolf (civil servant), 274
Bauer, Gustav (politician), 28
Baumeister (manager), 214
Bavaria: separatism flares up, 9; and separate peace, 10; breaks off relations with Reich, 131. See also Eisner
Beatty, Admiral, 280
Bebel, August (politician and author): founds workers' party, 18; ideas on general strike, 20; grows eccentric, 23
Berg, Baron von (Chief of Kaiser's Privy Council), 6

Berger (artist), 265
Berlin, 14
Bernstein, Eduard (politician and author): develops Reformist idea, 20; leader of opportunist wing, 21
Bernstorff, Johann Heinrich, Count of (diplomat): conversation with Scheidemann, 25; impressed by soviet telegram, 133 n.; dedication to destruction, 279
Bismarck, Prince Otto von (Reich Chancellor), 3
Bongard (civil servant): taken hostage, 180; released, 185
Braun, Otto (politician), 76
Brecht, Arnold (under-secretary), 151
Breithaupt, Wolfgang (deserter and traitor), 66. See also Union of Deserters
Breitscheid, Rudolf (politician), mediates in January, 207
Brockdorff-Rantzau, Ulrich, Count of (diplomat): and plea to make Wilson strong, 9; looks toward Russia, 260 n.; and struggle against capitalism, 279
Bussche, von dem, Major, 7

Capelle, Eduard von, Admiral, 67 n.
Centre Party: disagreeable past, 111; attitude toward centralization, 123; continues unchanged, 146
Central Council of the Navy, 177
Central Council of Workers' and Soldiers' Councils: elected, 173; accepts Hamburg Points, 174; insists on Hamburg Points, 188
Centralization: explained, 119; opposed by Junkers, 120; Pan-Germanism a substitute, 122; at Reich Congress, 125
Cohn, Adolf (trade unionist), 55
Cohn, Oskar (politician), 207
Commission of Nine formed, 236; Social Democrats resign, 238; and workers' demands, 243

287

Index

Communist Party of Germany, *see* Spartacus League

Constituent Assembly, *see* National Assembly

Constitution, Imperial: and war and peace, 1; changed, 8

Cossmann, Paul Nikolaus (publisher and publicist), 80

Council of People's Commissars: formed, 92; usurps legislative power, 103; agreement with Executive Council, 112; protests interference, 156; obtains legislative power, 167

Crasemann, Captain, 250

Däumig, Ernst (politician): represents Revolutionary Stewards, 51; arrested, 73; moves formation of central council, 111; moves formation of red guard, 114; warns against premature action, 204

David, Eduard (politician and theorist), 28

Dittmann, Wilhelm Karl (politician): joins action committee, 62; arrested and sentenced, 63; becomes People's Commissar, 92; resigns as People's Commissar, 188; mediates in January, 207

Dorrenbach, Lieutenant (navy): takes keys to Barth, 179; makes hysterical speech, 204; murdered, 249

Doyé (civil servant), 200

Ebert, Friedrich (politician and Reich President): chairman of Social Democratic *Fraktion*, 17; second in command of Reformists, 21; becomes leader of Majority Party, 26; becomes Chancellor, 26; on annexations, 28; swings Party to Prince Max, 29; disappoints Prince Max, 30; on Scheidemann's ultimatum, 33; first *tête-à-tête* with Prince Max, 33; refuses to withdraw ultimatum, 34; second *tête-à-tête* with Prince Max, 38; prepared to wreck his party, 41; takes office as Chancellor, 42; hedges about regency, 43; last *tête-à-tête* with Prince Max, 45; joins action committee, 62; and Magde-

burg Trial, 64; warns Wahnschaffe about riots, 71; becomes leader of revolution, 73; prepared to include Independents, 88; right of revolution, 89; becomes People's Commissar, 92; pact with Groener, 93; at Busch meeting, 97; chooses road back, 104; becomes dictator, 106; persuades Free States in favour of Constituent Assembly, 125; denies cable to U.S.A., 129; perturbed by Hamburg Points, 167; misgivings about Haeften Plan, 169; afraid of Barth, 171; pleads with Groener, 172; unable to resist military, 172; yields unreservedly to generals, 179; conversation with Radtke, 182; double game with loyalty, 224; elected President, 239

Economic demobilization, 273

Eglhofer (sailor): leader in mutiny, 67; dictator of Bavaria, 264; killed, 266

Ehrhardt, Captain (navy), 267

Eichhorn (politician): becomes police president, 197; character, 198; deposed by Prussian government, 200; refuses to surrender office, 203; dismissed by Central Council, 207; prominent in Brunswick, 254. *See also* Republican Security Wehr

Eight-hour day, 275

Eisner, Kurt (politician): attacks Solf and Erzberger, 131; tries to prove Germany's guilt, 132; Prime Minister of Bavaria, 256; assassinated, 257. *See also* Bavaria

Elections, general, 161

Epp, Ritter von, General: arrested, 257; commander-in-exile, 259

Erfurt programme: adopted in 1891, 18; interpretation of, 19

Ernst, Eugen (politician): attempts to become police president, 198; second attempt, 202

Erzberger, Matthias (politician): joins cabinet of Prince Max, 29; head of Armistice delegation, 86; makes Centre Party progressive, 111; favours centralization, 124; attacked by Eisner, 131; opposes Foreign Office, 138; establishes Reich income

288

Index

Index

Index

Index

Noske, Gustav (politician): goes to Kiel, 86; becomes People's Commissar, 189; opinion of Fischer, 202; appointed commander-in-chief, 206; success against revolutionaries, 214; called 'saviour of Berlin', 215; career, 225; ambiguous position in Kapp Putsch, 226; puts troops under Imperial officers, 232; issues rules concerning power of command, 234; bribes councils, 235; order to shoot revolutionaries, 246; and Press distortion, 251; feud with Brunswick, 253; congratulations to Oven, 269

Oberndorff, Count (diplomat), 127
Oerter, Sepp (politician), 253
Oldenburg-Januschau, Baron (Junker), 255
Oven, von, General: descends on Munich, 264; disobeys Noske, 269

Pabst, Captain: in command of Lequis's soldiers, 170; revolted by bloodshed, 181; connexion with murder of Liebknecht and Luxemburg, 229
Paderewski, Ignacius (pianist and President), 140
Pan-Germanism, 122
Papen, Baron (politician), 147
Particularism, 119
Patriotic Auxiliary Service, 57
Payer, Friedrich von (politician): suggests appointment of Prince Max, 6; Vice-Chancellor under Prince Max, 29; becomes leader of Progressive Liberals, 111
Peasants' Councils, 261
People's Marine Division, see Sailors
People's Wehr, 178
Pflugk-Hartung, von, Captain (navy), 230
Pieck, Wilhelm (Communist): member of Revolution Committee, 204; withdrawn by his party from Revolution Committee, 213
Poland: presents ultimatum to Germany, 137; fighting in Posen, 141
Progressive People's Party, becomes German Democratic Party, 143

Prussia: dominates Federal Council, 108; maintains three-class suffrage, 120

Radek, Karl (Russian revolutionary), 134
Radtke (sailor), 182
Rathenau, Walther (industrialist and author): recommends Koeth for office, 273; murdered, 277n.
Reformism, 20, 21
Reichert, J. (industrialist), 271
Reichpietsch (sailor), 67
Reichstag: government responsibility towards, 3; composition during war, 17; dissolved, 130
Reichswehr, 233
Reinhard, Colonel: attempts to become commandant of Berlin, 186; claims to be 'saviour of Berlin', 215; liquidates sailors, 248
Reinhardt, Colonel, 206
Republican Security Wehr: threatens to kill Wels, 183; insubordination, 199
Republican Soldiers' Wehr: organized by Wels, 152; unreliability, 199; last, appearance 247
Reuter, von, Admiral, 280
Revolutionary Stewards: connexion with Independents, 57; call April 1917 strike, 58; differ with Spartacists on tactics, 60; call January 1918 strike, 61; organization shattered, 64; character of membership, 68; reduced to insignificance, 91; revive from slump, 191; protest against Eichhorn's dismissal, 200
Rheinbaben, Rochus von (politician), 154
Roeder, von, Major, 32
Roehrig (civil servant), 236
Rosner, Karl (novelist), 80
Ross, Colin (author and spy): as soldiers' agitator, 114; ousted from Executive Council, 116; connected with putsch by Students' Guard, 155
Rühle, Otto (politician): votes against war credits, 47; advocates putschism, 191

292

Index

Runge (soldier), 230

Rupprecht, Crown Prince of Bavaria: flight, 13; on particularism, 118

Russia: first revolution, 57; despises Germans, 134

Sack, Alfons (lawyer), 154

Sailors: spread revolution, 86; move into Marstall, 175; receive reinforcements from Cuxhaven, 176; have pay stopped, 177; reach agreement with Prussia, 179; disbandment demanded by Hindenburg, 182; release Wels, 183; battle of the Marstall, 184; liquidation, 248-9

Schaefer, Heinrich (politician): helps Wels, 15; member of Executive Council, 98

Scheidemann, Philipp (politician): becomes leader of 'opportunists', 21; becomes deputy speaker of Reichstag, 23; apparent timidity towards governing, 25; on annexations, 28; becomes Imperial Secretary of State, 29; republican leanings, 30; fear of bolshevism, 31; suggests ultimatum to Prince Max, 32; pleads with Prince Max, 34; *Finis ultimati*, 35; resigns as Secretary of State, 38; Prince Max ignores resignation, 39; ignores his own resignation, 42; proclaims republic, 45; joins action committee, 62; becomes People's Commissar, 92; disparages masses, 93-4; misjudges councils, 95; advocates use of arms, 206-7; becomes Minister President, 239; resigns from office, 279

Scheüch, von, General: War Minister, 9-10; declares revolution irresistible, 36; reports troops will not fire on mob, 42; remains War Minister, 150; disclaims order to fire on Spartacists, 154; rejects Haeften Plan, 171; and rescue of Wels, 186

Schiffer, Eugen (politician), 116

Schleicher, von, Major, 173

Schleusinger (student), 267

Schlittenbauer (politician), 274

Schneppenhorst (politician), 261

Scholze (politician), 205

Schulenburg, Count Friedrich, General, 79

Separatism: Bavaria, 10; explained, 119

Severing, Karl (politician), 243

Simons, Walter (jurist), 155

Spiero (soldiers' representative), 150

Skoropadski (hetman), 14

Social Democratic Party of Germany: largest party in Reichstag, 17; divided into three wings, 21; becomes known as Majority Party, 26; joins government, 28; resolves to prevent revolution, 37; demands Chancellorship, 39; condemn power as undemocratic, 40; struggle against dissenters, 47-8; achieves compromise with Independents, 91; favours councils, 95; sees necessity to dominate councils, 96; favours centralization, 122; gives up centralization, 123; refusal to take hostages, 210; forbids members to join *Reichswehr*, 233

Socialization: debate in National Assembly, 240; danger overcome, 277

Solf, Wilhelm (diplomat): questions Ebert on his intentions, 42; attacked by Eisner, 131; forced to resign, 133

Spartacus League: connexion with Independents, 51; constituted, 53; fails to make headway, 54; differs from Revolutionary Stewards on tactics, 60; procession attacked, 151; issues ultimatum to Independents, 190; becomes Communist Party of Germany, 191; putschists gain upper hand, 191; revises programme, 193; protests against Eichhorn's dismissal, 200; withdraws from Revolution Committee, 213; refuses to join strike committee, 242; makes fantastic claims about role in 1919 upheaval, 244

Spartacus Letters, 52

Stab-in-the-back legend: prepared by Groener, 75; fostered by Cossmann, 80

Stampfer, Friedrich (journalist): on people and power, 99; praised by Baecker, 272

Stephani, von, Major, 213

293

Index

Stinnes, Hugo (industrialist): holds conversations with French, 251–2; dominates employers, 271; appointment to armistice commission sought by industrialists, 278

Stresemann, Gustav (politician): rejected by Prince Max, 27; becomes leader of German People's Party, 143

Stumm, Wilhelm von (diplomat), 155

Three-class suffrage, *see* Prussia

Thule Society, 262

Toller, Ernst (poet): becomes Soviet-Bavarian minister, 260; forms new government, 264; goes to prison, 267

Thyssen, August (industrialist), 252

Tost (worker), 175

Tyszka, Hasso von (informer), 211

Unification, 119

Union of Deserters, 192

Valentini, Rudolf von (chief of Kaiser's Privy Council): considers Hertling government unlikely to last, 4; replaced, 6

Vanselow, Captain (navy), 127

Vitschorek (sailor), 175

Vogel, Lieutenant, 230

Vögler, Albert (industrialist), 236

Vogtherr (deputy), 67

Vorwärts: has anti-war editorial staff, 48; suppressed, 49; resumes publication, 49; suppressed again, 62; becomes 'official gazette', 95; proclaims unity, 96; prints 'order by British Admiralty', 129; attacks Fehrenbach, 130; on battle of Marstall, 187; on task of socialization commission, 277; on Allies' demand for dissolution of councils, 280

Wadler (physician): becomes Soviet-Bavarian minister, 260; goes to prison, 269

Wahnschaffe, Arnold (Under-Secretary of State): and warning of impending riot, 71; exaggerates bloodshed in Berlin, 81; relays abdication report, 85

Watter, Baron von, General: commands in Ruhr, 237; negotiates with strikers, 238; involved in fresh upheaval, 243

Weimar, 239

Wels, Otto (politician): swings soldiers to revolution, 15; becomes commandant of Berlin, 16; at loggerheads with soldiers, 153; stops sailors' pay, 177; insists on receiving keys of Palace, 179; taken hostage, 180; deposed, 185

Wemyss, Admiral, 280

Weniger, Captain, 14

Wermuth, Adolf (civil servant), 36

Wilhelm, Crown Prince, 1

Wilhelm II, Kaiser: decides war must be terminated, 1; refuses to delay request for armistice, 7; abdication demanded by Junkers, 9; leaves capital, 10; civil list as King of Prussia, 24; abdication advised by Scheidemann, 30; Scheidemann's ultimatum on abdication, 32; *Finis ultimati*, 35; abdication proclaimed, 38; Groener on question of abdication, 76; considers rebellion unimportant, 78; makes last attack on Social Democrats, 82; declares King of Prussia cannot abdicate, 83

Wilson, Woodrow, 8

Winnig, August (politician and author), 138

Winterfeldt, von, General, 127

Wirth, Joseph (politician), 147

Wissell, Rudolf (politician): appointed People's Commissar, 189; presents socialization bill, 278

Wolff, Otto (merchant), 227

Workers' and Soldiers' Councils: spontaneous appearance, 91; elections, 95; Busch meeting, 97; confer executive power on government, 103; and proposed Red Guard, 114; 'parliament of the revolution', 158; agenda, 161. *See also* Executive Council of Workers' and Soldiers' Councils

Wrisberg, Ernst von, General: declares Berlin will be held, 36; connected with putsch, 155

Zetkin, Clara (Communist), 54

Zietz, Luise (Communist), 207